DAVID LIVINGSTONE

David Livingstone

Mission and Empire

Andrew C. Ross

Hambledon and London

London and New York

DT
1110
.L58
R67
2002

Hambledon and London
102 Gloucester Avenue
London, NW1 8HX

838 Broadway
New York
NY 10003–4812

First Published 2002

ISBN 1 85285 285 2

Copyright © Andrew C. Ross 2002

The moral rights of the author has been asserted.

All rights reserved.
Without limiting the rights under copyrights
reserved above, no part of this publication may be
reproduced, stored in or introduced into a retrieval system,
or transmitted, in any form or by any means (electronic, mechanical,
photocopying, recording or otherwise), without the prior
written permission of both the copyright owner and
the above publisher of the book.

A description of this book is available from the
British Library and from the Library of Congress.

Typeset by Carnegie Publishing, Lancaster
Printed on woodfree paper and bound in
Great Britain by Cambridge University Press

50125977

Contents

Illustrations

Plates

Between Pages 114 and 115

Maps

Text Illustrations

Introduction

On Saturday 18 April 1874 the *London Illustrated News* carried two striking full-page illustrations: one was of mourners following a hearse through the streets of Southampton which were thronged with spectators; the other was of a coffin and its bearers proceeding down the aisle of Westminster Abbey. The hearse which, to the sound of minute guns and muffled church bells, moved through Southampton from harbour to railway station was carrying the coffin of David Livingstone, who was to be laid to rest in Westminster Abbey. The long biographical editorial in the same issue began:

> 'A Peerage or Westminster Abbey!' was the celebrated saying of Nelson before plunging into the Battle of the Nile. No such aspiration, we may be sure, ever disturbed the simple mind of Dr Livingstone, whose mortal remains were a week ago consigned to the tomb. Probably, if he had been consulted, he would have preferred to be buried on the banks of one of the many rivers which he has discovered in Central Africa, and among the primitive negro races who, barbarous as they are, revered him as a father, rather than in the historical abbey, which is the mausoleum of so many British worthies, and of some unworthies. But the public funeral of Saturday last, if not quite in harmony with the antecedents of the great explorer, was a becoming national tribute of respect to a man whose life was one long service to the cause of missionary enterprise, practical philanthropy, and scientific discovery.

After reviewing Livingstone's life in some detail, the editorial ended with a repeat of the same note of caution with which it had begun; a questioning tone that did not appear in any of the long and detailed reports of the funeral in the *Times*, the *Scotsman* or other major newspapers. The *London Illustrated News* alone raised the question as to whether this tribute really did fit the man and what he stood for:

> It is nearly a year ago that, exhausted with hardship of travel, he pathetically enjoined his faithful native adherents, 'Build me a hut to die in, I am going home' – and there, at Ilala he slept the sleep of the just. His lifeless body was conveyed during many months of a toilsome and dangerous journey a distance of more than a thousand miles to the coast, by his humble body-guard, one and all liberated slaves – a grander and more touching momento of the great missionary explorer

than any tomb that can be raised in his honour in Westminster Abbey. The
devoted heroism of his followers was worthy of the chief they served.

The tone of this editorial was in contrast not only with the rest of the
press but with reports of the funeral elsewhere in the *Illustrated News* itself.
There much was made of the bouquet sent to deck the coffin by the Queen.
The fact that she and the Prince of Wales, as a further mark of respect,
sent their empty carriages to take part in the funeral procession, which went
from the headquarters of the Royal Geographical Society to the abbey, was
solemnly reported. The formal 'mourning carriages', filled by the Livingstone
family and Livingstone's friends among 'the great and the good', were
followed by the empty royal carriage heading a queue of carriages of
prominent members of the British establishment seeking to do honour to
a national hero.

In all the press notices there were very careful descriptions of exactly
where in the abbey Livingstone had been buried. His grave was, as they
pointed out, opposite the monument to Field Marshal Wade. The irony that
the great grandson of a Highland warrior, who had died fighting to over-
throw the very regime Wade represented, should be laid to rest beside Wade's
monument was lost on the commentators of the time

David Livingstone was proud of his great grandfather, who had died at
Culloden; a battle that had not only ended the last armed rebellion on the
soil of Britain but had also sounded the death knell of the last armed tribal
society in western Europe. Livingstone's grandfather Neil, like so many
Gaels, was forced to leave home by poverty and the new economic situation
in the highlands.[1] Many Gaels went to North America but the majority,
during the last decades of the eighteenth century and throughout the
nineteenth, went to the Scottish Lowlands. There the new industries which
were in the process of making Glasgow the 'Second City of the Empire'
absorbed them in their tens of thousands, along with thousands of their
Roman Catholic cousins from Ireland.

How did a young member of this essentially immigrant working class,
proud of his rebel great grandfather, come to be buried as a national hero
in Westminster Abbey? How was it that this man who spent half of his
working life in Africa as a British consul could be held up as the model
Protestant missionary? How was it that the European leaders as they
partitioned Africa between them invoked the name of this harsh critic of
the British settlers in South Africa, as well as of the policies and actions
of the British administration there – the name of a man who said that
obtaining firearms was the only hope African communities had of preserving
themselves?

In the last decades of the nineteenth century many people and groups wanted a mythic hero or a saint to invoke in justification of particular causes. David Livingstone, with his commitment to end the slave trade and his dedication to the Christianising and 'civilising' of Africa, could be used to fit many bills. He could be and at various times was presented as the ideal scientist and explorer, the dedicated missionary, the supreme example of British pluck, the dedicated campaigner against the slave trade, and the opener up of the way to the occupation of Africa by the Europeans powers for the good of its peoples.

David Livingstone did enough in his life to justify many descriptions. In some cases only a little can be challenged; in other cases later priorities and perceptions have imposed often unconscious distortions. While it is impossible to know someone completely over the gap in time between Livingstone and us, it should be possible to catch some idea of the man behind the image. Just as the famous Annan photographic portrait of Livingstone (plate 1) shows a hard yet striking face, a real face, in contrast with the softened and 'tidied up' face in the lithograph in *The Last Journals* edited by Waller, I hope to help the reader see the real Livingstone.

As a Scot who grew up in a pit village and who lived for three years in an African village only ten miles from Livingstone's base at the foot of the rapids he named the Murchison Cataracts, Livingstone has long intrigued me. When it was suggested to me that it was time for a new biography, after forty years studying southern African history I thought I was ready to attempt it. During these forty years many people have contributed to my understanding of Livingstone. The most important have been my friend and teacher, Professor George 'Sam' Shepperson and my Ngoni, Yao and Mang'anja friends with whom my family and I shared seven traumatic years in the history of Malawi.

More recently I would like to thank Rosemary Seton, archivist of the School of African and Oriental Studies, University of London, for her kindness and help. Mr Iain MacIvor of the National Library of Scotland has also been most helpful, as have the staff of the reading room there. New College of the University of Edinburgh and its Centre for the Study of Christianity in the Non-Western World have been for me, as for so many scholars, a base rich in vital resources to the researcher: archives, books and, above all, interested people. I would also like to express my thanks to Karen Carruthers of the David Livingstone Centre in Blantyre. Lastly, my thanks are due to Tony Morris and Martin Sheppard of Hambledon and London for their ongoing support, and to Martin in particular for his always helpful editing.

Note on African Names

The people I refer to as the Cape Folk, a translation of the name they call themselves in Afrikaans, die Kaapse Volk, were formerly designated 'Coloured' by the twentieth-century apartheid regime in South Africa. Whites often called them 'Hottentots', the name the original Dutch settlers gave to the indigenous population of the Cape, the Khoi. By the mid eighteenth century the Khoi had ceased to be an independent people and had become an Afrikaans-speaking servant class in Cape Town and on Boer farms. Many, but not all, of these Cape Folk families had some white ancestry. In 1834 the slaves freed under British legislation merged with them to form one Afrikaans-speaking community, referred to in some official documents as 'free people of colour'. Here they will be called Cape Folk, but in nineteenth-century texts they are referred to as Hottentots, for example in the material about Andries Pretorius and the 'Hottentot Rebellion' of 1851 in the Cape Colony.

In the Bantu family of languages a people was and are designated by the prefixes *a*, *ama*, *ba* or *wa*, their language by the prefixes *ci*, *se*, *si* or *ki*. Thus the language of the baTswana should strictly be referred to as seTswana, similarly that of the amaNdebele as siNdebele, that of the aNgoni as ciNgoni and that of the waNyamwesi as kiNyamwesi. While accurate, this convention would tend to confuse the general reader, so I have adopted the alternative convention of using Tswana for both the language and the people, Ngoni for the people and language and so on.

In Chapters 4 and 5 the Kgatla, Kwena, Ngwato, Fokeng and other peoples referred to were autonomous Tswana-speaking groups. The Tswana-Sotho speaking peoples did not have an overall political authority, as did the Xhosa and Zulu, though Moshweshwe did unite some of the previously autonomous units into the kingdom of Lesotho in the mid nineteenth century.

There is a further complication for readers of nineteenth- and early twentieth-century documents and books. It is that in the nineteenth and much of the twentieth century European writers and colonial governments referred officially to some peoples by the name used of them by another people in another language. Thus we find that the Ndebele were designated the Matabele, hence the province of Matabeleland in the old Southern Rhodesia. Matebele was how the Tswana and Shona referred to the Ndebele. Again the amaXhosa were called Caffres or Kafirs in the official documents of both Dutch and British. Kafir is the Arabic word for a non-believer, which was what the Muslim Malay slaves of the Dutch at the Cape called the Xhosa on their first encounter. The Xhosa homeland was designated in official British documents throughout the nineteenth century as Kaffraria. This was before the word Kafir in South Africa became an insulting designation for all Africans.

Lake Malawi was named variously by the Portuguese, Livingstone and others in the nineteenth century as Lake Maravi, Nyasa, Nyassa and Nyinyesi. The presently named Cabora Bassa Gorge in the nineteenth and twentieth centuries was variously referred to as Kebra Basa, Kebrabasa and Cabora Basa.

The Ndebele, Ngoni and Shangaan or Gazankulu were all Nguni groups who broke with the Zulu kingdom in the 1820s and marched northwards to find new lands for themselves. The Kololo of Sebitwane were the only group from among the Sotho/Tswana peoples who, like these Nguni groups, trekked north to find a new secure place to live, away from the turmoil caused by the creation and expansion of the Zulu kingdom by Dingiswayo and Chaka. This period of turmoil in southern African history is referred to in Xhosa as *difaqane* and in Sotho/Tswana as *mfecane*.

Nduna is an officer of a chief whose authority is solely that given by the chief, and is not personal to him through lineage. *Nganga*, *ngaka* and *sing'anga* are terms for the traditional healer in southern African society, someone Livingstone treated with respect. The often-used term 'witch-doctor' is wholly inappropriate when applied to such a practitioner. *Morafe* is a Sotho/Tswana term for an autonomous political unit. It is preferable to the English words, kingdom or state, which imply structures that simply were not there in a majority of traditional chieftaincies in southern Africa. There were two exceptions: the Sotho kingdom created by Moshweshwe and the Zulu kingdom of Chaka.

The Displaced Gael

David Livingstone was born on 19 March 1813 in a 'single-end' on the top floor of the tenement called 'Shuttle-Row' in the mill town of Blantyre, near Glasgow, the second son of Neil Livingstone and his wife Agnes Hunter.[1] Neil had been born in 1788 on Ulva, a small island off the west coast of Mull. Ulva is closely associated with Iona, the base from which St Columba launched his mission to Scotland, which, within a generation had under St Aidan led to the conversion of Northumbria and Mercia. David's grandfather was also called Neil Livingstone, and his father had been killed serving in the ranks of Prince Charles Edward's Highland army in their bitter defeat at Culloden in 1746.

There were two pieces of Highland oral tradition about this branch of the Livingstones of that time. The first, current in Mull, was that the redcoats drove the rebel Neil Livingstone's widow and her children from their cottage in the middle of a snowstorm. In nearby Appin another popular tradition, still being told well into the twentieth century, claimed that David Livingstone's great grandfather had not been killed at Culloden but had escaped.[2] He was then supposed to have turned up in Appin and have taken part, with other Livingstone men, in cutting down and taking away for burial the body of the executed James Stewart of the Glens, despite soldiers guarding it. James Stewart had been convicted of the murder of Campbell of Glenure in 1750, a killing central to R. L. Stevenson's novel *Kidnapped*.

This piece of oral tradition does not fit what facts we know of David Livingstone's family. David was clearly fascinated by the stories his grandfather told of their Highland past. He insisted that his grandfather could trace the family's story back for six generations, and was quite clear that the family was an Ulva not an Appin family, and that his great grandfather died at Culloden. It may be that the folk of Appin were claiming Livingstone for Gaeldom at a time, in the late nineteenth and early twentieth century, when he was written and talked of as an archetypal Lowland Scot. Most oral traditions that last have purposes other than simply telling a good story.

The failure of the potato crop in the early 1790s led most of the six hundred inhabitants of Ulva to leave Scotland for America or Canada, where many settled on Prince Edward Island. Those who went across the

Atlantic included all of Neil Livingstone's relations and the Morrison relations of his wife, Mary Morrison. Grandfather Neil, with his wife and their
children, John, Charles, Duncan, Donald, Neil, Kate and Margaret, left Ulva
in 1792 not for North America but for the Lowlands. According to church
records there was a third daughter but her name is now lost. Neil's standing,
in the eyes of the kirk session of the vast parish of Kilninian and Kilmore,
of which Ulva was part, was good and the family left with this letter of
recommendation:

> The bearer, Neil Livingstone, a married man in Ulva, part of the parish of
> Kilninian, has always maintained an unblemished moral character, and is known
> for a man of piety and religion. He has a family of four sons, the youngest of
> which is three years, and three daughters, of which the youngest is six years
> of age. As he proposes to offer his services at some of the cotton-spinning manu-
> factories, he and his wife Mary Morrison, and their family of children are hereby
> recommended for suitable encouragement.
>   Given at Ulva, this eighth day of January, 1792 by
>
>   Arch. McArthur, Minister [3]
>   Lach. Mclean, Elder
>   R. S. Stewart, JP, Elder [4]

The family settled in Blantyre, where Neil gained a position of trust with
the Glasgow firm of Monteith's in their Blantyre cotton mill. It appears to
have stood this incomer in good stead that he was literate in English, as
well as a Gaelic speaker, at a time of massive immigration by Gaelic speakers
from Ireland and the Highlands into the industrial central belt of Scotland.
All we know of his job is that one of his tasks was to convey large sums of
money weekly between the mill in Blantyre and the bank in Glasgow.

From what little else is available in the records it would appear his
grandchildren were fond of him and loved to hear him tell the old Highland
stories. Indeed David and his elder brother John, when in their teens, slept
at the cottage of old Neil and their grandmother Mary when their own
house became embarrassingly overcrowded. David Livingstone wrote of his
grandfather:

> Our grandfather was intimately acquainted with all the traditional legends which
> that great writer [Walter Scott] has since made use of in *Tales of a Grandfather*
> and other works. As a boy I remember listening to him with delight, for his
> memory was stored with a never-ending stock of stories, many of which were
> wonderfully like those I have since heard while sitting by the African evening fire.[5]

It is also clear that grandmother Mary Morrison was not at home in English
and that, towards the end of her life, when living with her son Neil, wanted
to have the Bible read to her daily in Gaelic. David's sister Janet remembered

a Highlander visiting their home regularly to help their father, Neil, learn to read Gaelic so as to be able to do this.[6] This remark by Janet has too often been taken to mean that Livingstone's father had somehow to relearn Gaelic. However it was in order to *read* Gaelic that Neil Livingstone needed help. He and his brothers and sisters had been brought up speaking Gaelic but their education had been in Blantyre, where they were taught to read and write in English. A Gaelic speaker who is literate only in English is not able to read Gaelic aloud in any sensible form without additional instruction. This was even more true in this case, as the Gaelic Bible that grandmother Mary wanted to have read was almost certainly the 1690 version. It was the only one that was available to her in her early and middle years. This was written in the Classic Gaelic of the 'learned orders', though printed in roman letters for use in Scotland.[7]

Livingstone's principal memory of his grandmother was of her singing Gaelic songs and then telling stories to the children about them. Telling stories handed down from the past and singing while doing chores in the home or on the land or while fishing was a strong Gaelic tradition, as it was and is in the Africa where her grandson would spend most of his life. Livingstone was through his grandfather and grandmother in contact with the old tribal, primarily oral, culture of the Highlands. Many thousands of men and women in Scotland at that time and in that same situation rejected that past as something backward and primitive. In stark contrast, he treasured it. It provides a clue to his ability to sympathise with and to enter into the different African societies with which he later came into contact.

David's father Neil was the only one of the sons of grandfather Neil who did not fight in the Napoleonic Wars. The others all volunteered to serve in one or other of the Scottish Regiments, a not unusual pattern for ex-Jacobite families. Old Neil was bitter about what happened to one son, Charles, who had risen to be chief clerk in the offices of Monteith's in Glasgow. He was no volunteer but was taken by the press gang while walking on Glasgow Green. It was no consolation to his family that his skills gained him the post of captain's clerk on the warship to which he was taken, a warrant officer rank in those days, for he died at sea in the Mediterranean.

Livingstone's father did not work in the cotton mill in which his grandfather was such a trusted employee but was apprenticed to David Hunter, a tailor, whose daughter, Agnes, Neil married in 1810. David Livingstone's sister, Janet, in the notes she provided Dr Blaikie for his biography of her brother, insisted that their father had been apprenticed against his will, which perhaps explains why he did not stay in the tailoring trade. Instead Neil Livingstone became a self-employed seller of tea. He did this from door to door and at the same time distributed Christian tracts and engaged folk in conversation about the Christian faith whenever an opportunity offered.

What is not clear is how Neil and his family came to live in Shuttle Row. These homes were specifically for the employees of Monteith's cotton mill. Did the family get this accommodation because of the prestige of grandfather Neil with the owners; or was it the need to qualify for this accommodation that sent father Neil's oldest son, John, to work in the mill at the age of ten, to be followed by David when he reached that age? The 'single-end' in Shuttle Row was only one room with two bed recesses, in which the family of seven lived, cooked, ate and slept. Truckle beds were kept under the beds in the bed recesses to be brought out at night. It was a situation where privacy was non-existent. There was a communal wash house across a yard at the back of the building and there were earth closets there also. All slops and other household rubbish were thrown out via sluice holes in the circular staircase that led to the various floors of the tenement. The common stairs and the yards were kept clean and tidy.

Harsh though Shuttle Row might appear to modern eyes, it was vastly superior to much working-class accommodation in central Scotland at that time. Families crowded into tenements intended to house a third of number that came to occupy them. To gain access to these buildings one walked through vennels down which open sewers ran and where rubbish and faeces lay around until swept away by the rain.

Livingstone's portrait of his father was an affectionate one

> my father remained at home, and, though too conscientious ever to become rich as a small tea-dealer, by his kindliness and winning ways he made the heart-strings of his children twine round him as firmly as if he had possessed, and could have bestowed upon them, every worldly advantage. He reared his children in connection with the Kirk of Scotland – a religious establishment which has been an incalculable blessing to that country; but afterwards he left it, and during the last twenty years of his life held the office of deacon of an independent church in Hamilton, and deserved my lasting gratitude and homage for presenting me, from my infancy, with a continuously consistent pious example, such as that the ideal of which is so beautifully and truthfully portrayed in Burns's *Cottar's Saturday Night*.[8]

Theirs certainly was a pious home, but the family piety was not static but one that reshaped itself a number of times and was the cause of conflict within the family. We have seen that Old Neil left Ulva in good standing with the Established Church of Scotland, the Kirk, and that his son Neil was also a good Kirk member and had all his children baptised in the local parish kirk. Young Neil, if we may call David's father so to distinguish him from his grandfather, became increasingly concerned about the strict Calvinist doctrine of election and the form of the doctrine of Limited Atonement as taught in Scotland at the time.[9]

After much agonising, Neil left the Kirk and began to attend an Independent congregation in nearby Hamilton. This congregation was a product of the Christianity shaped by the movement called in Britain the Evangelical Revival and in the United States the Awakening. For Neil Livingstone, the key issue was that the idea of Limited Atonement was done away with entirely in the beliefs of some groups within this new movement. Salvation was seen as available to all who would accept it through faith in Jesus Christ. The Livingstones, by joining this Independent chapel, moved out of the Calvinist tradition of the Kirk. This tradition, which dominated mainstream Scottish life in the nineteenth century, was not shaken when the Free Kirk broke away from the Established Church of Scotland, the Auld Kirk, in the Disruption of 1843, for the Free Kirk remained a Calvinist institution.

Before discussing the development of David Livingstone's faith, it is important to note that the Livingstone family were now 'outsiders' on a number of counts. First, the Livingstones were a Gaelic-speaking family who had migrated only recently to Blantyre. Now, added to that, they had deliberately joined an Independent chapel. Had Neil joined one of the old Seceder Kirks,[10] which were the products of peculiarly Scottish quarrels over what to outsiders appeared to be the minutiae of the Calvinist doctrine of church and state, that would not have been an exceptional step. The various Seceder groups were still within the tradition; indeed they saw themselves as the fundamental standard-bearers of the Calvinist faith in Scotland and of the tradition of the Covenants of the Kirk's conflicts with the Stuart monarchs of the seventeenth century. Neil, however, chose to join a group espousing a specifically non-Calvinist set of beliefs in order to resolve the tensions created in him by strict Scots Calvinism. Finally, the Livingstones set themselves apart also in ways that might appear superficial but in the life of a poor working-class community were very important. This was made clearer than she perhaps appreciated in Janet's reminiscence of her mother in her notes for Dr Blaikie:

> My Mother had the knack of making a little go a long way in comfort and respectability ... She was proud of her boys and liked to see them extra well dressed, she dressed them with frills around their necks. The Manager's wife, she kept a servant, said to my mother, 'I wonder ye can be fashed wi yer ruffles ti yer laddies, I'm glad ti gie them a clean sark.' My Mother said 'But woman, I like them baith – and they look sae nice and clean wi the frills.' [11]

It does not require a great deal of imagination to conceive what it was like

in the Blantyre of the day for 'laddies wi ruffles', even if it was only on the
Sabbath that they appeared in this finery.

The strong religious atmosphere of the Livingstone house in which David
grew up, and for which he often expressed himself to be deeply grateful, is
fundamental to any understanding of the person he became. As we have
seen, in the Livingstone household the simplicities of traditional Calvinist
piety and the controversies about the Covenants gave way to the piety of
the Evangelical Revival in a form that specifically rejected what were considered at the time central tenets of Calvinism. In this period of change in
the family's religious allegiance, Janet recorded that initially David did not
go with the rest of the family to the Independent chapel in Hamilton. 'My
brother David said he liked the Auld Kirk, and continued to attend it for
some time after. Then he took sittings in the Old Relief Church for the sake
of its fine library.' 12

This was a time in David's life when he was in rebellion against his father
on a number of issues. David's intense interest in nature and in science
drew him to read books on both, and he rejected his father's insistence that
he ceased to do this and instead read only books on the faith. Janet records
one such clash when David refused absolutely to read Wilberforce's *Practical
Christianity* at his father's behest and Neil took a stick to him. At this point
Janet reports that she 'grat sair' (wept uncontrollably). Neil was deeply afraid
that David's interest in science would endanger the young man's Christian
faith, as he had come to perceive science as inimical to Christianity. It was
David's membership of the Old Relief Church, with its fine library, that
brought back harmony to the whole family. It was in that library David
read the books of Dr Thomas Dick; books that reconciled modern science
and the Christian faith to David's satisfaction.

As a result of this resolution of his personal problems David applied for
membership of the chapel in Hamilton. This he felt able to do, not simply
because of Dr Dick's reconciliation of science and Christianity, but also
because his own personal fears and doubts had been resolved. These anxieties
were relieved by his accepting the belief, held by the movement of which
the Hamilton chapel was a part, that salvation was freely available to all
willing to receive it. He, like his father before him, was now free from the
fears created by traditional Scots Calvinist teaching on Election and Limited
Atonement. By the time of this resolution of the conflicts within himself
and with his father, David had been working in a mill for ten years. He
had begun work as what was called a 'piecer'. The piecers in all the cotton-
spinning mills had work to do that was essential to the success of the process.
Their task was to spot any flaw in the thread and 'piece' the ends together
so that no flaw was incorporated in the finished product. The children had

to be agile, dashing under the spinning jenny or climbing up on the frame to make the necessary repair. What was an even greater strain was that they had to keep their attention razor sharp every minute of their shift, a shift that lasted from six in the morning till eight at night, with a half hour break for breakfast and an hour for dinner.

Like many poor boys in the Scotland of that day, David had gone to the village school and had gained the basics of the three Rs before starting to work at the mill. His education did not cease. The millowners provided a schoolmaster and so the young piecers, when they finished their twelve and a half hour shift, could attend the mill school from eight until ten in the evening. When David was thirteen the village schoolmaster started a Latin class in the mill school during the two hours after the shift ended. It was attendance at this class that Livingstone described in a famous passage:

> With a part of my first week's wages I purchased Ruddiman's *Rudiments of Latin* and pursued the study of that language for many years afterwards, with unabated ardour, at an evening school, which met between the hours of eight and ten. The dictionary part of my labours was followed up till twelve o'clock, or later, if my mother did not interfere by jumping up and snatching the books out of my hands. I had to be back in the factory by six in the morning, and continued my work, with intervals for breakfast and dinner, till eight o'clock at night. I read in this manner many of the classical authors, and knew Virgil and Horace better at sixteen than I do now.[13]

How he managed to study, after an exhausting day followed by two hours class work, in a single room where his brothers and sisters as well as his parents were trying to sleep, is mind-boggling. There was a marginal alleviation of the strain when he and John were well into their teens and it was arranged that they slept at the nearby cottage to which grandfather Neil had retired.

David was again going along a road which made him even more of an outsider. This was his attempting to read books while at work. He was able to do this more readily once he was promoted to be a spinner. However, even as a piecer, he had tried and suffered from the other children throwing bobbins to knock his book off the frame of the loom where he had positioned it.

We see a picture here of a boy becoming a young man with singular determination and single-mindedness, and one who was dismissive of those who did not see things his way. There is a very revealing passage in a letter Livingstone wrote to his younger brother-in-law, John Smith Moffat, many years later. In it he said:

> When I was a piecer the fellows used to try and turn me off from the path I had

chosen, and always began with 'I think you ought etc', till I snapped them up with a mild 'You think! I can think and act for myself; don't need anybody to think for me'.[14]

This is, note, Livingstone being 'mild' when crossed. It is consistent with the youth who, rather than read other than what he believed worth reading, forced the issue with his father to the point of the beating which made Janet 'grat sair'.

There was, however, a side to Livingstone's boyhood and youth other than the picture of unrelenting toil and a grim determination to do what he held to be right despite all obstacles. He loved the beautiful Lanarkshire countryside and took every chance to roam through it. He very early displayed scientific curiosity and regularly went to a nearby limestone quarry to collect the shells which he found embedded in the stone. He also showed at that time a keen interest in botany, collecting specimens of plants which he related to those listed in W. Patrick's *The Indigenous Plants of Lanarkshire*.

> In recognising the plants pointed out in my first medical book, that extraordinary old work on astrological medicine, Culpepper's *Herbal*, I had the guidance of a book on the plants of Lanarkshire, by Patrick. Limited as my time was, I found opportunities to scour the whole countryside, 'collecting simples'. Deep and anxious were my studies on the still deeper and more perplexing profundities of astrology, and I believe I got as far into the abyss of fantasies as my author said he dared lead me ... These excursions, often in company with brothers, one now in Canada, and the other a clergyman in the United States, gratified my intense love of nature; and though we generally returned so unmercifully hungry and fatigued that the embryo parson shed tears, yet we discovered, to us, so many new and interesting things, that he was always as eager to join us next time as he was the last.[15]

David and his brothers were also keen on fishing and caught trout in the Clyde, as well as, on at least two occasions, a salmon. On one of the days of adventure, when they had caught a salmon (much more difficult to hide than trout), Charles was made use of by the other two. They thrust the salmon down one leg of Charles's trousers, causing passers by to comment sympathetically on the poor lad with the limp and the swollen leg. Although his early biographers attempted to show the lads were not really poaching, of course they were. Janet, though like her mother always aware of the need of the 'honest poor' to hold onto respectability, comes close to saying so in her reminiscences of her brother. She makes unambiguous references to her father's opposition to the Game Laws as 'unjust and demeaning', and she also writes of David's frequent gleeful return home boasting that he had 'jinked Sailor Jack', the gamekeeper on Lord Douglas's estate.[16] He was hardly going out regularly to 'jink' the gamekeeper simply for the fun of it, but surely rather for the fish.

There is a problem about our knowledge of Livingstone's early life. Although the sources are very limited, they all agree about his love of the countryside and the amount of time he spent roaming there. There is even a story about him spending at least some time as a cattle herd, a youngster sent into the field to keep an eye on the cattle. The farmer, when interviewed years later about this, was still clear enough in his memory of Livingstone to complain 'that he was aye on his belly reading a book'. The problem is to work out when he could have found the time.

After the age of ten he was in the mill from six in the morning to eight at night for six days a week. He attended church on Sundays. After he joined the rest of the family in going to the Hamilton chapel, this meant that they stayed at Hamilton till the early afternoon for another service. Some of the stories may relate to the period before he went into the mill, but many of them cannot be about a boy not yet ten years old. Even when we take account of daylight lasting in Scotland up till about eleven o'clock in the evening during the summer, when there was also no mill night school, and add this to free time that on Sunday, the amount of free time available was still very limited. It is also possible that for short periods at least, in times of economic slump, the management may have paid off piecers and spinners temporarily. The only source of free time that we know for certain did occur from time to time came from the rise and fall of the waters of the Clyde. Since the mill was water-driven, when the Clyde ran at a height inconvenient for the system of water wheels that drove the machinery of the mill, the management was forced to stop the water wheels and close the sluices leading to them. The employees then had a day or so of 'holiday'.

What can be seen, however, is that this pious family in the 1820s and 1830s clearly had no inhibitions about the boys roaming the countryside after services were over on the Sabbath. This is somewhat different from the popular image of what was supposed to be the normal pattern of behaviour of pious Scots on Sundays. This pattern of behaviour also helps to explain Livingstone's irritation in the opening months of the Zambesi Expedition with what he saw as Captain Bedingfeld's Sabbatarianism.

When Livingstone was twenty-one he read a pamphlet which his father had picked up one Sunday at their church in Hamilton. Karl Gutzlaff had published it the year before in Canton. Gutzlaff called for missionaries to come to China, emphasising that here was the largest unevangelised population in the world. This vision excited the young man – but Livingstone was intrigued even more by a startling new idea presented by Gutzlaff. He called for missionaries to train as physicians. Up till this time what was to become almost the stereotype of the Protestant missionary later in the century, the missionary doctor, did not exist. It was Gutzlaff, and Dr Peter Parker of the American Board of Commissioners for Foreign Missions,[17] who first presented this new concept to the Protestant missionary organisations of the United States and Europe.

Livingstone now approached his father with the idea of attempting to enter university to study medicine in order to become a missionary. Neil described the situation in a letter he wrote later to the directors of the London Missionary Society: -

> When he first mentioned to me his design of attending the University in order to study medicine I was much opposed to it, until he informed me that it was not to gain a livelihood he thought of doing so, his anxious wish was to be enabled to spend his life in the service of the Redeemer among the heathen; I no longer felt to oppose his design, but felt thankful that such a thought was in his heart.[18]

In answer to the thought that might have crossed the minds of the directors, and has certainly crossed the minds of others since, that this was a good way to get out of the unending drudgery of the life of a cotton spinner, Neil Livingstone pointed out in the same letter that his son had turned down opportunities to take up other employment. He made clear that one of these at least would have been paid more than the LMS paid missionaries. As he wrote in the same letter:

> His landlord – a Mr Dove, with whom he lodged in Glasgow – said to him one day, 'Well, Mr L., I admire your perseverance, and if you will leave the dissenters and become a Churchman, I will undertake to get you a situation as a Teacher worth £150 a year'; he replied he could not do that for any money. Mr Dove said one day afterwards: 'Well, if you give me leave, I will recommend you, and I think you will be accepted even retaining your principles as a dissenter.' David said he was grateful for his kindness, but that was not the object on which his heart was set.

It was decided that David should attempt to train as a physician. He began his medical studies at Anderson's College in Glasgow.[19] Although he only stayed two years at the Andersonian, as the college was often called, Livingstone was to make some lifelong friendships there and also received a thorough basic scientific training in possibly the liveliest centre of scientific education in the United Kingdom at that time.[20]

2

A Student in Glasgow and London

In regard to the provision of education for the general population, England and Scotland were very different countries in the first half of the nineteenth century. Since the Reformation Scotland had had some sort of national education structure which was supported by the state as well as the church. It was not complete geographically, and it did not always work well, but it was something Scots believed in and that Scottish society persistently attempted to implement. John Knox's ideal of every parish with a school had been achieved and worked well in the north east and the Lowlands before the middle of the eighteenth century.[1] These schools and their schoolmasters prepared their best pupils for university. Although rapid industrialisation and urbanisation reduced the effectiveness of the system in the first decades of the nineteenth century, in the 1830s the Scottish population continued to maintain a level of literacy that could be found elsewhere only in Prussia, some parts of Switzerland and New England.[2] The idea of a national education scheme from primary school to university developed in England only in the later nineteenth century. The lack of effective elementary education for the labouring classes in England was something that Livingstone noted and upon which, even while trying to win the English public for his African schemes in his *Missionary Travels and Researches*, he could not resist commenting.[3]

At the other end of the system, in the area of university education, the contrast between the two countries took a number of different forms. Scotland, with its much smaller population, had five universities, St Andrews, Aberdeen, Glasgow, Edinburgh and Anderson's, in contrast to England's two. Access to the university was radically different in the two countries. Robert Anderson in his magisterial discussion of Scottish education in the nineteenth century writes:

> For boys with talent but no resources, bursaries for university study were quite widely available ... universities were open to anyone who could scrape together a little Latin and mathematics, and this included men who decided to change course in adult life. The student body was a diverse one, and the universities were not hedged off by the kind of social barriers which made Oxford and Cambridge places of privilege. Their customs, indeed, recognized that many students would

combine university attendance with work of some kind, or would need to earn their living in the summer, for the university session ran only from late October to Easter.[4]

David Livingstone fits neatly into this picture of the Scottish student. Together, the village school followed by the mill school prepared him for entrance to Anderson's College. The problem he then faced was that studying at the Andersonian was dependent upon his ability to maintain himself by working at his old job in the mill from Easter to October each year. In consequence, he had to make sure of the agreement of the mill management to this arrangement before he could begin his course. Again in this he was typical rather than unusual among Scottish students.

Livingstone was also a typical Scottish student of the period in that he followed a mixture of classes, some relating to his desired qualification and others not. He studied medicine in order to qualify to sit the examinations of the Glasgow College of Physicians and Surgeons, as Anderson's did not grant medical degrees. He also undertook classes in chemistry at Anderson's. In addition he went along to the Congregational Church College to hear the theological lectures of Dr Richard Wardlaw, a Yale doctor of divinity and a passionate abolitionist. Blaikie, in his classic biography, says Livingstone followed a New Testament Greek class at Glasgow University, but that is not clear from the records and it would seem more likely that it was the Greek class at the Congregational College that he attended.

Just before the opening of the university session of 1836–37, Livingstone and his father walked the eight miles into Glasgow. A friend had given them a list of possible 'digs' for the new student. All of the suggested lodgings were visited but Neil and David judged them to be too expensive. Striking out on their own, they eventually found something they thought suitable. A landlady in Rotten Row was willing to take the young man for two shillings a week. This arrangement was not a success and, after a few weeks, Livingstone went out and found new lodgings with a Mr and Mrs Dove in the High Street, where he stayed for the rest of his time at Anderson's. Although in his second session at the Andersonian he walked home to Blantyre every Saturday morning, returning on Monday morning in time for his first class, in his first year he planned to go home once a month only. He decided this despite admitting to missing his close family circle very much. His sister Janet recorded his reasons. To modern ears they sound somewhat odd, but clearly they were deemed serious at the time. Apparently, a little while before, two young men from Blantyre who were students at Glasgow University and returned home every weekend were accused in Glasgow of slipping away each weekend as part of a resurrectionist gang. Livingstone did not want to risk a similar accusation.[5] Some time during his first year, however, he set aside his worries about being mistaken for a resurrectionist and got into the routine of walking home each Saturday morning. In any case, whether monthly or weekly, Janet tells of how the family longed for his visits and how much they enjoyed David relating his Glasgow adventures to them as they gathered round the fire on Saturday evenings.

Livingstone had saved as much as he could to provide the £12 annual academic fee and the money needed for food and lodging. Considering that his wage as a spinner was never more than four shillings a week, it was not surprising that he had to get help from his elder brother John to manage that first year. As ever, David in this new situation exhibited single-mindedness and a stubborn insistence on going his own way. David turned down the offer of a lift into Glasgow every Monday morning, just as he had turned down Mr Dove's offers of a career in teaching. As his father Neil put it:

> A kind gentleman, a member of our church, Fergus Ferguson, Esq. of Rosebank, would have taken him down to Glasgow every Monday morning in his gig, but he chose rather to walk on foot in all kinds of weather during the last severe winter, rising every Monday at five in the morning that he might reach Glasgow between 8 and 9 o'clock, as if he had waited on Mr F. he would have lost one lecture and part of another.[6]

Livingstone's utter disregard for his own health also appears in these first student years. When David finished his first year of study, Neil had wanted him to take a short break. David, however, insisted on starting at the mill the first day after the end of the examinations at college. Again his sister records another instance of this same dedication to the task at hand.

> Three weeks before the session closed in 1838 Mrs Dove wrote to my Father that his son was very ill that a doctor had been called who was treating him for inflammation of the bowels. My Father went immediately – found him relieved but very weak. My Father, ever serious about his children's immortal interests, said to him, said [sic] 'As you are very ill I would like to know if your mind is at rest.' David said 'I am so weak I can scarcely think, but I am just resting on "I will never leave thee nor forsake thee".' My Father said 'that's enough – if anything happened I just wanted your mother and me to be satisfied.' My Father hired a conveyance and brought him home. My Mother sat up with him for three nights but he soon came round and was able to attend the examinations of his classes.[7]

The head of the Department of Medicine, Professor Andrew Buchanan, became Livingstone's lifelong friend. Janet reported that, after the last of these examinations, Buchanan and Livingstone walked arm in arm along George Street, an unusual picture of a professor and a second year student at any time, let alone in the Scotland of that day. It was in the Chemistry Department, however, that Livingstone appears to have been most at home.[8] The head of department was Thomas Graham, later Professor of Chemistry at University College, London. His personal assistant was James Young and in the latter's small workroom a number of students used to gather for further instruction, George Wilson, later Professor of Technology at Edinburgh, and Livingstone among them. Under Young's guidance, Livingstone and Lyon Playfair constructed a galvanic battery on new principles, which was put on show by the Andersonian.[9] Young, who was to become an important figure in Livingstone's life, later was appointed to University College along with Graham. He did not stay an academic for long but found a commercial application for his scientific knowledge which made him a millionaire and gained him his reputation as 'Paraffin' Young.

While medical science was then only in an early stage of its development, so that the amount of what would be recognised now as good medical knowledge Livingstone received was limited, he was grounded very firmly in the scientific approach to nature. His youthful scientific curiosity, which he had indulged in his rambling in the Lanarkshire countryside, was now trained and disciplined. Throughout all his writings, whether published books, notebooks, journals or his thousands of letters, there runs a thread of careful scientific observation of African fauna and flora. Indeed in the notebook in which he made observations of all kinds in the last weeks of his life, in great pain and in the midst of difficult conditions, Livingstone recorded meticulous drawings of fish and insects that were new to him. This rigour he also brought to bear in his study of African languages. He used his thorough knowledge of Tswana as a base from which to study the other languages he encountered. This led him to make tentative suggestions about the structure of Bantu languages which provoked later linguistic scholars to lament that he had not left other interests aside and devoted himself to linguistics.

Limited though his medical knowledge was when he went to Africa, Livingstone tried to get medical journals sent to him and strove to keep up with new developments. He learned to use chloroform and quinine, and even made some scientific medical discoveries himself in the midst of his exhausting life in Africa. In 1848, before embarking on his treks northwards towards Lake Bangweulu and the Zambesi, he sent for the medical reports on the Niger Expedition of 1841, Dr James McWilliam's *Medical History of the Expedition to the Niger during the Years 1841–2*. Although he saw that McWilliam's treatment of malaria had not been effective, he paid particular attention to the reports of the eight autopsies McWilliam had performed. Beginning with this study, he developed his famous pill, made of a combination of quinine and a purgative. These pills proved an effective treatment for malaria when taken in large enough quantities 'to cause ringing in the ears'.

On these same journeys, between 1849 and 1851, he also studied Trypanoso-miasis. He worked out that carefully administered doses of arsenic might be an effective cure, but he ventured only to use this on horses with the equine version of the disease. Although he reported that this experiment had only limited success, he was still one of the pioneers in the use of arsenic in dealing with this disease, a form of medication that was to be used in treating Trypanosomiasis with some success well into the twentieth century. Of more long term importance, Livingstone was one of the first physicians to assert, as a result of careful observation, a causal link between a diet that was predominantly grain-based and chronic impairment of vision.[10]

The list of books he ordered from John Snow of Paternoster Row in London in 1853 gives some indication of his continuing intellectual interests and his keen desire to keep up with scientific advance. Against those who have dismissed Livingstone's 'classical' education as very limited, we should note his continued ability to make use of Hebrew and Greek in his Bible study. His request for Harriet Beecher Stowe's classic is a reminder of his continuing concern with slavery in the USA.

> Bloomfield's Supplement to his Greek New Testament
> Laycocks' Analeptics – was reviewed a few years ago in Forbes' Review
> Moral Aspects of Medical Life including the 'Askesis' of Prof. Marx.
> Daniel on the diseases of the coast of Guinea.
> Boyle's diseases of Western Africa
> Principles of medicine and therapeutics (latest edition) by Dr C. J. B. Williams
> The following volumes of Sir W. Jardines Naturalists library.
> Birds of Western Africa 2 Vols – Ruminating animals – Lions and Tigers – Elephants and Rhinoceros – Sun birds – Fly catchers – Entomology
> Uncle Tom's Cabin by Mrs Stowe
> Gesenius Hebrew Lexicon – there is a late edition with many improvements published in America – should prefer it.
> The remaining two volumes of Bunsen's Egypt's place in universal History
> First volume of Prof. Owen's lectures on the invertebrata.
> If you can get Hippocrates as printed by the Sydenham Society *second-hand* I shall feel obliged.
> A few more fasciculi of Maclises have come to hand. Send the whole.
> To the above may be added a Septuagint of clear type of the letters about the size of those employed in Bloomfield's Testament but the volume itself not very large.
>
> Believe me yours truly,
> David Livingstone.[11]

Livingstone and his father had thought that he should complete his medical qualifications before he applied to a missionary society. This plan changed completely when, during his second year at university, the manager of the Blantyre mill said that he could not expect to come back to work as a spinner after Easter. Livingstone now applied to the directors of the London Missionary Society, at that time the major missionary society in the United Kingdom, for an appointment. It was also, other than the very small Scottish and Glasgow Missionary Societies, the only one open to him. The Church Missionary Society was Anglican, and the Baptist and Methodist Missionary Societies were also clearly denominationally defined.

The London Missionary Society, founded in 1795, was firmly rooted in the tradition of the Evangelical Revival which saw denomination as a secondary issue for truly converted Christians. In 1796 the society famously declared its fundamental principle:

> As a union of God's People of various Denominations, in carrying on this great Work, is a most desirable Object, so, to prevent, if possible, any cause of future dissension, it is declared to be a fundamental principle of the Missionary Society, that our design is not to send Presbyterianism, Independency, Episcopacy, or any form of Church order and Government (about which there might be differences of opinion among serious Persons), but the Glorious Gospel of the blessed God to the Heathen: and it shall be left (as it ever ought to be left) to the minds of the Persons whom God may call into the fellowship of his Son from among them to assure for themselves such form of Church Government, as to them shall appear most agreeable to the Word of God.[12]

Livingstone applied to the LMS at the beginning of the university year, October 1837, but it was not until January that the directors of the LMS replied. They sent him their standard set of questions in booklet form which had to be answered by all candidates seeking to be taken on by the society. Livingstone also had to seek appropriate referees and write an essay on one of a number of suggested topics.

His answers are very revealing, particularly his essay on 'The Holy Spirit'. If one wants to understand the lives of Trotsky, Lenin or Rosa Luxemburg, and what separated as well as what united them, one has to study Marxism. The student must try to understand the importance of slight differences of wording or differences over the meaning to be attached to words in the philosophy that animated their lives. Similarly an observer has to try to come to terms with the different forms of words used to express the Protestant forms of the Christian faith in order to understand many people in the English-speaking world of the nineteenth century. In this light one paragraph of Livingstone's essay on the Holy Spirit, submitted to the directors of the LMS as part of their candidature procedure, is of crucial importance. In this essay, after a conventional description of the 'fallen' nature of humanity, he went on:

> The Bible treats him as a moral and accountable agent. Salvation is freely offered to him. Believe on the Lord Jesus Christ and thou shalt be saved – faith in the work of Jesus Christ is all that is required to shield him from everlasting punishment. Yet he will not believe it, unless the Holy Spirit exerts his influence over his will by convincing him of sin, shewing him the deceitfulness and desperate wickedness of his own heart, the folly and danger of living in sin and exhibits to his view the beauty of holiness.[13]

This is not classic Scottish Calvinism with its firm doctrine of Election and the concept of Limited Atonement, that is that Jesus having died only for the 'Elect'. Rather the young Scot is asserting that Jesus died for all and salvation is available to all, if they will only accept it. This was the belief that was so important to both David and his father, Neil. The second sentence about the aid of the Holy Spirit in making that decision is the conventional wording used by many in this tradition, which Livingstone had espoused, to protect themselves from the Calvinist accusation that they had turned salvation into 'the work of man'.

The faith espoused by Livingstone was, as we have noted, that of the 'Awakening' in the United States. Indeed the Christianity of the American Awakening, with its emphasis on transforming the world as well as the saving of souls, is an important guide to understanding Livingstone's faith, though this aspect of that tradition does not appear in his essay. This insistence on the essential relationship of saving souls and social transformation, associated especially with the American evangelist Charles G. Finney, had already been articulated clearly by a leader of the LMS, Dr John Philip, the resident director of the LMS in South Africa. It was on the basis of this particular theological understanding that Philip explained and defended his 'political' role in South Africa which offended so many. He summed up what it meant in his phrase 'Christianity and Civilisation'.[14]

We know that Livingstone read with approval works by Charles Finney, a passionate Abolitionist and the most famous preacher and leader in this theological tradition.[15] The 'Finneyite' approach insisted that slaveholding was not simply morally or politically wrong but that it was a sin that merited the breaking off of Christian fellowship with the slaveholder. This was far too radical an approach for most British evangelicals at the time but it was this tradition that played an important role in shaping David Livingstone's faith.[16] The terrible situation of Black slavery in America, a 'Christian' nation, was never far from his mind. This was very clear when, later, Livingstone talked about the potential of Central Africa for the production of cotton.

What excited him was his belief that Central Africa could supply the British market, the primary market for American cotton, and by replacing the slave-produced cotton would help to bring down American slavery by destroying its financial profitability.

Livingstone's essay and his answers to the LMS questionnaire received no reply at all from London. There is nothing in the LMS archives to explain why the officials of the society did not reply. His father, perturbed by this second long silence, eventually decided to write to the society on his son's behalf on 26 April 1838. Neil warned the LMS directors that this was done without his son's knowledge and that he wanted this to remain so. Again there is nothing in the archives to indicate how this letter was received, and there was yet another long interval without any word from London, which must have depressed the Livingstones. Finally, at the beginning of August 1838, David was invited to appear before the directors in London on 13th of the month to be interviewed.

Arriving in London on Friday 10 August, the young Scot went to the LMS boarding house at 57 Aldersgate Street. There Livingstone met a young man, Joseph Moore, who was also in London to be examined by the directors of the LMS. They wandered through the city on Saturday. On the Sunday, they attended a morning, afternoon and evening service in different churches in order to listen to three famous preachers, Anglican and Nonconformist. In a note Moore provided for Blaikie he went on to say:

> On Monday we passed our first examination. On Tuesday we went to Westminster Abbey. Who that had seen those two young men pass from monument to monument could have divined that one of them would one day be buried with a nation's – rather with the civilised world's – lament, in that sacred shrine? The wildest fancy could not have pictured that such an honour awaited David Livingstone. I grew daily more attached to him. If I were asked why, I would be rather at a loss to reply. There was truly an indescribable charm about him, which, with all his rather ungainly ways, and by no means winning face, attracted almost every one, and which helped him so much in his after-wanderings in Africa.[17]

Moore's remark about Livingstone's African life is conjecture since Moore was never in Africa. His witness to Livingstone's ability to attract the affection of people reinforces, however, what had happened at the Andersonian, where he had made lifelong friends of Professors Buchanan, Wilson and Graham as well as of 'Paraffin' Young. Moore was the first of the group of friends made by Livingstone during his time in London. Not everyone he met felt this 'indescribable charm' talked of by Moore; for others, Livingstone's stubborn determination not to be defeated, and his obsessive focus on what was to be achieved at any cost, was too much to bear. A failure on the part of others to be equally committed, and equally single-minded, too often led Livingstone to respond with scathing condemnation.

After a second set of interviews on 20 September, Moore and Livingstone were accepted as probationary candidates for service with the LMS. As was usual with such candidates for service as ordained ministers in the mission, they were sent for a three-month preparatory course to Chipping Ongar in Essex. There the students lived in a student residence but went daily to the Reverend Richard Cecil for classes. Under Cecil's instruction the students continued to develop their Latin and Greek and began the study of Hebrew. If, after three months or so, Richard Cecil pronounced himself satisfied, they were sent to a Nonconformist seminary, usually Cheshunt College. On top of the heavy burden of class work, the students were also supposed to preach regularly to nearby congregations. The form of instruction on the art of preaching given by their teacher was hardly in keeping with the idea of evangelical enthusiasm. The student was supposed to write out his sermon in full, have it corrected by Mr Cecil, commit it to memory, and then deliver it without notes as a sort of recitation. Livingstone was notoriously unsatisfactory in the eyes of the authorities in performing these exercises. On one occasion, at a church in nearby Stanford Rivers, he simply 'froze' and, after apologising to the congregation, left the pulpit.[18] He was considered rustic and somewhat uncouth by many, though enough Scots had already passed through the training programme of the LMS to have got rid of the attitude that equated a Scots accent with backwardness. After all, Livingstone had had a scientific training superior to that available to most other candidates. Yet class, nationality and the arts bias of British culture all combined to make him even more of an outsider in Essex and London than he had been in Glasgow.

Moore writes of both himself and Livingstone being reported to the board of directors as unsatisfactory, but insisted that someone at the board pleaded for them each to have a second chance. Nothing in the records confirms this. The three month report sent in December 1838 by Mr Cecil is no longer in the records of the LMS. Cecil wrote to the board again on 26 January 1839 and again on 23 February. In the first letter Cecil refers to his previous report of the unsatisfactory aspects of Livingstone's performance, but then goes on

> but he has sense, and quick vigour; his temper is good and his character substantial; so that I do not like the thought of his being rejected. Add to his stock of knowledge, and then I trust he will prove, after all, an instrument worth having ... If the decision now were coming on I should say accept him.[19]

In the February letter Cecil continued to support Livingstone's worthiness but was still doubtful as to whether he was ready for the classical theological course at Cheshunt. In June 1839 the society decided to accept Livingstone. The directors wisely acceded to his request that they allow him to continue to study with Mr Cecil until the end of the year and then to support him not at Cheshunt but in London, while he undertook to further his study of medicine.

The directors, before agreeing to this course of action, initially suggested that he might go to serve somewhere in the West Indies. Livingstone was not written to directly on this matter but was first sounded out by Cecil. In response Livingstone wrote to the directors:

> Having been informed a few days ago by Mr Cecil, that there had been some intimation of a wish on the part of the Directors, that I should be employed in the West Indies in preference to South Africa, and being desirous to enter upon that sphere of labour, and, I trust, that only, in which I may be able most efficiently to advance the great cause of our Blessed Redeemer; permit me to state, the following particulars for their consideration, previous to coming to a final decision in my case.[20]

He went on to point out his initial scientific and medical training would be wasted if he was sent now to the West Indies, as there were plenty of properly qualified doctors there and he could not practise in competition with them. In any case going to the West Indies was far too like a settled pastorate at home, which was exactly what he did not want. He also wanted to study medicine further, as he had already requested.

In London he went to stay again in the missionary boarding house at 57 Aldersgate Street. The landlady there, Mrs Sewell, with whom Livingstone was to correspond regularly for many years, was another of those who recognised the 'indescribable charm' that some saw in the young Scot.[21] It was at 57 Aldersgate Street that Robert Moffat, a veteran of twenty years service in southern Africa, first met the man who was later to become his son-in-law. Moffat recalled meeting him on a number of occasions when his young fellow Scot took the chance to ask him questions about Africa. In an article on Livingstone, in *Sunday at Home* in July 1874, Moffat said that at that time he found Livingstone 'preparing to go forth as a medical missionary to China'. Again in his notes sent to help Blaikie with his biography of Livingstone, Moffat wrote of this budding relationship

> By and by he asked me whether I thought he would do for Africa. I said I believed he would, if he would not go to an old station, but would advance to unoccupied ground, specifying the vast plain to the north, where I had sometimes seen in the morning sun the smoke of a thousand villages where no missionary had ever been. At last Livingstone said: 'What is the use of my waiting for the end of this

abominable opium war? I will go at once to Africa.' The Directors concurred and Africa became his sphere.[22]

Livingstone himself wrote, in the opening chapter of his *Missionary Travels and Researches*, as if he had been waiting for the ending of the Opium War in order to enter China until turned to Africa by Moffat. This seems an excellent example of how friends' memories can come together to agree on a version of events that is not quite what appears to be the case to later investigators.

In the letter which Livingstone wrote to the directors on 2 July 1839, several months before he moved to London, he declined the society's suggestion of sending him to the West Indies 'in preference to South Africa'. Undoubtedly the situation in China, which became a formally declared war in September of that year, had already led the LMS to put an embargo on sending new missionaries there. It is also clear, however, that five months before he met Moffat, Livingstone had already opted for South Africa. His repeated questioning of Moffat about Africa, and his eventual asking the veteran whether he was suited for Africa, is in keeping with this earlier decision as well as with the recollection in the minds of both men years later.

When Livingstone left Ongar after his extra months of classical theological training he went to London to continue his medical studies. The LMS had agreed to support him while he was taking classes at the British and Foreign Medical School in London. At the Andersonian Livingstone had worked primarily, though not exclusively, at what would now be called 'pre-clinical' subjects, and therefore lacked significant clinical training. He began to rectify this by getting in as much clinical practice as possible, attending the classes of Dr J. Risdon Bennett at Charing Cross Hospital medical school as well as two of Bennett's clinics. He also went to the Hunterian Museum, where he studied comparative anatomy under Professor Richard Owen. Bennett's father was a famous Nonconformist preacher whose church Livingstone attended later in the year when pressure of work forced him to give up trying to take services himself every Sunday. He had attempted this on coming to London, taking services on Sundays at Tyler's Green or Blackmore, but on top of his medical work it became too much for him.

Risdon Bennett described Livingstone's initial workload in the notes he sent to Blaikie, a workload that was over and above classes at the British and Foreign Medical School.

> I was at that time Physician to the Aldersgate Street Dispensary, and was lecturing at the Charing Cross Hospital on the practice of medicine, and thus was able to

obtain for him free admission to hospital practice as well as attendance on my lectures and my practice at the dispensary. I think that I also obtained for him admission to the ophthalmic hospital in Moorfields.[23]

When Bennett's class was finished at the end of April Livingstone sought to register for other clinical classes at St Bartholomew's. He now ran into difficulty. Barts took the line that a missionary candidate could take as many classes as he could fit into the time, but he had to pay the class fee for at least one. So, late in April 1840, Livingstone wrote to Arthur Tidman, one of the secretaries of the LMS, asking the society to pay this fee. He pointed out that he has chosen the cheapest course on the Barts list as the one for which he had opted to pay.[24] The LMS paid the fee and Livingstone continued his studies at the same frenetic pace, he and another medical student working at their books together after their clinical work was over and trying to get by on four hours sleep in the twenty-four. In July Livingstone fell ill and his friend Moore thought he might never see him again after escorting him onto a boat for Glasgow. After a few weeks in Scotland, however, he returned to London and his studies with as much vigour as ever.

When he had completed what was then held to be the full medical curriculum, Livingstone felt depressed, since it was clear to him that the society would not pay for him to take the examinations of the Royal College of Surgeons in London. As he wrote to another Scottish student at Ongar, Henry Dickson from Edinburgh, who was to die on the way to his first posting in Samoa, 'but its no great matter I shall be able to practise medicine amongst the Bechuana as well without as with the Licence of the Royal College of Surgeons'.[25] The LMS did agree, however, to pay the much lower examination fees of the Royal College of Physicians and Surgeons of Glasgow, the body whose examinations he would have undertaken in any case had he stayed on at Anderson's. On 15 November 1840 Livingstone was examined by the college and passed. Something very typical of the man took place at the examination.

> Having completed the medical curriculum and presented a thesis on a subject which required the use of the stethoscope for its diagnosis, I unwittingly procured for myself an examination rather more severe and prolonged than usual among examining bodies. The reason was, that between me and the examiners a slight difference of opinion existed as to whether this instrument could do what was asserted. The wiser plan would have been to have no opinion of my own.[26]

On this visit to Glasgow he was able to spend only one night with his family in Blantyre. David felt that they had so much to speak about they should sit up all night, but his mother would not hear of it. Sister Janet remembered well that cold November morning when he left Blantyre for the last time before setting out:

> On the morning of the 17th November, we got up at 5 o'clock. My mother made coffee. David read the 121st and 135th Psalms, and prayed. My father and he walked to Glasgow to catch the Liverpool steamer.[27]

Livingstone was back in London for his ordination as a 'minister of word and sacraments', to use the old Scottish Presbyterian wording, at the Albion Street Chapel in Finsbury on the evening of 20 November. The Reverend J. J. Freeman, later to be home secretary of the LMS, and Livingstone's old tutor at Ongar, Richard Cecil, conducted the service. William Ross, who went to South Africa with Livingstone, was ordained at the same service. The ordination is clearly recorded and it is therefore surprising that some of his biographers have implied that Livingstone was not a minister of religion.

A number of books on Livingstone have referred to his relationship with a young woman, Catherine Ridley, during his time at Ongar. Some have portrayed this as a frustrated love affair, Livingstone being seen as in love with Miss Ridley and being devastated by her choosing a fellow student at the LMS establishment at Ongar, Thomas Prentice; so much so that it affected his life for years to come.[28] There is no doubt that Livingstone had an affection for her. The evidence upon which to build the story of a life-shaping love affair consists, however, of one letter to her and six to Prentice, together with some short references to her in letters to others. All six of these letters were written after Thomas and Catherine had become engaged to be married. The references certainly make clear that Livingstone thought that part of Prentice's appeal to her had been his intention of becoming a missionary, which he did not fulfil because of ill health.[29]

What is clear from the letters is that Livingstone never declared his feelings to Catherine and that, as early as May 1840 he knew that she had accepted Prentice's proposal. Livingstone says so in May 1840, in a letter to his ill-fated fellow student Henry Dickson. At one time Livingstone had given her a book and she had given him one, Charles Bridges's *Reflections on the 119th Psalm,* but there is no reason see this exchange as especially significant when one reads his opening words to her in the one letter that we have. The letter was written from the ship on which he was travelling to the Cape soon after leaving Rio de Janeiro. At this time he presumed Prentice was coming to work for the LMS in South Africa.

> My Dear Friend, You must not be surprised at the liberty I take in addressing you so for I can claim relationship to you through a third party whom we both consider a dear friend.

He then went on to describe his visit to Rio and the countryside around the city. He encouraged her to write to him for information about the missions in South Africa and what she might expect there, and he promised to tell her 'plainly'. The letter ends

> I have your 'Bridges' by me in my berth and often get my heart warmed by his heavenly minded reflections. Many thanks for it.
>
> May every blessing attend you is the prayer of
> Yours affectionately,
> David Livingston

There is no doubt he was upset that she and Prentice did not come out as missionaries – Prentice gave up any idea even of the home ministry and became a wool merchant. This did not prevent David from continuing to write to Prentice and from expecting letters back from him. The last of his extant letters to Prentice was written on 9 October 1843. It ends

> How is old Mr Ridley and Susan and all? I like much just to hear how it is with everyone I ever knew. Is Elizabeth pious now? Will you present my Christian salutations to Mr W. Ridley. Could he spend a thought or two on being a missionary to the Brazils and the immense population there?
>
> May His presence be with your dear Catherine and comfort her as only He can. I hope your little boy will be a missionary. Please give him a press to your heart for me. Please present my affectionate salutations to Catherine. I can't think of her as Mrs P. and will always name her as she was when I first saw her. To your Father, Mother and Brothers. Surely Fison might as easily give me a note as write some nonsense from Greek plays.
>
> Ever affectionately yours,
> David Livingston [30]

How much longer their correspondence continued we do not know, but the letters to Prentice do not differ in tone from the many letters he wrote to others who had been fellow students at Ongar. In any case these letters can hardly be seen as coming from a man struggling to cope with losing the love of his life.

While in London we know that Livingstone took time off from the frenetic rush to complete the medical curriculum in order to attend a massive public meeting at Exeter Hall on 1 June 1840.[31] At this meeting Fowell Buxton, Wilberforce's successor as leader of the antislavery movement, set in motion a chain of events that produced the Niger Expedition of 1841. The prestige of the meeting can be measured by Queen Victoria's consort, Prince Albert, choosing to make attending it one of his first public appearances after his marriage. Buxton's message was that it was Christianity and commerce that would solve Africa's problems: above all, these two together would eliminate the slave trade. Africans had a hunger now for European manufactured goods; and, in order to obtain these, chiefs sold other Africans as slaves. If legitimate European commerce could only penetrate Africa and promote the cultivation of products Europe wanted to buy, then these could be exchanged for European goods, uplifting African standards of living and ending the slave trade. At the same time, the work of Christian missions in preaching the Gospel and in developing schools would aid the process and in turn be aided by it.

This was a version of what Livingstone was to urge on the British public later. Although it has been asserted that Livingstone got his vision at the Exeter Hall meeting, this is very unlikely. The relationship of civilisation and Christianity had been debated hotly in missionary circles from the 1790s onwards. The form that the argument took in Buxton's linking of Christianity and commerce had already been clearly articulated by Dr John Philip. In his *Researches in South Africa*, published in London in 1828, Philip had insisted on the creative relationship of what he called 'civilisation' with Christianity. Philip pointed out that civilisation need not bring Christianity, but he insisted Christianity would always bring civilisation. Philip's concept of civilisation encompassed education to the highest available level but also what can only be called 'commerce', with great emphasis on the creative impact of free trade and free labour upon any society.

This is in the last analysis the same argument that Buxton made at the great rally. There is a good possibility that in the months of consultation between Philip and Buxton during 1827 and 1828, while Philip was writing his *Researches*, it may have been Philip who presented the idea to Buxton. Whatever the case, Philip's book was undoubtedly the product of a relationship he developed with Buxton during the two years that he spent in England. At the well-publicised Exeter Hall event Buxton gave his imprimatur to a precise understanding of the relationship of civilisation and Christianity that had been the subject of lively controversy in missionary circles for years. Though Buxton at Exeter Hall did not introduce Livingstone to the idea of the combined power of Christianity, civilisation and commerce, this enormously impressive event may well have etched it yet more strongly on his mind.

On 8 December 1840 Livingstone set sail from London, along with Mr and Mrs Ross, for the Cape of Good Hope on the barque *George*. Livingstone had been used to steamships in the British coastal waters taking him to and from Scotland. Steamships were not yet used, however, for long haul voyages to places like Cape Town. Although there were not the fearful risks and the loss of life that such long voyages had entailed in the seventeenth and eighteenth centuries, every voyage in a wooden sailing ship, even in the

1840s, was still an adventure. What would this voyage hold for the young cotton-spinner become physician and pastor, and what lay ahead of him at the Cape of Good Hope?

3

The LMS and Southern Africa

When David Livingstone arrived in Cape Town in March 1841, the LMS had been in southern Africa for forty-two years.[1] The first party of LMS missionaries, led by Dr Johannes van der Kemp, had arrived in Cape Town on 31 March 1799 and found that all the peoples south of the Zambesi were in the midst of major political and social changes. By the time of Livingstone's arrival, this had had a severe impact on society as far north as what are now Zambia and Malawi.

In order to understand the situation one has to go back to one of the principal roots of this period of almost continuous change in southern Africa. First one must go back to April 1652, when Jan van Riebeeck raised the flag of the Dutch East India Company on the shore of Table Bay, where Cape Town was to develop. Van Riebeeck claimed part of the Cape peninsula for the Dutch East India Company. His primary concern was to control Table Bay for the benefit of the company's fleet. The bay had been used for many years by Portuguese, Dutch, English and French ships going to and from the Indies. The Netherlanders, having claimed the land for themselves, started to build a permanent settlement but did not close the anchorage to ships of other nations. Instead they made a profit from allowing foreign ships to use Table Bay as a revictualling station, gaining Cape Town its nickname of 'Tavern of the Seas'. On shore the sick from these ships (and until well into the nineteenth century there were always many of these) could regain their health and the ships could be cleaned, repaired and restocked with food and water. Meanwhile the hotels and inns of the town flourished as passengers stayed on shore.

At first the company had not wanted to extend its authority inland. The Dutch traded for cattle and sheep with the local African population, the Khoi,[2] and, in addition, a few whites were allowed to farm vegetables and grain. The area that these new permanent white residents farmed expanded slowly but steadily, and the arrival of Huguenot refugees in the 1690s added vineyards to this expanding world of the white farming and stock-raising community. These permanent settlers of Dutch, Huguenot and German origins began to call themselves Boers (Dutch for farmer) or

Afrikaners, in order to make clear who they were over against the people of Cape Town and company officials.

Who were the Africans that were there before the coming of van Riebeeck and the growth of this white community? In what is now called the Western Cape and northwards into present-day Namibia were the Khoisan peoples. The Khoi, called Hottentots by the whites, were light-skinned cattle herders, though further north some lived as hunter-gatherers. The San people were physically smaller and lived mainly as hunter-gatherers and were called by the whites 'Bushmen'. Unknown to those aboard the ships visiting Table Bay, and at first ignored by the inhabitants of the small European settlement, there lived to the east and north east a much denser population of peoples speaking languages that belong to the Bantu family of languages as classified by modern philologists.

Throughout a large part of the twentieth century one school of scholars asserted that these Bantu-speaking peoples were newcomers to southern Africa. When the whites in the Cape expanded northwards and eastwards and, in the eighteenth century, met these peoples, they insisted that it was a meeting of two different groups of recent invaders who had arrived in southern Africa at roughly the same period. By the 1970s this hypothesis had been set aside because of the mass of evidence that showed that, though the Bantu-speaking peoples did come from further north: they had arrived in southern Africa centuries before van Reibeeck, indeed before the end of the first millennium.

These Bantu-speaking peoples belonged to one or other of two groups which are linguistically distinct. The first group, which was and is the larger numerically of the two, is made up of those usually referred to by scholars as the Nguni. The Nguni are today divided into two closely related language groups, Xhosa and Zulu. The Nguni occupied the lowlands and foothills that run from Delagoa Bay round to the Sunday's River in the Eastern Cape. The Great Escarpment, which follows the curving South African coast at a distance varying from forty to nearly a hundred miles, separates the lands of the Nguni peoples from the inland area of the high veld. This rolling savanna land of the high veld, varying in altitude from three to over six thousand feet, with a number of mountains reaching much greater heights, stretches northward through eastern Africa as far as Kenya. The valleys of the Limpopo and the Zambesi rivers cut across the high veld as do the Great Lakes, Malawi and Tanganyika.

South of the Limpopo the majority of the peoples inhabiting this high veld country spoke languages of the Sotho-Tswana family, all of which are mutually intelligible. The population density, though lighter than among

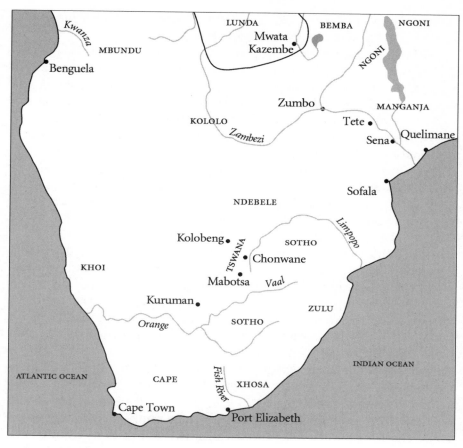

1. Southern Africa.

the Nguni, was heavier in the east and became gradually thinner the further westward one travelled towards the Kalahari Desert.

All of these Bantu-speaking peoples were cattle herders who also pursued hoe cultivation. Their social structure was sophisticated and the Nguni, in particular, were militarily efficient, using the shield, throwing spears, the war axe and the short stabbing spear. The Nguni had long been in contact with the Khoi and had absorbed them rather than conquered them. In the first two decades of the nineteenth century European observers in the eastern Cape indeed commented on the way certain Khoi clans were in the process of becoming the Gqunukhwebe subdivision of the Xhosa. The existence in both Xhosa and Zulu of three of the 'clicks' characteristic of the Khoi language, the 'click' is a phenomenon which appears in no other Bantu language, is very clear evidence of the longevity of this two-way process of absorption.

In the eighteenth century the white population of the Dutch East India Company colony gradually divided into three groups, though there was always some degree of overlap. The first group was made up of the Dutch East India Company officials, and the innkeepers, merchants and craftsmen who made up the white population of Cape Town, which always had a cosmopolitan flavour because of the stream of ships of all nations that used Table Bay. The second group developed in an area of land enjoying a Mediterranean climate, in what is now called the Western Cape. In this area a community of rich farmers had grown up by the second half of the eighteenth century, producing citrus fruit, grapes, wine and brandy as well as wheat. They had built solid farmhouses at the centre of their large estate farms. These were worked by slaves, indentured Khoi and mixed race servants. They had also begun to build small towns such as Stellenbosch and Swellendam. Beyond them, spreading out further and further from Cape Town, were the families who were stock farmers and hunters. These men and women were the third group, the *trekboers* always seeking the *lekker lewe* – the sweet life – over the next ridge. They had few slaves but always a large following of Khoi servants, many of whom were related by blood to the core white family of the group. It was these trekboers who first referred to themselves as 'Afrikaner', rather than the usual Boer, to distinguish themselves from other whites. It was among these communities, dominated by whites but including Khoi and mixed race servants who greatly outnumbered them, that there developed the new much simplified and more flexible form of Dutch with a vocabulary expanded by African borrowings. This language, originally called *die Taal* – the Tongue – was the root of modern Afrikaans.

During this same period the Khoi people of the Cape ceased to exist as an autonomous people. By the 1770s the vast majority constituted a rural working class serving the settled farms of the west or the trekboer communities of the north and east. This change had been greatly accelerated by two destructive outbreaks of smallpox in 1713 and 1755. These wreaked an appalling loss of life among the Khoi, who had no in-built resistance to the imported disease. By the end of the eighteenth century the Khoi community had become a new people, speaking Afrikaans and having a strong admixture of European ancestry among many but not all families. They were becoming the 'Cape Coloureds', though they came to refer to themselves as *die Kaapse Volk*, the Cape People or Cape Folk. When the slaves, those of Indonesian as well as African origin, were freed in 1834, they merged into and became part of the Cape Folk. Many whites still called the whole community 'Hottentots' until the last quarter of the twentieth century.

The Dutch East India Company made little or no attempt to oversee the slow but steady advance of the trekboers to the east and north east throughout the eighteenth century. So long as they presented no problems to the administration, they were left alone. The company was totally dependent upon them to supply the almost insatiable demand of Cape Town and its busy harbour for beef and mutton. In return the trekboers were happy to be left alone so long as they could get coffee, tobacco and ammunition in return for their cattle and sheep. In addition they wanted to be in touch with a minister of the state church (the Nederduits Gereformeerde Kerk) from time to time, the gap sometimes extending as long as three years, in order to have children baptised and marriages solemnised. When he later ran into this among the Transvaalers, Livingstone categorised it as hypocrisy.

In the 1770s the company could no longer turn a blind eye to the expansion of the trekboer communities. This was for two reasons. First in the north east the trekboers had become engaged in bitter fighting with San groups who had organised a bloody guerilla campaign against the farmers in the Sneeuberg Mountains. So effective were the San that they provoked the most savage reprisals against them by trekboer commandos. The reports of many horrifying acts, with women and children shot down like game animals, forced the authorities in Cape Town to call on the local leaders to explain themselves. These men sent to Cape Town a document explaining their conduct, though they did not take company authority all that seriously. As the company had no troops on the frontier, and did not intend to send any, as long as the company did not cut off their supply of ammunition, the trekboers did not need to pay much heed to the officials in Cape Town.

The second reason for company concern was that a much more serious situation had arisen to the east of the colony. Officials in Cape Town had long known that beyond the Gamtoos river lay the frontier communities of the Xhosa people. They knew the Xhosa were formidable militarily. As early as the 1730s they had wiped out a large party of well-armed elephant hunters from the Cape who had challenged Xhosa authority. By the middle of the century the Cape authorities had issued instructions that no one was to enter Xhosa territory, even for purposes of trade. This edict had only affected a few adventurers until about 1770, when trekboer groups brought their cattle to the Gamtoos river and contemplating crossing it. This would have brought them into conflict with Xhosa chiefs who saw this area of the Zuurveld as potential additional pasturage for their herds. The company now declared that the boundary of the colony was a line drawn from the Bruintje's Hoogte Mountains to the mouth of the Gamtoos river. The company in this case, as in the case of the Sneeuberg frontier, did not have the resources to make their proclamations effective. Some trekboer groups had indeed already crossed the Gamtoos. In an attempt to catch up with the vanguard of the trekboers and keep them under company authority, the governor in Cape Town in 1775 declared that the frontier was now the Bushman's River. There then followed a period of a few years when Xhosa groups and trekboer groups mingled in the Zuurveld, on the whole peacefully. Trouble, however, was inevitable since the trekboers were by then insisting that the Great Fish River was the real frontier and that therefore legally the Xhosa presence in the Zuurveld was transitory and ought to be prohibited. On the other hand, the Ghunukwebe division of the Xhosa, citing their Khoi antecedents, claimed correctly that the Zuurveld was their ancestral land. In 1780 serious fighting broke out between the trekboers and the Xhosa and the authorities in Cape Town were drawn into the fighting. The one hundred years of white-Xhosa conflict on the eastern frontier had begun.

Initially sporadic fighting led to no clear resolution. This was changed when in 1795 the British seized the Cape in order to protect their connections with India in the war against France. At the peace of Amiens in 1802 they handed it over to the Batavian Republic, as the Netherlands was known at that time, only to occupy it again in 1806 and then retain it permanently in accordance with the peace settlement decided upon at the Congress of Vienna in 1815.

The main difference that British rule brought was not its endorsement of urban liberal attitudes that clashed with the very old-fashioned values of Afrikaner society, as has often been suggested. What they did bring was the desire, and more important the will and power, to make their rule effective up to the recognised frontiers. There was to be no more *lekker lewe* where the trekboer communities were free to pursue their own policies. There was to be effective British rule throughout the colony. The Xhosa were the first to feel the effects of this new power with bloody defeats in 1809 and 1812.

The firepower of redcoat infantry and grapeshot from cannon brought a devastating and completely new dimension to warfare to southern Africa.

The stamp of firm British government authority also profoundly affected the trekboers. It led them to become keenly aware that their way of life was threatened. When British legislation in 1809 and 1811 gave some minimal recognition of civil rights 'for all His Majesty's subjects' in the Cape, the seeds of open conflict were being sown. This legislation allowed the so-called 'Coloured' indentured servants to bring cases against their masters in court. Up till then people of Khoi ancestry had no standing whatever in a court within the colony. To many Afrikaners this legal recognition given to the 'Coloureds' was an intolerable affront to their own dignity as a people.

The missionaries of the LMS who first arrived in the Cape in 1799 made this situation worse in the eyes of the trekboer community by their consistent assertion of the equality before God of all peoples. In keeping with their belief that equality before God bore some relationship to equality in this life, the leading LMS missionaries Johannes van der Kemp and James Read helped many Cape Folk bring their masters to court to face charges of ill treatment under the new legislation. Van der Kemp died before most cases came to court, but Read carried on his work after his leader's death.

Soon after Dr John Philip arrived in Cape Town in 1819, as resident director of the LMS in South Africa, his policies contributed to this situation becoming even more tense.[3] Philip has remained celebrated in South African history for his insistence that the preaching of equality before God must be made actual and manifest in the laws of the colony. When in 1828 the British government, by an order in council, made equality before the law a reality in the Cape Colony, a result of Philip's influence with the aged Wilberforce and his successor, Fowell Buxton, as head of the Antislavery Society, many trekboers saw this as the last straw.[4] They were joined in complaints against Philip and the LMS by the new British settlers who had arrived in 1820 and been settled by the British government on the eastern Xhosa frontier. When, in 1834, all the slaves in the British Empire were made free the tension reached fever pitch, as by this act there were two free 'people of colour' for every white in the Colony.

In response many Afrikaners, about one third of the total, gathered together in well-organised and well-prepared parties. They had sent out reconnaissance groups as early as 1830, and the leaders of these parties then began to lead their people out of the colony in a mass migration.[5] This trek, the Great Trek or Voortrek, led to the settlement of well-armed Boer communities beyond the Orange river in what is now the Orange Free State and beyond the Vaal river in what is now the Transvaal. It was, in effect, a rebellion by removal against what they considered the oppressive nature of British rule. These new communities in the north soon began to see the missionaries of the LMS as their enemies and became determined to restrict any move by the LMS into what they came to see as 'their' lands. Their occupation of these lands on the high veld was greatly aided by the turmoil and loss of life among the peoples of the area during the previous twenty years. Chaka's creation by 1818 of a unified Zulu military state was at least partly to blame for the fighting and famine that distressed the Sotho-Tswana peoples on the high veld at that time. Various militarily formidable groups including Zwangendaba's Ngoni, the Maseko Ngoni and the Ndebele of Mzilikazi fled before Chaka and fought their way across the high veld through the Tswana-Sotho speaking peoples, some of whom in turn, like Sebitwane's Kololo, joined them on the move to find new lands. These peoples settled in what are now Zimbabwe, Zambia and Malawi.[6]

In 1834–35 there also took place a particularly bitter war between the colony and the Xhosa, during which Philip and many LMS missionaries again became the object of bitter criticism from the British settlers, even more than from the Afrikaners. These settlers had been placed by the British government on land that the Xhosa considered theirs, and from which they had only recently been driven, so the British settlers bore the brunt of the Xhosa attack. The settlers were furious with Philip because, although he called on indigenous Christians to support the colony while the fighting lasted, he also insisted publicly, in words widely reported in the British papers, that the Xhosa had not been to blame for the war. He asserted that British policy and the behaviour of the frontier farmers had led to such injustice for the Xhosa that war had become inevitable. The Xhosa, he insisted, were not the 'irreclaimable savages' that the Governor, Sir Benjamin D'Urban, and the editor of the *Grahamstown Journal* had deemed them.[7] Philip at this time worked with his son-in-law, John Fairbairn, and the radical Afrikaner Andries Stockenstrom in seeking racial justice within the colony and a peaceful settlement with the Xhosa. Their activities were the beginnings of what some have called 'Cape Liberalism'. This movement had probably its greatest triumph early in its development. This was when Fairbairn and Stockenstrom, while Philip lay dying, led a successful campaign which guaranteed a low-qualification non-racial franchise for the new Cape Parliament which met for the first time in 1853.

In this context David Livingstone made two important contributions to affairs in southern Africa. He brought to the attention of the British public the danger that the Transvaalers might attempt to block any missionaries going to the north. Secondly, for a few months in 1852, he took the place of Philip, who died in 1851, as the leading critic of British policy in South Africa.

Outside the colony to the north, the LMS had from the beginning begun work among the Tswana-Sotho peoples of the high veld as well as in the two small Griqua states north of the Orange River.[8] John Philip had also, during a visit to Europe in 1827–28, persuaded the Protestant Paris Missionary Society and the Rhenish Mission Society to send missionaries to South Africa.[9] At his suggestion the French Protestants went outside the colony to settle with Moshweshwe as he built a powerful Sotho kingdom.

The furthest north of all the mission stations outside the colony was Kuruman. This area was first evangelised by James Read and Cupido Kakkelak, but it was to be made his own by Robert Moffat. He arrived there at the station among the Tlhaping division of the Tswana under chief Mothibi in 1820. Moffat and his wife, Mary, spent the first eight years there, creating well-irrigated and productive gardens and putting up the basic buildings of a permanent mission station. By 1829 Kuruman was considered a success; a success that led to Moffat being considered by many in Britain as the African missionary par excellence, to be surpassed by Livingstone only after the latter's death. In that year Moffat completed the construction of the new permanent school building, he baptised the first converts, and work on his church building was begun. He also completed his translation of the Gospel according to Luke into Tswana and paid the first of his visits to Mzilikazi, chief of the Ndebele, the leader of the most powerful military force in central African affairs until they were finally crushed by Rhodes in 1896.

The majority of LMS missionaries worked with Cape Folk communities within the colony, though a substantial minority worked with the Griqua and Tswana groups outside the colony to the north and others among the Xhosa to the east. Under Philip's leadership, as resident director of the society, they had been allowed a great deal of individual autonomy in their work. On the eve of Livingstone's going to southern Africa, however, the LMS board in London decided that southern Africa should be divided into areas, and that each area should have a missionary committee which would control the work in the area. This was something that neither Philip nor Moffat had wanted. The board of directors in London had long been aware of deep differences of opinion among the missionaries on many subjects. Some felt that Philip was too concerned about politics and was pro-African in an unbalanced way (the 'Colonial Party' Livingstone was to call them); others resented the prominence of Philip or Moffat or of both. The committee structure, the directors believed, would help bring better order to the varied activities of the society as well as better relations among the staff, as this structure would make manifest the essential equality of all staff. This was to ignore the fact that the new structure did nothing to alleviate the tension between artisan missionaries and those who were ordained. It was this tension which accounted to a significant degree for the bad relations that were to develop between Livingstone and his colleague Rogers Edwards when they set up the mission station at Mabotsa together.

4

Kuruman and Mabotsa

When Livingstone embarked on the brig *George* with the two other missionaries, William Ross and his wife, they were starting a voyage that was to
take them to Rio de Janeiro before they reached Cape Town four months
later. Their passage was very different from what was to become the norm
only forty years later, a swift passage on a powerful steel steamship in
conditions that were comfortable even in third class. Travelling to South
Africa on a wooden sailing brig in 1840 was still a very uncomfortable,
tedious experience in cramped accommodation with minimum privacy that
lasted many months. It also continued to involve real danger, even if there
were no longer pirates off Rio, as there had been in 1800 when a ship
carrying fifteen LMS missionaries had been taken by sea rovers. Livingstone,
believing that his friend Prentice with his bride Catherine would soon be
following him out to South Africa, wrote to warn them of what to expect
on such a voyage.

> Get a swinging cot to sleep in instead of a mattress – a swinging tray. Take no
> edibles except perhaps a few oranges or apples, some seidlitz powders and a few
> lemonade and soda. Not more than two trunks for the cabin. Let those contain
> all you need for the voyage, part of them of easy access. Have all your other goods
> in airtight boxes and don't open them while at sea ... Expect to be sick and take
> nothing from your trunks until that is over ... you will need a lantern for your
> berth. A folio is perhaps better than a writing desk. Get your bedding and
> everything else arranged previous to sailing and you need not be downcast, though
> I have told you of the disagreeable ordeal through which you have to pass.[1]

After crossing the Bay of Biscay in continuously stormy weather, an even
fiercer storm off the Cape Verde islands drove the *George* westwards and
split her mainmast so that she was in danger of foundering. The captain
decided to head for Rio de Janeiro, the nearest port where the necessary
repairs could be made. Livingstone's description of these storms showed
both his insouciance in the face of danger and the somewhat acid sense of
humour that would characterise him all his life. He wrote:

> Our little vessel went reeling and staggering over the waves as if she had been
> drunk, our trunks perpetually breaking from their lashings were tossed from one

side of the cabin to the other, everything both pleasant and unpleasant [a reference to seasickness] huddled together in glorious confusion. You have been on board a steamer; that is nothing to a little sailing vessel in a stormy sea such as we had when, about the Bay of Biscay, she writhed and twisted about terribly. Imagine if you can a ship in a fit of epilepsy. My nervous system not being over sensitive enabled me calmly to contemplate the whole scene and certainly I never beheld such a mess before, it might well be called 'the world turned upside down'. The storm I won't attempt to describe. It went beyond description and I hope you will see one yourself.[2]

While the ship was in Rio, Livingstone was the only passenger who ventured ashore. He not only visited the sights of the city, such as the cathedral, but also went out beyond the city limits into the forest. There he stripped off his clothes and took a shower by standing under a small waterfall. He told Prentice that such a shower 'with a flesh-brush and perhaps a pair of horse-hair gloves' would do more to maintain his health than all the medicines in his medical bag.[3] In the forest he also made friends with a peasant family with whom he shared a meal, all this in an area that he was told was too dangerous for sensible people to enter.

He was very unhappy about the British and American sailors in Rio who, unlike those of other nations, appeared to be constantly drunk and were frequently involved in brawls. He decided to try to do something about this and ventured into a notorious dockside pub to distribute tracts and appeal to the sailors there to behave better. While it might be thought that he was lucky to get away with this, and that his actions were brave but naive, this ignores Livingstone's background in working-class Blantyre and Glasgow. He was no middle-class innocent wandering into a situation beyond his ken.[4]

While all the other passengers appeared apprehensive about going ashore in Rio, Livingstone loved the place and, what is remarkable for an evangelical Protestant of the mid nineteenth century, expressed his admiration for the Catholic Church there, even if somewhat lightheartedly. In the rhetoric of many of his Protestant contemporaries, Rome appears more the enemy than Islam, paganism or irreligion. In contrast Livingstone wrote to his old friend Watt saying:

> I did not regret going into Rio. It is certainly the finest place I ever saw. Everything delighted me except man. Even the 'church establishment' there is beautiful, they really do things in style there. If ever I join an Establishment it won't be either of the poor degenerate 'sisters' at home but the good old mother herself in Brazil.[5]

This is Livingstone free to express himself, even if half in fun. In the thousands of letters of his that have survived we see someone somewhat different from the Livingstone of his speeches and works prepared for publication. In these latter he was usually addressing the British public at large to gain their support for projects that he believed essential to the success of the Christian mission and to the development of Africa. What he wrote was shaped to achieve those ends, though even there, as we shall see when we look at his *Travels*, he could slip in some sharp pricks that reveal feelings usually unexpressed. A typical example is when he wonders in the first chapter of the *Travels* why the poor are left without school provision in England, unlike Scotland.[6]

On the long voyage Livingstone began the study of Dutch and Tswana, one the language of the majority of the population of the colony, white and black, and the other the language of the people north of the Orange where he was to work. He also spent a great deal of time with the captain of the brig; indeed Blaikie says that Captain Donaldson was 'his chief friend' on the voyage.[7] The length of the voyage enabled Donaldson to give Livingstone a thorough grounding in navigation. This was not a skill of any great use to someone who is going to settle down and work for a lifetime at creating a well-structured missionary base as Moffat had done at Kuruman.

The ship with the three missionaries on board made land at Simon's Town in Table Bay on 15 March 1841. It was to stay there for a month before going to Algoa Bay, where Port Elizabeth now is, and where the missionaries would disembark again and start their long journey to Kuruman. Livingstone's instructions from the society had been to go to Kuruman and there await the arrival of Moffat, who was still in Britain. Meanwhile, at Cape Town, Livingstone and the Rosses were guests of Dr and Mrs Philip in their house in Church Square.

While still in London, Livingstone had been aware that many in LMS circles in England, including the Moffats, were very critical of Philip. He was relieved to find that the resident director of the LMS in southern Africa was not as he had been pictured. The gossip he heard, however, was the first indication he received of the deep divisions among the missionaries in the field. It appeared to him that those among the Griqua were often at loggerheads with Moffat and his colleagues among the Tswana further north. While these same two groups, working outside the colony, were united in asserting that the work of the majority of the missionaries within the colony was not real missionary work, they resented Dr Philip's obdurate defence of the colonial missions. Those in the north thought that most of the men in the colony should be moved out to take up the task of extending the frontiers of mission. This was a position that Livingstone would come to adopt and express strongly later, when he criticised Philip in the evangelical press in Britain for his conservatism on the issue.

Livingstone discovered, however, a more important division running
through the mission community that was the basis, often hidden, of the
almost perpetual criticisms of John Philip in this period. On this matter he
took Dr Philip's part and, although he changed his first opinions on a
number of matters over the years, on this count he never changed. The
issue was race. He explained Philip's position to Prentice in a long letter
written after he had reached Kuruman:

> He has been the means of saving from the most abject and cruel slavery all the
> Hottentots and not only them but all the Aborigines beyond the Colony. The
> Boers hate him cordially. Many would think it doing God service to shoot him.
> They have an inveterate hatred of the coloured population and to him as their
> friend and advocate; you can't understand it, it is like caste in India. Can you
> believe it? Some of the missionaries have imbibed a portion of it. I name none
> but you will find none of that feeling among the friends of Dr Philip. It is entirely
> confined to the Antys [sic] party. However you will understand what is meant by
> 'Colonial feeling' when you come.[8]

He was soon to learn that it was this issue of race which had also brought
about the attacks on Philip from the British settlers on the eastern frontier.
He wrote to his friend D. G. Watt that all, or at least all whom he had met,
of Dr Philip's missionary critics shared the anti-black attitude of the British
colonists.[9] The British settlers were not only bitter about Philip's defence of
the Xhosa position over land, they went so far as to blame Philip for their
failure to achieve their war aims in the 1835 conflict with the Xhosa.[10]

At Algoa Bay Livingstone and the Rosses were held up again for a month
before they could begin the long journey by ox-wagon of over 500 miles to
Kuruman. Finally, on 19 May, they set off and reached Kuruman on the
last day of July, just over seven months after leaving London. The traveller
in an ox-wagon in those days rarely achieved more than ten miles a day,
and some have described that kind of trekking as tedious, but for Livingstone
it was not tedious but a continuously enjoyable experience. In these ten
weeks he fell in love with travelling through the bush. He loved the freedom
that it gave him and his letters are full of details about the landscape. At
first, in the foothills and then the mountains of the Drakensberg, he likened
the scenery to Scotland. As they approached the Orange river, however, the
dry plains broken up by rocky kopjes and yielding not forest but only thorn
scrub presented a landscape new and strange to him. It nevertheless fascinated him and he busied himself gathering specimens both of fauna and
flora to be sent to Professor Owen at the Hunterian Museum.

On this journey Livingstone began to talk of travelling to the north beyond
where other whites had gone. In his letters to Prentice and Watt he talked

of the stories of a freshwater lake some two months travel to the north of Kuruman and how many missionaries were excited about being the first to see it. In the same letter to Watt of 7 July he wrote:

> If they gave your humble servant a month or two to learn the colloquial language they may spare themselves the pains of being first 'in at the death'. I can acquire the language while travelling, without this ponderous vehicle, as well as by remaining at Kuruman, perhaps better for I shall live as they do and mix constantly with them and I can obtain information respecting the population etc. at the same time.[11]

Later in this letter he wrote prophetically about his future. He exposed to Watt a speculative idea about his future that in spirit though not in detail forecast his future career. He went on to undertake the exhausting toil of building a new mission station three times, he married and had children, yet all the time another vision of himself was challenging him to action. He wrote to Watt

> What do you say to my going up to Abyssinia? This is talked of by many of the missionaries as a desirable object, and some propose doing it. Would it not promote our cause by making known to the churches the awful degraded state of an immense population? Look at the map published by the Society for the diffusion of K[nowledge] you see far beyond us 'very populous country' etc. I think one may be quite safe if alone and without anything to excite the cupidity of the natives. I should cost the society nothing during these years I should be away. It might be for six or seven years before I should return but if the languages are dialects of the Bechuana I should soon make known a little of the liberal plan of mercy to the different tribes on the way and if I should never return perhaps my life will be as profitable spent as a forerunner as in any other way.[12]

From time to time this dream can also be seen in letters to a number of different people. A particularly telling example is in a letter after his marriage to Mary Moffat, which was a marriage of love and affection; yet he was able to write to Watt, possibly his closest intimate friend:

> I have read about the Jesuits in different parts lately – although quite happy and content in the married state I think I should like to commence being more of a Jesuit than I was when a batchelor [sic] and that I could begin again. I would correct many errors into which I have fallen.[13]

What he found when he got to Kuruman contributed further to his public and constant insistence on the need to explore to the north. In the barrenness of this semi-desert country, Moffat had created an oasis of luxuriant green vegetation and of European civilisation. To Livingstone's surprise, however, Kuruman was in the midst of a Tswana community of no more than two thousand people. In addition, the wider surrounding territory was also very sparsely populated. Moffat's famous remark of seeing the smoke of a thousand villages certainly did not refer to a vantage point anywhere within a hundred miles of Kuruman.

Although Livingstone agreed with the missionaries north of the Orange that too many missionaries were tied up within the colony, he began to criticise a policy which placed so many resources in the midst of such a scanty population. While waiting at Kuruman for the return of Moffat, he speculated as to whether there were more populous areas further to the north, perhaps where the much talked of freshwater lake was. In any case he began to prepare himself by trying to achieve fluency in Tswana and by gaining some understanding of the culture of the people. He did this by undertaking three long journeys away from Kuruman. On these journeys he soon came to the conclusion that missionaries were better received by people whom European hunters or traders had not yet reached.

Despite the vast distances that Livingstone was to travel in Africa, the many different peoples he encountered all spoke languages belonging to the Bantu family of languages. The cultures of these peoples, like their languages, also all shared a number of fundamental traits. They supported themselves by hoe agriculture together with herding, hunting and fishing. In the areas where the tsetse fly was present, goats took the place of cattle for the herders, who were always men or boys. It was the men who cleared new ground for cultivation but cultivation itself was the domain of the women, as were all domestic tasks. As well as hunting and fishing, the men made tools and weapons. In some areas the men smelted copper or iron and traded their surplus output with neighbouring peoples. In other areas it was canoes that the men crafted for their own use and for trade. In what are now the northern Cape and Botswana, the beautiful skin cloaks or karosses was sewn together by the men, but the skins used to make the cloaks were first prepared and softened by the women. The kaross was the characteristic Tswana garment but they were also sold to traders from the Cape Colony, where they were highly valued.

The Bantu-speaking peoples of central and southern Africa also shared key elements in their non-material culture. They shared a belief in one creator God who was just and beneficent but very far from the lives of ordinary people. This God was called by a surprisingly limited variety of names, given the many languages involved; Molimo, Mulungu, Leza and Cautu were the predominant forms. The religious activity of the people was, however, focused on the ever-present ancestors, not on Molimo, who could only be called on in moments of great emergency. This religious life presented many problems to European observers because of their sense of the duality of the spiritual and the material; a duality which simply did not exist in the understanding of reality in the culture of Bantu-speaking peoples.

All of the peoples shared a tradition of open discussion which shaped the role of the chief. A chief, whether of the Xhosa of the Cape, the Ngwato of Botswana or the Lozi of Zambia, ruled only with the cooperation of the elders. In many communities the chief could be a man or a woman. There was no primogeniture among any of the peoples; the elders chose as chief he or she they deemed most suitable from a particular generation in the chiefly lineage. In their management of the community, chiefs discussed every important decision, whether judicial or administrative, with the elders in a public place. This tradition, variously referred to as *kgotla*, *mlandu* or *baraza*, shaped the political structures of the various peoples, great and small, from the Cape to Lake Tanganyika. Paramount chiefs, chiefs whose authority stretched over a large area, rarely took executive style decisions for all their people. Only in a grave crisis would he or she act in that way. In more usual times the paramount chief's role was to adjudicate between the minor chiefs over issues they could not resolve themselves. Thus paramount chiefs like Sandile of the Xhosa, whom Livingstone so admired, or Shinde of the Lunda, with whom he stayed on his trans-Africa journey, were more akin to a chief justice than to an absolute monarch. The authoritarian kingship created by Chaka among the Zulu was the exception in central and southern Africa.

That all the peoples of southern and central Africa shared these fundamental aspects of culture was enormously to Livingstone's advantage. It meant that when he immersed himself in Tswana life, in order to try to learn the language and appreciate the people's ways of thinking, Livingstone was learning what would stand him in good stead both on the fertile shores of Lake Malawi and in the semi-desert of Botswana.

The first journey he undertook was with Rogers Edwards, who had served as an artisan missionary at Kuruman since 1830. Edwards had been told by Moffat to explore the possibility of setting up a new station to the north of Kuruman and was happy to take Livingstone with him. The two missionaries with two African companions set off on a 750 mile trek, though they reached no further than 250 miles north of Kuruman. On this trek they were favourably impressed with a well-wooded and well-watered area called Mabotsa and began to plan the setting up of a new station there.

At the end of this journey, which lasted from September to the end of December 1841, Livingstone sent off a large number of letters to friends and to officials of the LMS.[14] In all of them he was insistent that only what he called 'Native Agency' would bring about the conversion of Africa, that is only Africans would convert Africa. In these letters he also insisted that it was necessary to extend the work northwards and eastwards where there were many more people to be evangelised than could be found in the area around Kuruman. He made clear that this task was one he felt ready to undertake. He insisted on this hope again two years later in a letter to the officials of the LMS, asserting that he 'always felt an intense desire to carry the gospel to the regions beyond'.[15] His letter to Dr Risdon Bennett was somewhat different from the others, in that he spent a great deal of space describing the landscape in detail and discussing the possible use he could make of African medicines. In this letter he also raised the possibility that southern Africa had entered into a period of long term of desiccation.

While waiting for Moffat to arrive, Livingstone undertook two further extensive journeys. On these journeys he travelled with African companions only. The first of these journeys lasted from 10 February 1842 until end of June 1842. The second began in mid February of 1843 and ended with his return to Kuruman on 20 June 1843. With Paul and Mebalwe as his two principal companions, he visited a wide range of the Tswana groups, including the Kwena of Sechele, with whom Livingstone would later stay, and the Ngwato of Sekhomi, father of the famous Christian leader Khama and great-grandfather of the first President of Botswana. He was accompanied for part of the latter trek by a number of Kwena sent by Sechele to help him. These two journeys were accomplished to a large extent on foot or riding on an ox. They were not primarily to seek out new sites for possible mission stations, as Livingstone had no authority to do that and the LMS had no plans for stations further north. They were a means of Livingstone getting to know the language and the people. He did, however, talk with a number of chiefs to the north about sending an African teacher to stay with them, in his mind a better way of spreading the message than a European missionary, as well as cheaper. These journeys appear to confirm that he was preparing himself, with at least part of his mind, for the role of pioneer he had talked of in letters he had written as he trekked from Algoa Bay to Kuruman.

He also gained considerable insight into the thought and culture of the Tswana. The measure of how far he had succeeded can be seen in his certainty (contrary to what Moffat had asserted) that they were not bereft of a knowledge of God, of a concept of the afterlife and of a moral conscience. He expressed these ideas clearly for the first time in a letter to H. M. Dyke of the French Mission among the Sotho.[16] On these journeys his lifelong interest in African traditional methods of healing was aroused. All of this already marked him out from most other missionaries in Africa at that time, who showed neither serious interest in nor any sympathetic understanding of African culture.

Back at Kuruman in June 1843 he found the staff were still awaiting the return of the Moffat family and the two new missionary families who were accompanying them. Their caravan did not reach Kuruman until February 1844. Livingstone was almost driven to distraction by this delay. He also felt compelled to ask in letters to the LMS in London what all these missionaries were meant to do at Kuruman, where, to his mind, only two missionaries were needed.

Relief came when Edwards received a letter saying he could go ahead to start a new station in the north. Livingstone got Edwards to agree to let him accompany him to build the new station at Mabotsa. What Edwards did not know was that Livingstone was clear in his own mind that he did not see Mabotsa as his Kuruman, and that he did not see his future as building a station and giving his life to it on the Moffat model. Edwards meanwhile was delighted because he was going to escape from what he had seen as his status as an underling to Moffat over the previous decade.

Chief Mosielele of the Kgatla granted the use of land at Mabotsa to the two missionaries. He also agreed to move his main village to Mabotsa, where there was more than adequate pasture for their herds and flocks. The Kgatla were ironworkers and the trust that Livingstone engendered among African people was early shown when, on the first journey, Livingstone had been allowed to join the iron smelters at their work in the Molopo Hills. This work was usually hidden from all except initiated unmarried men and was protected by sorcery.

Edwards and Livingstone plunged immediately into the sheer drudgery of building a dwelling house, a dam and a canal to irrigate their land. The produce of the land was an essential element in the ability of the missionaries to live with reasonable comfort given their meagre salaries. Edwards and his wife initially appeared to get on well with Livingstone and he with them. There was, however, plenty of potential for difficulty. Edwards was at last getting the chance to act independently, away from the shadow of Moffat, so he was apprehensive that the newcomer, a doctor and an ordained minister, might see the mission as his own, making Edwards again the assistant. Livingstone's closeness to Chief Mosielele, and to the African evangelists Paul and Mebalwe and their families, was also a point of potential conflict. Had Livingstone made clear to Edwards that Mabotsa was not meant to be his permanent place but only a stepping-stone to the north, all might have gone well between them.

Whatever was going on in Edwards's mind, Livingstone was initially oblivious to any difference between them and they worked well together. Then in January 1844 word came that the Moffats were at last on their way to Kuruman. Livingstone, who was at Kuruman at the time, rode down to meet them at the Vaal river. He travelled back on the Moffat wagon, sitting on the box seat with Moffat and talking for hours on end. It was here that the close relationship between the two men began, a deep and lifelong friendship which did not prevent them from expressing strong differences of opinion. It was also on this long slow trek that Livingstone first got to know the Moffats' eldest daughter Mary. With the Moffats settled again in Kuruman, Livingstone returned to the hard manual labour of building and gardening at Mabotsa.

It was soon after his return to Mabotsa that on 16 February 1844 there took place an event forever associated with Livingstone. He was mauled by a lion. This dramatic event has been sketched and reproduced in so many publications, serious and popular, that for many it has been the abiding image of Livingstone. It was an event that at the time Livingstone did not make much of; indeed he appeared to have been somewhat embarrassed by it. He and Mebalwe had gone to the aid of neighbours whose sheep had been attacked by lions. Livingstone wrote:

> I saw one of the beasts sitting on a piece of rock as before, but this time he had a little bush in front. Being about thirty yards off, I took good aim at his body through the bush, and fired both barrels into it. The men then called out 'He is shot! He is shot!' Others cried, 'He has been shot by another man too; let us go to him!' I did not see any one else shoot at him, but I saw the lion's tail erected in anger behind the bush, and, turning to the people, said, 'Stop a little, till I load again'. When in the act of ramming down the bullets, I heard a shout. Starting, and looking half round, I saw the lion just in the act of springing upon me. I was on a little height; he caught my shoulder as he sprang and we both came to the ground below together. Growling horribly close to my ear, he shook me as a terrier does a rat. The shock produced a stupor similar to that which seems to be felt by a mouse after the first shake of the cat ... Turning round to relieve myself of the weight, as he had one paw on the back of my head, I saw his eyes directed at Mebalwe, who was trying to shoot him at a distance of ten or fifteen yards. His gun, a flint one, missed fire in both barrels; the lion immediately left me, and, attacking Mebalwe, bit his thigh. Another man, whose life I had saved after he had been tossed by a buffalo, attempted to spear the lion while he was biting Mebalwe. He left Mebalwe and caught this man by the shoulder, but at that moment the bullets he had received took effect, and he fell down dead ... Besides crunching the bone into splinters, he left eleven teeth wounds on the upper part of my arm.[17]

Edwards reported the terrible agony Livingstone suffered as the uniting of the shattered bone was complicated by a secondary infection which led to severe 'purulent discharge'. The incident brought out the differences between Livingstone and Edwards. There is no doubt Edwards dealt with the injury immediately after the event, but his claim to have nursed Livingstone with his wife's help until he was wholly well was somewhat overstating

1. David Livingstone being mauled by a lion.

things. Livingstone felt so unhappy about the attention he received, even if this may have been an irrational response due to fever, that he moved out of the house he shared with the Edwardses. He spent the rest of the time he needed to recover in a small traditional Tswana house which the Kgatla put up for him, nursed by Mebalwe, Paul and their families. He felt well enough in April to go to Kuruman for the meeting of the district committee, a new structure for the administration of the LMS missions which he disliked intensely. On his return to Mabotsa he indulged again in hard physical work, which led to more trouble with the arm. When the break finally healed fully it left a large lump in the middle of the humerus, one of the key signs which allowed the doctors in London in 1874 to declare the mummified body that had so recently arrived from Africa was Livingstone's.

At the beginning of July he went to Kuruman for three weeks of real convalescence in the care of Mrs Moffat, MmaMary as she was known among Tswana speakers from the tradition of renaming a woman after the birth of her first child. At the end of that time, under an almond tree in the garden of the Moffats' house, he proposed to Mary Moffat and was accepted.

Was this a marriage of convenience for both of them as has often been asserted? That convenience was probably part of it does not mean there was no affection between them, nor does it mean that this affection did not grow and deepen into something very powerful. On Livingstone's part he had stated to the society in his application that he was not married and had no plans to marry. Indeed he had refused to accept the insistent advice of Mrs Moffat in London that he should marry before going out to Africa. As late as September 1843 he had written to his friend Watt:

> There's no outlet for me when I begin to think of getting married but that of sending home an advertisement to the *Evangelical Magazine*, and if I get very old, it must be for some decent sort of widow. In the meantime I am too busy to think of anything of the kind.[18]

Marriage had now crossed his mind, though when he wrote he clearly had no hopes in that direction. Three very different considerations influenced him. The first was the appalling difficulties he faced when he was so ill after the encounter with the lion. The second consideration was that he had by then a sufficient understanding of Tswana culture to realise that an unmarried male stranger had much greater difficulty in being accepted by a local community than a married couple. There was a third consideration which he never explicitly mentioned; it was a subject rarely referred to in nineteenth-century missionary circles: human sexuality. Livingstone was clearly a man of strong passions in most aspects of life and there is no reason to suppose him in some sense deficient sexually. St Paul's famous phrase about it being better to marry than to burn was undoubtedly an aspect of Livingstone's decision to marry. Another aspect of this issue of sexuality was the suppressed sexual tension within the missionary community. He got on well with Africans, women as well as men. He was often close to them in ways that some other missionaries were not; typical of him is this report:

> We found our way up to the palace, and entering we found some of the chief's wives eating porridge. Being hungry and wishing to gain their confidence, I squatted down beside them and put my hand into the dish too. They were highly amused and, the porridge being too warm, at my complaint one of them spread it up the side of the dish with her hand ... On turning up my shirt, the horrid whiteness of my skin made them stand aghast; and the queen, after she had become a little better acquainted, ventured to put up her hand to my nose, to feel if it were really so far elevated from the level of my face and not like her own little flat thing.[19]

Something as innocent but undoubtedly intimate as this incident was more than enough to raise sexual scandal among mission circles in southern Africa. Indeed only a little over twenty years before, the LMS in the colony had been torn apart with claim and counter-claim about sexual irregularity between missionaries and local women. That there was sexual tension among the missionary community itself relating to single men is also clear. This affected Livingstone directly when, at different times, both Ross and Edwards asserted impropriety in Livingstone's relations with their wives, neither of them beauties and both older (in Mrs Edwards's case much older) than he. Of the accusation by Ross, which was occasioned on the voyage out by Livingstone attempting to help Mrs Ross with her devastating seasickness, Livingstone wrote to his teacher, Richard Cecil, that he would rather have flirted with his grandmother.[20] Altogether there were plenty of reasons for Livingstone to get married.

What of Mary? Was this marriage for her simply a welcome escape just when she feared she was going to end up on the shelf? Whether she met Livingstone when he visited her parents in London we do not know. The first time she saw him in Africa was when he appeared galloping on horseback across the veld to meet the Moffat wagons just after they had crossed the Vaal. All the Moffats were surprised and delighted by this unexpected welcome. His dramatic arrival was by any standards a romantic moment. Although, as we have seen, Livingstone appears to have spent most of the rest of the trek in conversation with Robert Moffat, the young tanned Scot could not have avoided being also in close and constant contact with Mary for the seventeen or eighteen days of the ox-wagon journey. Her next meeting with him was when he came, the wounded hero, to convalesce at Kuruman for three weeks, at the end of which he proposed.

Mary was the first child of Robert and Mary Moffat, born at Griqua Town. She had spent the first part of her childhood at Kuruman. There she grew up speaking Tswana as well as she spoke English, the oldest white child in an African community. At ten she was sent to school in the Methodist institution at Salem in the eastern Cape. Then at fifteen she went to Cape Town to train as a teacher. She was almost immediately withdrawn from the course for a time when she had return to Kuruman to take over running the home when her mother was ill for some months. Then in 1839 she had had to give up her education again, to accompany the rest of the family to Britain. Before their ship had cleared Table Bay, she helped deliver her mother's new baby and almost immediately afterwards she acted as her father's and the other children's main support in the last hours of her brother Jamie's life: he died three days after the birth of his sister.

She had difficulty in adjusting to life in Britain. She disliked the cold and she appears to have spent these four years as her mother's domestic assistant. At the end of four years in the United Kingdom the family had an enormous amount of material to take back to Kuruman. It was young Mary who supervised the packing and labelling of two tons of luggage to be shipped to Africa. Back at Kuruman she taught in the school and assisted her mother in a household which was the centre of the whole community and which provided it with leadership and purpose. It appeared as if the pattern of her life was set as the senior helper to her mother and father in the home and in the school.

Mary Moffat and Livingstone must have appeared to each other as the answer to their problems. Mary could now be mistress in her own house and with Livingstone strike out in partnership into the Africa that she loved. Livingstone needed a wife and here was a devout young woman who could speak Tswana, and knew Africa and how to live in the bush. No one from Britain could have filled the bill so well. They had spent two periods of three weeks during which they were in each other's company almost constantly, and they had certainly came to like each other before he proposed. It was a better basis for marriage than that of many marriages in Victorian Britain.

After their engagement, Livingstone went off to Mabotsa to build a house for them. He wrote to her of his plans, which were for a house as big as that of the Moffats at Kuruman, though at Mabotsa Livingstone built in stone only to breast height and completed the walls with wattle and daub. It is from there during this period of waiting to be married that he wrote her letters that show there was more than mere convenience in the marriage. First, in a letter of the first August 1844, he tells her that if her father forgets to get the special licence from the nearest British magistrate at Colesberg they will just go ahead and license themselves.[21] More revealingly he wrote in September with a drawing of the plans of the house:

> The walls will be finished long before you receive this, and I suppose the roof too. But I have still the wood of the roof to seek ... Baba has been most useful in making door and window frames. Indeed if he had not turned out I should not have been so far advanced as I am. Mr E.'s finger is the cause in part of my having had no aid from him. But all will come right at last. It is pretty hard work, and almost enough to drive love out of my head. But it is not situated there; it is in my heart, and won't come out unless you behave so as to quench it.[22]

As we have seen, Edwards had for some time been uneasy about his situation with Livingstone at Mabotsa, although the latter seems to have been unaware of these feelings. When Livingstone moved out of the Edwards's house to be cared for by his African friends in a little wattle and daub hut there could not, however, have been a more visible rift between them. Yet when he returned with news of his intention to marry and started to build his house, Livingstone seemed surprised at the furious attack Edwards made on him.

It is understandable from Edwards's point of view. He had started a new station with the chance of being his own man after years of being Moffat's assistant. Now this young ordained doctor was bringing Moffat's daughter to the station as his wife, building her a formidably big house, and clearly consistently undermining Edwards's status and authority with Africans. This last must have appeared so to Edwards, first when Livingstone moved out of their house while very ill and again, after his return, when Livingstone in Edwards's eyes took the side of Mebalwe and his wife in a difference they had had with Mrs Edwards. It seemed to the Edwardses that Livingstone and the Moffat connection clearly wanted to take over Mabotsa from him, even though Livingstone had no such intention.

There is still an unresolved puzzle. Why did Livingstone go to the trouble to build such a substantial house? Was it to impress the Moffat parents? As it is not clear why he built it, the house can be seen as making Edwards's fears excusable. We know Livingstone was already planning to go north to work with the Kwena of Chief Sechele.[23] Almost immediately after his return to Mabotsa, he had begun regular visits to Sechele on which he took young trees and seed to plant at Sechele's. He then usually talked with the chief and preached to his people. It was at the end of January 1846 that Livingstone and Mary left Mabotsa for good and settled at Chonuane with Sechele and his people.

The move was not achieved without trouble. The missionary committee initially attempted to forbid it. It was only when Livingstone agreed to leave his newly-built house to Edwards and to build anew at Chonuane at his own expense that they agreed to his going. It was still an irregular move, as the LMS directors in London had not sanctioned expansion to the north. This all fitted into Livingstone's constant complaint about the refusal of the society to reduce the number of men among the sparse population of the southern Tswana and move the frontier of mission forward to the north where there were reputed to be more people. He had now achieved his aim to be the missionary furthest into the continent from Cape Town and he certainly was not building on other men's foundation.

One cloud hangs over Livingstone's stay at Mabotsa: the quarrel with Edwards which brought out the worst aspects of Livingstone's character. When, after Livingstone's return to Mabotsa, Edwards had shown him the letter he intended to send to the directors in London outlining what Edwards considered the various incidents of unacceptable behaviour by him, Livingstone was astounded. He also learned at that time that Mrs Edwards had already written to Mrs Moffat warning her of the disreputable nature of her new son-in-law. In fact Edwards never sent the letter but Livingstone did not know that and his response was by any standards excessive. He bombarded Moffat and the directors with long letters defending himself and attacking Edwards. Not only then but years later he would still refer to Edwards with what can only be called venom. It was a fault in his own nature that Livingstone recognised when he asked Arthur Tidman, the LMS secretary, to pray for him that he might not take offence so readily and aggressively.[24]

While it is no excuse, this extreme reaction has its roots in Livingstone's family and class background. In Livingstone's eyes his apparent friend and colleague had attacked him completely out of the blue. This was a terrible betrayal. To this betrayal was added Livingstone's lifelong readiness to take offence, making a poisonous combination. Livingstone's readiness to take offence and to maintain a feud-like antagonism towards those who, in his eyes, had betrayed him can be explained by some consideration of the culture that helped shape him. The culture of the working class in the industrialised areas of the west of Scotland did not produce any understanding of shades of grey. Things were either black or white: he who is not with me is against me. It was a culture that produced, and still produces, men ready to take offence at the least sign that their honour is impugned or their dignity undermined.[25] It was a culture where men could switch from bonhomie to aggressive anger in an instant.[26] Ransford, who saw these things in Livingstone as signs of a clinical case of manic-depressive personality, clearly had never been in a pub in Coatbridge or Sauchiehall Street.[27]

5

Kolobeng and the North

Sechele had decided he wanted a missionary and, although he knew that Chonuane could not be a long-term centre for his people because of the annual threat of drought, he helped Livingstone to settle there. Any talk of the need to move might have made Livingstone, whom he had got to know and like, hesitate about coming to join him. Sechele wanted a missionary whom he could trust, having learned how a missionary could bring advantages to a chieftaincy. Sechele was in touch with Moshweshwe, the creator of the powerful Sotho kingdom. Moshweshwe had welcomed the Paris Evangelical Mission into his kingdom and the mission had become an ally in his drive to extend his authority over a widening area. Moshweshwe also got the missionaries' cooperation in his desired modernisation programme and the mission was, in turn, an effective mediator, through its links with Dr Philip, between him and both the voortrekkers and the Cape Colony.[1]

Although it has been suggested that Livingstone also knew that there was no future at Chonuane, this can hardly be so when we consider the sheer physical effort he put into building a house and trying to raise crops there. This was work that he had begun during his many visits to Sechele while still at Mabotsa. He had to rush the last stages of building to get the house ready for Mary, while she waited at Mabotsa for the arrival of their first baby. The baby, born in January 1846, was a boy and his parents named him Robert after his maternal grandfather, breaking with the Highland tradition that would have named him Neil after his paternal grandfather. This may have been a mark of the close bond that had grown up between Livingstone and his father-in-law: he addressed Moffat as 'My Dear Father' in letters. Alternatively, it may have been that he could not bear being called by the Tswana, Rra-Neili? Instead Livingstone now became Rra-Rrobati, which sounds to ears used to a Scottish 'R' more like La-Lobati.

At Chonuane Livingstone planted the seeds for a large vegetable garden and also planted wheat, which had grown well at Mabotsa. The vegetables shrivelled and died since there was little rain that year and the nearby stream dried up; the wheat fared no better and was entirely burnt up. Sechele then indicated that he and his people were ready to move to a better-watered place as soon as Livingstone was ready to go. In total Livingstone and Mary struggled on for eleven months with the help of Paul, his son Isaac and Mebalwe and his wife. The Livingstones' African helpers shared the suffering produced by the failure of their new-planted gardens. They were all given a respite when, in the middle of 1846, Mrs Moffat arrived with a wagonload of supplies.

Despite the frustration and hard labour of finishing off a house to make it tolerable for his wife and family, and the exhaustion of subsistence farming, Livingstone and Mary with their African helpers also attempted to preach and to set up a school. In a letter to his mother, in which Livingstone again insisted that his parents should emigrate to North America, as he had been doing in almost every letter ever since his arrival in Africa, he went on to described his life succinctly:

> Poor Joseph, 'separate from his brethren', has been farrier, builder, carpenter, glazier, doctor, minister, man-midwife, blacksmith, boardsmith, tinsmith, shoe-maker, waggon mender and painter, gunmender, hunter and fisher, and I don't know what else, but would not refuse his aged parents a place at his fireside.[2]

In the midst of all this backbreaking and mind-numbing physical work, perhaps even as an escape from it, Livingstone was busy planning the expansion of the mission to the east and into the much denser population to be found there. He had already set up contacts with Mokgatle of the Fokeng and with Paul had gone on treks in that direction as far as the Limpopo.

He used the first of these journeys to placate the voortrekkers of the Transvaal, who were deeply suspicious of the LMS and who had also warned him that they were coming to disarm Sechele. Then, in November 1846, he set off again, this time with Mary and baby Robert as well as Mabelwe. They certainly found a much denser population in this area than anywhere the LMS was then working north of the Orange. Many of the chiefs were willing to set up relations with the mission. The leaders of the new white state that was being formed by the voortrekkers made clear that they were not going to be persuaded readily to allow the LMS to begin work in their territories. They saw the presence of an LMS missionary, white or black, if not as an extension of British power, certainly as a form of spying by the British as a prelude to that extension. In a way the Transvaalers were right to be suspicious, given the history of the connections of the LMS in the Cape Colony with humanitarian circles in Britain. Livingstone did indeed report on the nature of the new state, unfavourably and in some detail to the LMS in London, which information was passed on to the British government.[3] By that time, however, the impact of the humanitarian lobby in Britain had weakened considerably and the government was enthusiastic about building good relations with the voortrekkers and wished no extension of its commitments in southern Africa.

Sechele, his people and the Livingstones finally agreed to move to a spot on the River Kolobeng that was supposed never to run dry. In August 1847, leaving Mary at Chonuane, Livingstone set out with Paul and many Kwena to start building at Kolobeng. They quickly built wattle and daub dwelling houses for the Livingstones and for the various Christian African families who were working with him, those of Paul, Isaac, Mebalwe and Modukanele. The main body of the Kwena also moved to a site close by. Late in September Sechele insisted that a meeting house must be raised and cooperated with the mission party in completing a building fifteen feet by forty feet. Unlike most mission developments of the time, this building, which doubled as school and church, was not built by paid labour but was a cooperative effort of mission and community. This period of Livingstone's life has been seen as unmitigated failure, but this way of working was one in which he believed firmly and it was the way ahead if the church and school were ever going to belong to the people. It was the pattern of development later in Malawi and Uganda, where grassroots African Christianity was to grow very rapidly at the end of the nineteenth century. Livingstone also received unpaid community cooperation in making a dam and cutting a channel for irrigation. This work was vital to produce the food essential for the subsistence of the missionary families, since Livingstone now had no money, though he did promise the six most prominent Kwena helpers in clearing the land for the family plot a heifer each when he could get them from Kuruman. He was in debt largely because his moves had never been authorised, so there was no grant from the LMS for the Chonuane buildings and the transport costs, let alone for this new development at Kolobeng, all of which he had to bear from his meagre salary of £100.

Despite the sheer exhaustion from which he suffered at this time, Livingstone was still continuing to develop a Tswana vocabulary, telling Moffat of many new words and also of different usages in the north from those around Kuruman. He also insisted in letters written at this time that, if a grammar of Tswana was to be written, all ideas of relating it to classical grammatical structures, as had been attempted previously, had to be scrapped. He had rightly understood that the languages of southern Africa had their own very different grammatical and syntactical structures. On top of all this he also continued to gather evidence for his theory of the progressive desiccation of southern Africa.

Before the Livingstones left Chonuane for the last time, Mary was delivered of a girl, Agnes, or Nanee as she was always called as a child. Now the family faced the sheer toil of creating a new homestead all over again. Livingstone

was so short of resources that door frames and window frames were ripped
for the house at Chonuane and reused, but even more drastic measures
were forced on him. He in fact burnt down the house completely so as to
recover the nails from the ashes. Even so he was soon begging Moffat for
nails and tools. It took another year of hard work before he had completed
a permanent house with breast-high stone walls finished with wattle and
daub. During this time he had a variety of mishaps. Once he slipped and was
left hanging from the roof beam by his bad arm, another time he cut himself
with an axe. All the while he was so careless of the sun's power that his lips
were cracked for days on end.

He described their daily life after the house was completed to his most
intimate confidant, D. G. Watt:

> We get up as soon as we can, generally with the sun in summer, then have family
> worship, breakfast and school; as soon as these are over we begin the manual
> operations needed, sowing, ploughing, smithy work, and every other sort of work
> by turn as required. My better half is employed all the morning in culinary work
> or other; and feeling pretty well tired by dinner time, we take about two hours
> rest then; but more frequently without the respite I try to secure for myself she
> goes off to hold infant school, and this, I am very happy to say, is very popular
> with the youngsters. She sometimes has eighty but the average is sixty. My manual
> labours are continued till about five o'clock. I then go into the town to give lessons
> and talk to anyone who may be disposed for it. As soon as the cows are milked
> we have a meeting and this is followed by a prayer-meeting in Sechele's house,
> which brings me home about half-past eight, and generally tired enough, too
> fatigued to think of any mental exertion.[4]

He went on to bemoan that this prevented him from getting on with real
missionary work. What did mean by that? After all what he described to
Watt was a description of the life that Moffat had led for his first ten years
during which he had laid the firm foundations of Kuruman, which everyone
regarded as a great success. It would appear that what Livingstone meant
as real missionary work was what he called 'itinerating', travelling ever
further to find new peoples and bring them into the orbit of Christian
missions; an effort of pathfinding which would lay a trail that future
missionaries, European and above all African, would follow.

Livingstone had hoped that this development would have been to the east
in what is now the Transvaal and parts of southern Zimbabwe, but the
power of the new voortrekker state with its capital at Potchefstroom stood
in the way. The alternative that he began to consider was to go north where
the desert held no promise, but beyond it there was this much talked of
freshwater lake and the promise of the dense population that water should
be able to support. If a readily followed road to the lake could be opened

up, perhaps future expansion lay there. What was unclear was how Livingstone could put together the resources for even a basic expedition to go north when he was in debt, having spent his own resources and some of Moffat's on making the two recent moves. The role of Mary and the children in any such venture was also unresolved.

It was the relationships that by this time he had built up with men of a class with whom Livingstone had never before had dealings that made possible the implementation of these ideas of expansion to the north. These connections had begun while the Livingstones were still at Mabotsa. Sometime early in 1843, Captain Thomas Montague Steele, ADC to the Governor of Madras, and J. R. Pringle, a Collector in the same Indian Province, came through Mabotsa on a hunting trip.[5] Livingstone travelled with them for some days and was of service to them through his knowledge of the people and the language. Steele and he became friends. Indeed Livingstone wrote to Steele often throughout his life but particularly in the years before the Zambesi Expedition. These letters were usually long and full of ideas as well being very frank.[6] Livingstone regretted Steele and Pringle's slaughtering of animals for sport and not for food but found them courteous, and he appreciated their good relations with Africans, which were in marked contrast to many other European travellers who came that way.

Back in India, Steele talked of the attractions of the area and the helpfulness of Livingstone. As a result Captain Frank Vardon of the 25th Madras Light Infantry and William Cotton Oswell of the East India Company's Civil Service both made trips to the area and struck up friendships with the Livingstones. Oswell was to go on to become one of the main supports of Livingstone's family during the rest of the missionary's life. After his first visit with Vardon in 1846, Oswell left a wagon as a gift to the Livingstones, a symbol of the constant support he would afford them in the years ahead.[7]

Livingstone and all three 'Indians' had talked about trying to get to the fabled lake in the north. Livingstone came to realise that it was only with their help that the journey could be accomplished and perhaps a new missionary road opened up. It was Oswell, however, who promised to come back and help set up an expedition to the lake. He, with a friend, Mungo Murray of Lintrose, arrived at Cape Town to begin preparing the expedition in the first months of 1849. Livingstone had hoped that Steele would come too, but he was unable to join them. When the expedition arrived at Kolobeng it had been joined by J. H. Wilson, a trader who hoped to bring back ivory. Sechele was interested in this venture. He did not go himself but sent a party of his men whose task it was to help Livingstone but also to bring back ivory. Mary stayed with the children at Kolobeng.

Because of his knowledge of the country and the people, as well as his fluency in Tswana, Livingstone took the lead after the party reached Kolobeng, but the expedition was still Oswell's. There had been two previous attempts by Europeans to reach Ngami but the Kalahari Desert had defeated them. Livingstone and his companions were the first Europeans to see Lake Ngami, but this discovery was not what really moved him. The discovery that Central Africa was not a great desert, as many in Europe had thought, but a well-watered and populous area excited him.[8] He could not explore further because the local chief blocked their crossing of the Zouga river, cutting them off from getting to the Zambesi and to Sebitwane of the Kololo, a friend of Sechele's. In any case, they had been away so long that Livingstone had become worried about Mary. When Oswell promised, however, to come back in the next cool season and mount an expedition to reach Sebitwane, Livingstone was content to return to Kolobeng.

Livingstone immediately reported his journey to the LMS headquarters in London. Tidman passed the information on to the Royal Geographical Society, whose new President Sir Roderick Murchison was seeking publicity for the society. Both the LMS and RGS benefited in terms of public interest and support from this story of the 'discovery' of Lake Ngami. Oswell and Murray made no attempt to write up their part in the expedition and the glory was all Livingstone's, including a half share in the annual royal premium of £25 presented by the RGS.

Livingstone was by this time obsessed with the need to go back north so as to make contact with Sebitwane. The chief's desire for a missionary was aroused by reasons similar to those that had first inspired Sechele. The difference was that a Moffat connection was seen by Sebitwane as important in relation to the great military threat posed to his people by the Ndebele kingdom of Mzilikazi. He knew that Mzilikazi had great affection and respect for Robert Moffat and would not harm Moffat's daughter.

When the hot season ended and Oswell had not appeared, Livingstone took off to the north again; he was only able to do this because of the money Oswell had already made available to him for the new expedition. This time Mary, already pregnant again, came with him bringing along the children, Robert four, Nanee three and Thomas (named after Steele) only one year old. This was a very drastic decision since this trip would entail crossing a stretch of the Kalahari, then entering an area where there were patches of tsetse fly which might wipe out their oxen and leave them stranded. Beyond the Kalahari the travellers would be exposed to malaria in a way they were not at Kolobeng. Livingstone had, however, studied the literature on malaria and took quinine with him on the trip.

When the Livingstones did reach Ngami, the chief who had obstructed their further progress on the last visit agreed to let them go on, but they

2. Arrival at Lake Ngami.

3. Lake Ngami.

could not. The children were unwell and Mary's pregnancy was advanced. They returned to Kolobeng after an appallingly difficult crossing of the Kalahari in the middle of August 1850. A week later Mary gave birth to a little girl. All the children caught a bronchial infection prevalent among the Kwena at that time and the baby, Elizabeth, died of it. Livingstone wrote to Moffat:

> Have just returned from burying our youngest child. Never conceived before how fast a little stranger can twine round the affections. She was just six weeks old when called away to see the King in his beauty ... She is home now, yet it was like tearing out one's bowels to see her in the embrace of the King of Terrors. She was a very active child, about the same size as Robert was at her age. Had very fine blue eyes. Was smitten by the epidemic which is raging here, viz. inflammation of the lungs. I could not apply the usual remedies to one so young ... We administered quinine with the barely formed hope that she might come through, but yesterday evening the beautifully formed countenance began to set in death. The pulse at the wrist vanished several times, then returned quite strong. Then at one o'clock she opened her beautiful eyes and screamed with a great effort to make her lungs work, and instantly expired. That scream went to our hearts, and will probably not be forgotten in Eternity.[9]

Mary was also ill, indeed she suffered from paralysis of some of the facial muscles, and Mrs Moffat insisted that Mary, David and the children go to Kuruman in order to recuperate. They stayed there from November 1850 to February 1851.

The close friendship of Moffat and Livingstone appeared unaffected by what had happened but Mrs Moffat was very unhappy about the whole situation. She became very upset indeed when she discovered that David and Mary were already planning to go north yet again with Oswell in order to try to reach Sebitwane, who had sent word that he would welcome Livingstone's visit. In a very angry letter to her son-in-law she made clear that she knew that her husband had tacitly agreed to the plan but that she had not. She wrote:

> Was it not enough that you lost one lovely babe and scarcely saved the others, while the mother came home threatened with Paralysis? And will you again expose her and them in those sickly regions on an exploring expedition? All the world will condemn the cruelty of the thing, to say nothing of the indecorousness of it.[10]

Many commentators have continued to condemn this risking of the lives of his children, yet it is clear that Mary wanted to go with him. That the children suffered serious hardship on these journeys cannot be denied, but many Victorian parents in comfortable surroundings lost more than one child to disease. It does seem, however, to have been the cause of an estrangement between Mary Livingstone and her mother, in addition to Mrs Moffat's profound and continuing anger with her son-in-law.

What was not clear to Mrs Moffat, understandably since Livingstone had not told anyone, was that he and the family intended to stay with Sebitwane for about a year in order to set up a mission station there.[11] Again he was striking off on his own, irrespective of any plans by the LMS, which, like the Moffats, knew nothing of his intentions.

Oswell and the Livingstones set off for the north on 24 April 1851. At first things went very well, Oswell going ahead to open up the waterholes in the Kalahari for the main cavalcade. However, instead of going via Lake Ngami after they had crossed the Botletle river, they went straight north across the saltpans there and only narrowly escaped death by thirst. They were saved only when they freed their oxen from the yoke and the beasts led them to a spring. It was fouled by debris and rhinoceros dung but it was water and they survived. They then entered the well-watered area between the Chobe and Zambesi rivers. This was the borderland of Sebitwane's kingdom but also of the tsetse fly; Livingstone's reports were one of the earliest attempts at scientific reporting on this insect, whose presence was fatal to cattle and horses. Tsetse were, however, not present everywhere but limited to specific areas and local people were able to warn the travellers where these were.

Messengers from Sebitwane contacted them immediately and said that the chief was coming to meet them. Livingstone and Oswell left Mary, the children and the rest of the party in a tsetse-free spot and went off down the river in a canoe to meet the great man. They met him on 21 June 1851. Both Oswell and Livingstone were deeply impressed with this veteran warrior. He had successfully led his Sotho-speaking people far from their home in what is now the southern Orange Free State, first to escape the destructive impact of the *difaqane* and then to escape the raids of Mzilikazi and the Ndebele. Only one thing depressed the two travellers, which was their discovery that the Portuguese were already present in the area and were trading for slaves. There were also hints that Swahili slave-traders had reached a point not too far away to the east.

Sebitwane almost immediately fell ill and died on 7 July, but not before he had spent a night by the fire with Livingstone and Oswell relating his long and adventurous life to them, a story which Livingstone recorded in his journal.[12] Sebitwane's heir, his daughter, Mma-Motsiasane, insisted that she would still welcome a mission being set up among her people. Indeed she promised that they would begin a garden for Livingstone so that there would be food waiting when he returned to stay. This was not to be because a new vision had gripped Livingstone. South Central Africa was a densely populated area and it was not gripped by the desiccation process so apparent further south. Tragically it was being invaded by a destructive disease, the slave trade. Only the twin pronged weapon that Fowell Buxton had so passionately recommended for west Africa, 'Christianity and Commerce', could save the people. The arrival of honest traders and missionaries would enable the people to exchange ivory, in an area where it was lying around in abundance at that time, for the European trade goods they now desired. This would soon undercut and end the slave trade, leaving the possibility of the growth of Christianity and the development of a more prosperous African society.

Livingstone was convinced by this time that he was called to open up a route into the area, which would enable the honest trader and missionary to travel there readily. This route could not begin in South Africa. It had to begin from the east or west coast. Livingstone was so excited that he even talked to Oswell about setting out immediately for the west coast, though remembering Mary and the children still waiting on the Chobe with the wagons brought him up sharply. Livingstone therefore made up his mind to go back with the family, and to make suitable provision for them, but then to return to the north and explore a possible route from the west coast for the entry of Christianity and commerce. He decided that the best thing was for Mary and the children to go to Scotland and stay with his family, an arrangement Mary appears to have accepted without demur.

On the way back to Kolobeng the caravan had to stop on the banks of the Botletle and stay for four weeks, to allow Mary to have her new baby, a boy named William Oswell.[13] Also on this return trip they ran into a young English traveller, William Frederick Webb, who had fallen ill while on a hunting trip. They took him back to Kolobeng with them and he became another of the group of wealthy upper-class Englishmen who became lifelong friends and supporters of Livingstone.

When Livingstone arrived at Kolobeng he found that Sechele and his people had moved. At Dimawe, ten miles away, they had found a spot much less affected by the recent droughts. On their arrival Sechele came over to visit and presented them with an ox, even though, by this time, he knew that Livingstone was not going to stay. For more than two years Livingstone's whole concern had been focused on the north. He had indeed spent so much time travelling that one has to wonder what had been happening at his station.

From the arrival of Livingstone at Chonuane, Sechele had been an eager learner. He quickly learned how to read and had soon began regular prayer and Bible-study sessions at his house. His wives had been eager learners, except for his senior wife, an ironic situation given that at that time only the senior wife could be seen as a true wife in the eyes of missionaries.[14] The terrible drought first at Chonuane and then at Kolobeng was explained by many of the Kwena as being the result of Sechele's straying from the old ways because of Livingstone's influence. When Sechele decided that he wanted to be baptised, and to put away his junior wives, his people were desperately upset. These wives, whom Livingstone admitted were the best pupils he and Mary had, represented alliances between the Kwena and their fathers, who were chiefs. Livingstone appreciated these difficulties but saw no way out. He had not attempted in any way to oppose the elaborate male and female initiation ceremonies, *bogwera* and *bojale*, which most missionaries at that time saw as essentially evil. In contrast he saw them as traditional and vital social customs; but with polygamy he felt there could be no compromise.

Sechele was baptised and admitted to communion on 1 October 1848, an event that most of his people deplored. It also left a group of literate young women attracted by Christianity feeling that they had been betrayed. One of these junior wives remained behind because she had no place to go, since in her home district her family was out of favour with their chief because of the divorce. Sechele and she resumed marital relations for a time and the news of this devastated Livingstone. He appeared to see this lapse as evidence of his failure as a missionary. Many writers and biographers since have referred to this as 'Sechele's apostasy'. It was, of course, no such thing. Moral failure such as Sechele's was a matter of church discipline. Such lapses were dealt with by suspension of the sinner from communion until full proof of repentance was shown, when the penitent sinner could then be allowed to receive communion again. This was, and still is in Africa, the Presbyterian and Congregationalist equivalent of the Catholic sacrament of penance. Apostasy is an explicit rejection of the beliefs of the Christian faith.

Sechele never apostatised and throughout his life, as he moved his chief village to different sites to accommodate his growing authority, he built a church in every new location and usually preached in it himself regularly. Robert Moffat and others judged what he preached to be a strange mixture of Christianity and paganism. Many theologians in the second half of the twentieth century have seen it, however, as an attempt, if an inadequate one, to develop an African Christianity: what has come to be referred to as the inculturation of Christianity. In this enterprise of Sechele's, which saw the majority of his people become baptised members of the Christian church, he got little understanding from the various missionaries who worked with his people during these years. However, Bessie Price, Mary Livingstone's sister, who with her husband Thomas Price worked among the Kwena for many years from 1866, came to like and admire him. She complained, however, that when he differed from them he would quote scripture in his defence and if that failed he would simply insist 'Well, David did it'.

At Kolobeng the family prepared to go to Cape Town, where Mary and the children would set sail for Britain. They stopped off at Kuruman for a fortnight on the way south. It is surprising that Mary and David Livingstone did not decide that Mary and the children should stay at Kuruman. After all the children knew and loved their Moffat grandparents. Mary and the children did not know Scotland or the Livingstone family. They spoke Tswana better than they spoke English; and, despite all its hardships, theirs was a very free life in the sun and Mary was used to being the mistress of her own household. To send them to live with strangers in a crowded industrial village in a strange cold grey land was a puzzling decision to make. If it was a matter of the children's education, their early education would be undertaken well enough at Kuruman and there were opportunities for secondary education in the Cape Colony.

It has been argued that the bitter complaints Mrs Moffat had addressed to Livingstone about taking the family on the treks to the north meant that their staying at Kuruman was impossible. Yet Robert Moffat and Livingstone were as close as ever, and Livingstone had restored relations with Mary Moffat to some extent, as can be seen in a letter to Moffat, whom he continued to address as 'My Dear Father':

> From the way Mrs M. has written to us for some time past, I expect to be obliged to pull down my breeches as soon as we reach Kuruman and get my bottom warmed with the taws.[15]

It was also Mary, not he, who would have stayed at Kuruman. It could hardly have been that he was embarrassed to be beholden to the Moffats, as he had begged tools and supplies from them for the previous three years without hesitation. Part of the explanation may be that Livingstone thought that the family was to be without him for only two years, not the four and a half years that were to prove so miserable and humiliating for Mary.

The answers to these questions remain a mystery. There is nothing in the mass of correspondence and publications by Livingstone and the Moffats – Mary Moffat was almost as active a correspondent as Robert – which explains what proved to be a tragic decision. It is certainly wrong to conclude that Livingstone was indifferent to his family. While he was a complex man, and had even ruminated at one time that it might have been better had he started in 'a more Jesuit way', and often talked as if he were indifferent to human companionship, he could also write emotionally about those he cared for if they were taken from him. There is no doubting his agony when baby

Elizabeth died. The strength of his attachment is clear from what he wrote at Cape Town after he saw Mary and the children set sail:

> How I miss you now, and the dear children! My heart yearns incessantly over you. How many thoughts of the past crowd into my mind! I feel as if I would treat you all much more tenderly and lovingly than ever. You have been a great blessing to me. You attended to my comfort in many ways. May God bless you for all your kindnesses! I see no face now to be compared to that sunburnt one which has so often greeted me with its kind looks. Let us do our duty to our Saviour and we shall meet again. I wish that time were now. You may read the letters over again which I wrote at Mabotsa, the sweet time you know. As I told you before, I tell you again, they are true, true; there is not a bit of hypocrisy in them. I never show all my feelings; but I can say truly, my dearest, that I loved you when I married you, and the longer I lived with you, I loved you the better . . . [16]

6

South African Politics

Livingstone and his family arrived in Cape Town on 16 April 1852, eleven years and one month after he had first arrived there. Dr Philip had died in August of the previous year and had been succeeded as the LMS agent for southern Africa by William Thompson. Thompson, who became a lifelong friend of Livingstone's, was the son-in-law of a noted Glasgow preacher and antislavery activist, the Reverend Ralph Wardlaw, Dr Philip's friend and admirer. The Livingstones presented a strange sight to the sophisticated citizens of Cape Town, as they straggled into town on their old dilapidated wagon surrounded by their Tswana attendants. Livingstone, Mary and the children were all dressed in worn and patched clothes bearing no relation to what was fashionable in Cape Town then or at any time. As Livingstone himself said, 'We were a queer looking lot on coming to Cape Town'.

The Thompsons warmly welcomed this wild-looking family, more at home in Tswana than in English, into their house on Church Square, the same house in which Dr Philip had entertained Livingstone eleven years before. In addition to this hospitality Livingstone also found £200 awaiting him, a gift from Oswell to allow Mary and the children be kitted out for the trip to Britain. This money, the equivalent of two years' salary for a married missionary of the LMS, also allowed Livingstone to rent a house as their base while they prepared for the family's journey to Britain and for his trek to the north.

After Mary and the children left, Livingstone found time amidst his preparations to take classes from Thomas Maclear, Astronomer Royal at the Cape. Maclear taught Livingstone how to make accurate plottings of latitude and longitude. From then on Livingstone's cartography clearly distinguished his travels in Central Africa from those of earlier Portuguese travellers and of his contemporaries.

Livingstone also found time to write about the political situation in the colony. He had recently published a number of articles in the *British Quarterly*. In them he had attacked Philip's policy on the maintenance of the mission stations within the colony. Livingstone had written that they should be abandoned, so that the local 'coloured congregations' would be forced to survive on their own resources as normal pastorates. The editor seemed so willing to publish what Livingstone wrote that the latter believed the *Quarterly* provided him with the means of letting the British public know the real situation in the Cape Colony. He was to find that the *Quarterly* was in fact only too pleased to publish articles in Britain critical of Philip, but not ones critical of British policy in South Africa. This was part of Livingstone's education about what he could and could not publish when attempting to influence the British public.

On his arrival, Livingstone had found the colony yet again at war with the Xhosa. He set himself to understand the roots of this conflict which the colonists called the Eighth Kafir War and the Xhosa called the War of Mlanjeni. Livingstone saw that the new war was simply the resumption of the fighting between the Xhosa and the colony begun in the War of the Axe of 1845 and 1846, which had ended unsatisfactorily for either side. The difference in 1850 was that some of the 'Hottentot' veterans of that war had gone over to the Xhosa in what the whites called 'The Hottentot Rebellion'. The veterans' actions were a result of the unjust treatment all the Cape Folk soldiers had received at the end of the previous conflict, particularly those from the Kat River – where the majority of prosperous Cape Folk lived.[1]

When still at Kolobeng Livingstone had commented, in letters to his family in Scotland, on the War of the Axe in terms unfavourable to the Xhosa, his comments being based on very little hard information. He was now much better informed and began a campaign to gain the sympathy of the British public as a whole, not just the evangelical circles in Britain and North America, both for the Cape Folk rebels and for the Xhosa. He did this by writing to the LMS directors and by attempting to have a speech of Sandile, the principal chief of the Xhosa, translated and published in evangelical magazines in the United States and the United Kingdom.[2] To achieve his wider aim Livingstone relied on the enthusiasm the editor of the *British Quarterly* had shown to publish his earlier thoughts on South Africa. He wrote a long analytical essay on the war and on white-black relationships in South Africa and sent it to the *British Quarterly*.

In mounting his campaign Livingstone was filling a gap left by the death of Dr Philip for a spokesman for the cause of equal rights in South Africa, but his adoption of this role was only temporary. Livingstone had no intention, despite the passion that informed what he wrote, of staying in the south to take up Philip's mantle. He did not, on this occasion, interpret the situation in which chance left him as a providential calling to a new task, as he so often did in other circumstances.

On arrival at the Cape the publications and actions of Henry Calderwood had particularly shocked Livingstone. Calderwood, who had come to the Cape as an LMS missionary, had later become government commissioner among the Xhosa. Livingstone was upset by Calderwood's public assertion of the guilt of Andries Botha, an officer on trial for his life. Botha had led Cape Folk levies in the War of the Axe and had been decorated for bravery in an action at Burnshill where he and his levies saved the whole of the British army's commissariat train from capture or destruction. After the so-called 'Hottentot Rebellion' at the beginning of the new conflict, however, Botha was charged with fomenting the dissension that led to some Cape Folk soldiers going over to the enemy. Livingstone wrote

> Well, that is a fine letter from his Riverence Calderwood. I look upon it with mingled feelings of scorn and shame. With scorn, when I think of an English professor of Christianity so unutterably mean as to join in the hue and cry against a poor Hottentot, and so dead to the shame of infamy as to confess at the same time that it has been his practice to act the part of a common informer, a salaried government spy.[3]

Livingstone also complained about the fact that Botha, a poor man, was not provided with a defence counsel at the expense of the state as he would have been so provided in a capital case in Scotland. That Calderwood, also a Scot, should have said that it was a good thing that this Scottish precedent was not followed in the Cape, as it was a morally and socially harmful thing in Scotland itself, left Livingstone doubly angry. His bitterness spills out in an exclamation in his letter to Thompson: 'From Commissioners who can play the fool for £600 per annum, with the Bible in one hand and the sjambok in the other, Good Lord deliver us.'[4] His angriest comments, however, were reserved for Sir John Wylde, Chief Justice of the Cape Colony. Livingstone referred to him with contempt in a number of letters to various friends and LMS officials. In his private journal Livingstone wrote of Wylde's conduct at Botha's trial:

> The Lord Chief Justice is an infamous hypocrite and gave ample evidence of having prejudged the case. The conduct of the court was extremely indecorous through, and at last a bottle of wine was brought in. Sir John Wylde took several swills, pretending he was so much fatigued he needed it, pursed up his mouth after each glass as if he did not like it, and then when he passed sentence, which had been previously written, he brightened up till even the foam came out at the corners of his mouth. His tirade in passing sentence was half an hour in length, and was the most horrid exhibition I ever witnessed. Old Botha made a sensible speech afterwards[5]

Wylde sentenced Botha to death despite the jury's recommendation of mercy. The Governor, who recognised both Botha's outstanding service to the crown and the faulty procedures of the trial, commuted the sentence to that of a short period of imprisonment.

What appears to have had the deepest effect on Livingstone, however, was the speech the Xhosa Chief Sandile had made to Henry Renton, a United Presbyterian minister from Scotland who was visiting the missions of the Glasgow Missionary Society. Livingstone sought to make its effect felt in church and missionary circles in Britain and the United States. He copied out passages from it and summarised other parts of the speech in his private journal and referred to it in letters to LMS officials as well as to friends and family. He also sent a translation of the whole speech into English to his brother Charles in the United States to have it published there. He was particularly touched by a passage that he copied out in a number of different notebooks and letters. It was a passage where Sandile had said

> No white man is without a book [the Bible]. Is it God who gave this book bids them think of blood? Some white men come and say the Caffres steal. God made a boundary by the sea and you white men cross it to rob us of our country. When the Son of God came into the world, you white men killed him. It was not black men who did that, and you white men are now killing me. Send this over the sea that they might know my mind. I was not made a chief by Englishmen, your Queen makes men chiefs. She made Smith a chief, God made me a chief. How is it that you are breaking the law of God? I do not know who will make peace in this country. I have given up my life and God may preserve it. I will never give up fighting. If you are able you may take me. If you drive me over the Bashee I will fight there also. If you kill me my bones will fight and my bones' bones will fight ... I am angry with the English, I am tired of the English on account of their bad conduct.[6]

The most significant piece about the situation in South Africa of all that Livingstone wrote was the long article he prepared for the *British Quarterly* and the *Morning Herald*. This article remained unpublished in Britain or the United States at the time.[7] Its ideas are, however, fundamental to understanding Livingstone and without consideration of the attitudes expressed in his letters at that time, which were summed up in this draft article, a great deal of what Livingstone said later can be, and indeed has been, misunderstood.

It could be argued that, in the feverish rush and emotional turmoil of seeing his family off and preparing to go north, Livingstone had no time for considered thought. He did not complete the essay in Cape Town at this time, however, but during the weeks of leisurely ox-wagon travel to Kuruman and his subsequent fifteen-week stay there, which gave him ample time to go over his thoughts and to express them with some care.[8]

In the essay he described the tension between the settlers in the eastern and western sections of the Colony and how they refused to turn out for commando service in the war. He then went on:

> In the meantime England is paying at the rate of £120,000 per month. England, prepared to shed her own blood for liberty, imagines that this money is expended in defence of her children. The mass of the English people sympathize with the triumphs of liberty throughout the world. In no other country was there such a general wish for the success of Kossuth and the Hungarians. Our Queen, as in everything else of the good and generous, partook of the feelings of her people. But while England had been sympathising with the struggles for freedom which she herself knows so well how to enjoy, she has been struggling to crush a nation fighting as bravely for nationality as ever Magyar did. In so far as the Queen and country are concerned the attempts to crush have been made unwittingly. The Government has been hoodwinked into the belief that by foul means or fair it must crush the Caffres.

Livingstone then went on to outline Sandile's speech and contrasted it with a speech made by Sir Harry Smith at a dinner given in Smith's honour by the corporation of Portsmouth with its bombast about victories won over the savages. If Smith had been correct in his claims, why was Sir George Cathcart still involved in a bitterly fought campaign with these same defeated savages, Livingstone asked. He continued:

> We are no advocates for war but we would prefer perpetual war to perpetual slavery. No nation ever secured its freedom without fighting for it. And every nation on earth worthy of freedom is ready to shed blood in its defence. In sympathising with the Caffres we side with the weak against the strong. Savages they are but surely deserving of independence seeing they have fought right gallantly for it for upwards of twenty months ... Hints were given during the anticonvict struggle [a struggle by white settlers against a government plan to make the Cape a penal colony] about the possibility of England employing the same means of crushing as are now brought to bear upon the Caffres. The answer was 'Never', the whole civilized world would cry out against it. 'But we are men and they are savages.' Is this the feeling in the fashionable 'law of Providence by which the black must disappear before the white'?

This last query was provoked by the widespread development in educated circles in Britain of ideas of 'progress' and 'race' that would later in the century come to dominate thinking in the English-speaking world. This school of thought was made all the more persuasive from the 1870s when apparently confirmed in its objective truth by the development of 'Scientific Racism', a movement involving scientists as distinguished as T. H. Huxley.

William S. Hogge, one of the two imperial commissioners who negotiated at that time the Sand River Convention with the Voortrekkers, which recognised in practice the independence of the Transvaal Boers, was an exponent of this new fashionable thought. He had written to Earl Grey, the Colonial Secretary:

> The history of the Cape is already written in that of America, and the gradual increase of the white race must eventually though slowly ensure the disappearance of the Black. Providence vindicates this its unalterable law.[9]

John Mitford Bowker, leader of the British settlers in the Eastern Cape was another exponent of the now fashionable and very convenient understanding of progress. He had insisted in a notorious speech that, just as the great herds of springbok had disappeared before the onward march of progress, so must the Xhosa.[10] When Livingstone was in Cape Town, a brilliant and radical Ulsterman, William Porter, the Attorney General of the colony, had recently attacked this intellectual understanding of Providence and Nature in public, the two terms tending to be used interchangeably by supporters of the new intellectual position. His words had so impressed J. J. Freeman, the secretary of the LMS, on his visit to South Africa that he referred extensively to them in the published version of his report, *A Tour of South Africa*. Porter had said with regard to the opinions of the English settlers in the Eastern Cape:

> Their profound contempt of colour, and lofty pride of caste contains within it the concentrated essence and odious principle of all the tyranny and oppression which white has exercised over black. But the Cape-frontier Englishman is not alone. A member of the British House of Commons, in one of the New Zealand debates, has lately said, that the brown man is destined everywhere to disappear before the white man, and such is the law of nature.[11]

By the end of the nineteenth century that extraordinary amalgam of ideas produced by Social Darwinism and Scientific Racism, and the Anglo-Saxonism of the historians of Oxford, Harvard and Columbia, had become the intellectual orthodoxy of the English-speaking world.[12]

This was Livingstone's first reference to it. Although he did later make occasional but always scornful references to it, he at no time attempted to deal with this intellectual position head on. Typical of his references was a passage in his private journal in 1853 where he discussed two very popular books of the day which attempted to show the gulf between the different races and the inferiority of the dark races of the earth, J. C. Prichard's *Researches into the Physical History of Mankind* and A. Guyot's *The Earth and Man*. In a very few words he disposed of them to his satisfaction by common sense, pointing out a fundamental flaw in their methodology. They both attempted to affirm their assertions about the races of humankind by means of drawings and photographs taken of people of various 'races' from around the world. He wrote:

> I have often been struck by meeting countenances the facsimiles of renowned statesmen in everything except as to colour. One of Sekhomi's courtiers was the picture of M. Guizot. Another among the Bamapela, could be the ruddy colour of the original been imparted, might have sat for the likeness of Professor Agassiz of Neufchatel ... The plates selected by M. Guyot if coloured dark find ready counterparts among the dark tribes. Even the Caucasian and Captain Cook may be found. By selecting the ugliest or the best looking of different races anything may be proved which the writer wishes.[13]

That he rarely took on this developing stream of ideas on race was due to his being concerned with communicating his own positive message without the distractions of arguing about what appeared to him to be a side issue. How could he have viewed these various writers and their ideas as constituting a side issue? He did so because when he left Britain for the last time, in August 1865, the race-oriented family of ideas had not yet achieved the intellectual hegemony it was to achieve in the later decades of the nineteenth century and the early ones of the twentieth.[14] These were the foundations upon which, in the 1930s, the Nazis built their science of race even as the hegemony of race thinking over the western intellectual world had elsewhere begun to disintegrate.

To return to the long essay, which the *British Quarterly* ignored, Livingstone showed unambiguously that he shared with John Philip a belief in the oneness of humanity and the equality of all human beings in terms of human rights. Culturally the Xhosa were savages but they were human beings and, as such, had 'certain inalienable rights' in the words of the Declaration of Independence. This concept of inalienable rights was an Enlightenment idea but it was also deeply rooted in many sectors of Protestant evangelicalism. Witness one of the founders of the Evangelical Revival, John Wesley, writing about slavery: 'Liberty is the right of every human creature, as soon as he breathes the vital air: and no human law can deprive him of that right which he derives from the law of Nature.'[15] It was on this basis that Livingstone insisted the Xhosa had the right to fight for the freedom of their homeland. He insisted their struggle was on a par with the much lauded struggle of Kossuth and the Magyars for the freedom of Hungary in 1848. There could be no more unambiguous expression of his belief in the oneness of humanity.

It was a belief he held all his life, which was not contradicted when he called the Xhosa 'savages' or the Kololo 'degraded'. He wanted them all to become Christian and to also to become more 'civilised', as well as to have a better quality of life in terms of what we would now call development. The key issue is that the quality of being a 'savage' in his view was a culturally conditioned one, not an irremovable genetic characteristic as the scientific thought of the last decades of the century would have it. However degraded or objectionable from a European or Christian perspective a culture might appear, it could not take away the genuine humanity of the peoples of Africa nor remove their inalienable rights. Livingstone was, after all, fully aware that his own great-grandfather had been a member of a tribal society which, before the Victorians romanticised it, had been seen by Lowland Scots and the English as 'degraded' and 'savage'. He is also quite clear that his white contemporaries could be 'savages' and called the Transvaalers such because of their stealing of Kwena women and children as slaves after the battle with Sechele at Dimawe. His references to the British settlers around Grahamstown at that time were of a similar nature.

This combination of ideas, shared by Livingstone and so many evangelical humanitarians in the first half of the nineteenth century, was almost to disappear later.[16] The language Livingstone and others used was misunderstood when in the intellectual climate of the 1880s 'savage' and 'degraded' had become code words for those darker peoples supposedly fixed on the lower levels of the genetically conditioned hierarchy of races. They became peoples whose the best hope was that the dominant Anglo-Saxons, destined by Nature or Providence to rule the world, would listen to Kipling's call 'to take up the whiteman's burden' rather than adopt the attitude that led to the genocide of the Aborigines in Tasmania.

It was this misunderstanding of Livingstone's language and ideas that allowed him, a passionate defender of the rights of Xhosa to fight for their freedom from British rule, to become, after his death, an icon of liberal imperialism of the Kiplingesque kind. This confusion and misunderstanding also allowed many apologists for the European powers when they conquered Africa, in the astonishing decade between 1885 and 1895, to claim that they had done so to fulfil Livingstone's dreams.

Livingstone's last involvement in South African politics came about in response to the attack upon Sechele and the Kwena by a commando of Transvaalers. The Transvaal authorities in Potchefstroom had been threatening to bring Sechele to heel for some time. Indeed their threat had appeared so imminent to Livingstone in 1849 that he had sent his wife and children to Kuruman, though, he says, Mary would have preferred to go westwards with the Kwena women.[17] That threat passed but things changed for the worst when the Sand River Convention of January 1852 made clear to Transvaal voortrekkers that they were now free to do what they wanted north of the Vaal, as far as the British government was concerned. The token gesture to British humanitarian concern in the Convention had been a clause forbidding slavery in the new white state. This did not worry Potchefstroom in the least, as the British were clearly not going to enforce it. The Transvaalers had also been negotiating with Commissioner Hogge. From his opinions and attitude towards Africans and African rights, it was clear to them that the era of Dr Philip and the power of the 'humanitarian lobby' to influence British policy in South Africa was over.

Livingstone graphically described what happened at Dimawe in a letter to William Thompson, Philip's successor in Cape Town:

> From it [a letter Livingstone had sent to the Lieutenant Governor] and Mr Moffat's letter you will have a pretty clear idea of the doings of Dr Robertson's converts, and may fancy that the reverend sinner turning up the whites of his eyes and saying to them at the Communion table, 'Eat, O friends! Drink, yea drink abundantly, O beloved'.[18] They went the whole hog – attended church on Sunday, hearing Mebaloe preach, and then made the parson flee for his life on Monday. He ran the gauntlet, some of them calling out, when they saw him with clothes on, 'Here is the chief', and then the bullets whistled over, behind and before him. He seems to have become terrified, ran through the midst of the Boers, and so fast his feet were dreadfully bruised. He has lost all he had, viz. twenty-seven head of cattle and his furniture, etc. His house was burned by the *Christians*. He it was who stood by me when bitten by the lion and got bit himself. He has been with me ever since I came into the country, but I fear this will be a settler for him. He is now on his way out here. Some fine young men whom I knew and loved have fallen. My heart is sore when I think of them.[19]

He went on to add a sentence of great significance: 'There is not a native in the country but knows now for certain on whose side I am.' This has often been seen as a reference to the struggle between Africans and the Transvaalers, but it is clear from his letters, and what he wrote in the essay which the *British Quarterly* refused to publish, that he was on the side of all Africans who fought to remain free of foreign rule. As he said:

> We are no advocates for war but we would prefer perpetual war to perpetual slavery. No nation ever secured its liberty without fighting for it. And every nation on earth worthy of freedom is ready to shed its blood in its defence. In sympathising with the Caffres we side with the weak against the strong. Savages they are but surely deserving of independence seeing they have fought right gallantly for it for upwards of twenty months.[20]

His ideas would have been seen as subversive in Nairobi, Johannesburg or London in 1952, let alone 1852. After all when President Roosevelt and Prime Minister Churchill drew up the Atlantic Declaration in 1941, Churchill insisted to Roosevelt that, of course, paragraph 3 did not apply to the populations of the European colonies. (The paragraph asserted that the two nations respected every people's right to choose its own form of government and wanted sovereign rights and self-government restored to those forcibly deprived of them.)

Although Livingstone, while still in Cape Town, had rightly rejected the accusation made by Dr Robertson and others that he had been arming the Kwena, there is no doubt that he repaired guns for them and that he was in favour of them arming themselves with guns. He saw that guns were their only hope of maintaining their independence. As he wrote to his relations in Scotland:

I had no hand in procuring the guns of the Bakwains, but felt very pleased when they did get them. Moral suasion and the law of love are very fine in their places, but they would not do if introduced to Newgate, the doors being left open. The Boers with whom we have to deal are similar characters to those in Newgate ... About three weeks ago one of our people bought a tusk from another tribe, and when carrying it home in order to barter with it was met by a Boer, who immediately fell upon him with a whip made of rhinoceros hide and thrashed and compelled him to carry the tusk to his waggon. The native had never seen the Boer before and the Boer knew nothing of the tusk. The Native passively endured all. Fancy an appeal to arbitration instead of war between the Natives and the Boers, the latter being firm believers in the idea that the former are no more men than the baboons are. I have been told by them quite seriously that I might as well try to convert baboons as Natives.

All the tribes which have no firearms are reduced to a state of bitter slavery and a missionary who lately went to them was forcibly obliged to return [a reference to Boers driving away a missionary from the Mapela people]. The Boer referred to above sent to Sechele for a number of people to conduct his sons to hunt elephants. Sechele civilly requested payment for the people, but the Boers said no, they were not accustomed to pay anyone. The people were of course not given and now the Boers are more anxious than ever to attack us. We know what takes place at their meetings, and they declare to each other that there is danger in going against Sechele, 'for he has guns'. They attack and kill hundreds of other tribes and reduce the children to slavery without the smallest fear, because they can do so without the smallest danger to themselves; they sit on their horses and murder in cool blood, and the Natives cannot approach them ... Resistance to such tyrants and murderers is I think obedience to God, and Charles will no doubt enlighten you on the point. The only means which with the divine blessing have preserved *our independence as a people* are those very guns which you think our people would have been better without.[21]

It is also clear that he gloried in the courage of the Kwena and their willingness to defend themselves. As he wrote to Arthur Tidman, the LMS secretary in London:

The Wanketse and Bakhatla followed the usual course of tribes in that quarter:

they fled without attempting to strike a blow on those who were wantonly killing them. But Sechele fought a whole day; therefore, say the Boers, 'that horrid doctor must have taught them to fight'. It is remarkable that those who evinced most inclination to learn to read have shewn the most bravery, and the leading opponents of the gospel found their hearts melting with fear as soon as the Boers approached.[22]

Even before news of the attack on Sechele had reached Cape Town, the complaints of the Transvaalers had clearly affected the attitude of the officials in Cape Town towards Livingstone. The Cape authorities were most insistent that he could not take with him the amount of powder he had requested and needed; an amount, they implied, that showed he intended to sell or give it to Africans, which was forbidden. In the circumstances it was understandable that Livingstone publicly and vehemently denied arming Sechele, which was true in a literal sense but untrue in spirit.

Eventually the authorities in Cape Town allowed him to purchase and take with him the amount of powder he had originally requested. He was then ready to go north. He aimed to go far beyond where any European had gone before.[23] He aimed to reach the Kololo kingdom in the Zambesi valley and there seek a suitable base from which Christianity, civilisation and commerce could play their role in transforming Africa without the violence, injustice and slavery which he believed had characterised the meeting of European and African heretofore.

7

Coast to Coast

When Livingstone finally left Cape Town, on 8 June 1852, his wagon was so loaded with goods he had promised to transport for people further north that at times he was afraid one or other axle would break. Despite some desperately near things he got to Kuruman without mishap, but, having arrived, not an axle but one of the wheels broke. Previously Livingstone had arranged with the prominent Cape Town merchant, H. E. Rutherfoord, for George Fleming, a West Indian ex-slave, to accompany him to the Kololo country with a wagon of merchandise. Fleming's task was, apparently, to test the market for European goods and to act as the commerce side of the enterprise of Christianity, civilisation and commerce for which Livingstone was seeking an entry route to Central Africa. Since, however, Livingstone already knew that the Kololo were eager for European goods and that the trans-Kalahari route they were about to follow was impracticable for regular and routine trade, it is not clear what function Fleming was to fulfil except the simple one of getting a load of ivory to take back to Cape Town.

As always with African journeys by wagon, the pace was slow. Livingstone did not reach Kuruman until 27 August 1852. He was then detained at Kuruman for over two months, not simply because his wheel broke. This delay occurred because wagon drivers were nervous of going north for fear of the Transvaalers who had defeated Sechele at Dimawe. Livingstone himself did not wish to risk being captured by either of the two Transvaal commandos still operating on the edge of the Kalahari. In different letters and publications Livingstone mentions one or other, and sometimes both, as the reason for the delay.

He took advantage of this delay to finish his *Analysis of the Language of the Bechuana*. He left this in draft with Robert Moffat but did not have it published until he had twenty-five copies printed to aid the European staff of the Zambesi Expedition in 1858. In this work he insisted that traditional classical grammar could not be applied to languages of what came to be called the Bantu family. In the little book he attempted an alternative approach as well as reiterating his belief that ancient Egyptian culture had been an African culture.

The Sichuana absolute verb, like that of the ancient Egyptian is often expressed by the same words which express the absolute noun: a peculiarity which, according to Bunsen, may be explained in a philosophical point of view by the inseparable union, and therefore apparent identity, of the two ideas of personality and existence. I have often been struck by the similarity the structure of this language bears to Sichuana.

A bird's-eye view of the structure of the language is easily obtained by classifying the particles or signs of nouns, and by separating the roots or radicals from all their flexions and combinations with prefixes, suffixes, and other signs, whereby relation, determination, demonstration, reversion, causation, distribution, &c. &c., are expressed. Radical nouns and verbs are then seen to constitute the hard skeleton of the language, and these, in learning to speak it, are to be mastered by the exercise of memory alone.

In believing that there exists a resemblance between the African languages and the ancient Egyptian, we are guided by affinity in structure. There has been nothing done until now to fix the former, while the latter appears before us unchanged in its state of primitive development, though thousands of years old. The system, however, of affixes, prefixes, formation of the verb, &c., which may be said to form the scaffolding of the two languages, continues essentially the same. A remark of Dr Lepsius, quoted in vol. 1. p. 276 of the Chevalier Bunsen's work, that the vowel forming the termination of certain polysyllabic Egyptian words, in Coptic always forms part of the sound of the first syllable, seems to contain the germ of the system of signs now so largely developed in Sichuana. Reduplication, in order to impart intensity, is also perpetually employed, thus *ma*, mother; *mamaisa*, to nurse, to comfort: *tlola*, to remain; *tlolatlola*, to remain some time; *tlogo*, the head; *tlogotlogo*, the heads of people = the elders; or in the following ditty spoken to the fire in kindling it:

Fire / catch-catch / wood / brothers / mine / they / tremble-tremble
Molelo/ cuara-cuara / logon / bo / nake / bo / roroma-roroma.

Fire, do catch the wood; my brothers are trembling much.

Adjectives too, are used as verbs; thus: *molemo*, good or goodness; *lemohala*, become good; *molatu*, guilt or guilty; *latuhala*, become guilty; *latuhatsa*, cause to become guilty = accuse; *iñtle*, beautiful; *iñtlahatsa*, make beautiful; *lele*, long; *lelehatsa*, make long. The nouns are formed from these again, thus: *temohala*, a becoming good; *tatuhalo*, a becoming guilty = *latuhaco*, accusation; *telehaco*, a making long; *tsepha*, cleanse or purify; *tsepho*, purity; *itsepha*, cleanse oneself; *itsephisa*, make oneself pure; *boitsepho*, holiness. It is also worthy of observation that the insertion of the letter s into a verb converts being into action. It forms the causative, the stimulus to activity of the predicate. The letter l too, engrafted onto the root plays an important part in the expression of relationship.[1]

It was also at Kuruman that he completed and sent off his article on British policy at the Cape to the *British Quarterly*. He also hoped to get it published in either the *London Gazette* or the *Morning Herald*.[2]

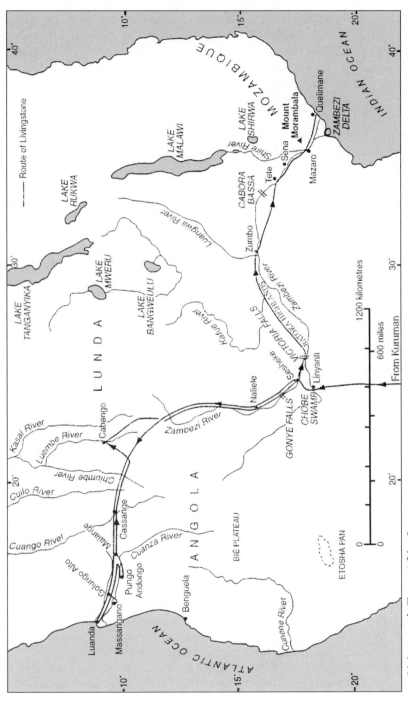

2. Livingstone's Trans-Africa Journey, 1853–56.

By this time Livingstone was practising a much more accurate recording of latitude and longitude than heretofore. The maps he made of the upper Zambesi were models of accuracy and surpassed the existing Portuguese charts, about which in any case he knew nothing at that time. Portuguese slave-traders had already entered the lands to which he was going, and in the seventeenth century a few Portuguese travellers had indeed penetrated the upper Zambesi valley and the Lake Malawi area. Outside a small circle of scholars in Portugal no one in Europe seems to have had knowledge of these reports and it was widely held that the interior of central Africa was a large desert similar to the Sahara in West Africa. Although he was also preceded by a handful of eighteenth-century Portuguese travellers, Livingstone became the first person to map the area with accuracy and thoroughness.[3] Portuguese cartographers in the eighteenth century had, however, produced tentative maps of what are now Mozambique, Zimbabwe, Malawi and Zambia. Admittedly they were sketchy with large blank areas and some of what detail they had was inaccurate, but they did show a Lake Maravi reasonably close to the position and to the dimensions of Lake Malawi. What is strange is that the RGS and the educated British public accepted that nothing was known of the area other than it might be desert, despite the fact that three books were published in Britain between 1817 and 1834 replicating these Portuguese sketches and placing Lake Malawi reasonably accurately. In each case the author indicated by broken lines that the upper half of the lake as drawn was an unconfirmed suggestion of its shape and size.[4] One can only presume that these were discounted as mere speculation and as coming from the 'armchair geographers' that Murchison and Livingstone later scorned without naming whom they meant. The authors of these three books had never been in Africa but were working from old, mainly Portuguese records which were not the products of mere surmise. Their publications, however, appear to have had no impact on the level of the knowledge of African geography in Europe.

The outline of the continent had been known since the sixteenth century, though the Royal Navy was still far from completing the process of producing accurate charts of the African coastline. These were much needed since, for example, though the Portuguese had been at Quilemane since the sixteenth century, they had not mapped the Zambesi delta. Even more surprisingly they still did not know which channel in the delta linked the main stream of the Zambesi with the sea. What lay inland of the coast of Africa south of the Gulf of Guinea and north of the Limpopo was still *terra incognita* in Europe, despite the reports of the early Portuguese travellers.

Livingstone's relations with Robert Moffat continued to be close. He never ceased to address Moffat as 'My Dear Father' in letters, but the stay at

Kuruman was an uncomfortable one since Mrs Moffat was still angry with him. She had been appalled at his taking Mary and the children on his treks to the north. She had written to Livingstone about her daughter Mary complaining of the terrible suffering to which Livingstone had exposed her and the children for the sake of 'exploring'. She was equally unhappy about his sending them to Britain so that he could go off on his 'wanderings', as she referred to his projected trek. As late as the end of September 1855 Livingstone still had to defend himself and his actions to his mother-in-law in a long letter. Anger, though it was being suppressed, was clearly near to the surface in his opening sentences:

> I have just read over again your note enclosed in the parcels which lay a twelve-month on an island in the Zambesi or Leeambye, and I am sorry to see you so much distressed on my account, and the more so as you appear perplexed at 'not knowing my plans'. I have been labouring under the impression that those plans were thoroughly well known to all my friends, inasmuch as the proposition I made to the Directors and their assent thereto, were published in the *Missionary Chronicle*.[5]

Had there been no communication between Livingstone and his mother-in-law during these ten weeks or so that he had been waiting at Kuruman to begin the journey? When he eventually did get off to the north it must have been a relief to all concerned.

These criticisms by Mary Moffat have contributed to the widespread questioning of Livingstone's affection for his children. Livingstone's letter to Moffat on the death of little Elizabeth should dispel all doubt about his love. In this connection a letter he wrote to the children, after he had arrived at the Kololo capital, reveals both his love for the children and his understanding of the divine which was far from the scary all-seeing judge that is so often set out as the typical Victorian idea of God.

> Here is another little letter to you all. I should like to see you much more than write to you, and speak with my tongue rather than with my pen; but we are far from each other – very, very far. Here are Sepione, and Meriye and others who saw you as the first white children they ever looked at. Meriye came the other day and brought a round basket for Nannie [Agnes]. She made it of the leaves of the palmyra. Others put me in mind of you all by calling me Rananee, and Rarobert, and there is a little Thomas in the town, and when I think of you I remember, though I am far off, Jesus our good and gracious Jesus, is ever near both you and me, and then I pray to Him to bless you and make you good.
>
> He is ever near. Remember this if you feel angry or naughty. Jesus is near you, and sees you, and He is so good and kind. When he was among men, those who heard Him speak said, 'Never spake man like this man', and now we say, 'Never

did man love like Him'. You see little Zouga is carried on mamma's bosom. You are taken care of by Jesus with as much care as mamma takes of Zouga.[6]

His first stop after leaving Kuruman was to spend some time with Sechele and the Kwena. He helped Sechele compose a list to be sent to the British authorities of over 130 children who had been captured by the Transvaal commando and taken off as slaves, though called 'apprentices' by the Transvaalers. Livingstone, however, tried to dissuade Sechele from going to Cape Town to appeal to the British authorities for aid against the Transvaalers. Sechele was even hoping that he might go to London. Despite Livingstone's pleas, Sechele insisted on going and Livingstone commented in a letter to his brother Charles:

> Sechele has gone South to implore the English to assist him to regain his children. I fear he might as well have remained at home. He abstained from all acts of retaliation lest the English should be offended.[7]

Clearly Commissioner Hogge and the Sand River Convention had left Livingstone feeling that, despite the apparent differences between them, 'English' and Boer were as one with regard to African rights in southern Africa.

To travel from Kuruman northwards, up what was beginning to be called the 'English Road', entailed for Livingstone the same agonising trek across the desert as in the three previous journeys. A Mr McCabe had made good time through the Kalahari the previous year because heavy rains had produced a rich crop of desert melons that made up for the lack of water for both men and beasts. Livingstone and Fleming had no such luck.

On the journey Livingstone recorded in his journal one of those prayer-cum-meditations which he produced at various points in all his diaries and journals. This one starts off with him wondering whether he would ever see Mary and the children again, and whether he would die in Sebitwane's country. He finishes,

> O Jesus, fill me with thy love now, and I beseech thee accept me and use me a little for thy glory. I have done nothing for thee yet, and I would like to do something. O do, do I beseech thee, accept me and my service and take thou all the glory.[8]

This last is typical of a style of prayer centred on Jesus which recurs in his diaries and journals all his life, indeed one such is among the last entries he ever made in 1873 on the eve of his death. These contrast starkly with the Providential God who appears in so many of his religious statements made in things written for publication. These latter statements would appear to be his genuine enough acceptance of the formal theological conventions of his day while his prayers in the private journals were products of a more personal and private faith.

On the journey Livingstone spent a great deal of time gathering and noting all kinds of information about the insects, animals and people of that arid stretch of Africa. For example, he described in great detail the technique of the white ants or termites in building their 'anthills', and sought to understand how they communicated with each other as they surely did in order to work in such elaborate concert. Again he made a careful study of the diet of several of the animals they encountered, such as the rhino and the wildebeeste. No other European traveller in southern and central Africa in this period commented on the fauna and flora in such detail or with such scientifically trained accuracy of observation. He distinguished four kinds of rhinoceros and his notes on the white rhino contradict the often-asserted aggressiveness of this animal.

The White Rhinoceros is partially gregarious, being met with occasionally in groups of five or seven. They feed on coarse long grass and have no incisor teeth. He deposits his droppings in particular spots, always excavating the centre of his heap when he comes to it. The undigested grass appears in them, and a kind of solaneum generally springs up from the part. It is the most inoffensive of all the large animals. Elephants sometimes assault a village at night, overturning the huts and killing inhabitants, or enter gardens and when the women attempt to drive them off kill them. But a Mohohoo [white rhino] never molests anyone. The males occasionally break in the front sinuses of each other in their affairs of gallantry, but that is a private affair between themselves. He is a placid good-natured fellow and almost always fat. He may often be seen sauntering along the banks of rivulets in the afternoon, having spent the heat of the day in some shady bower. His sight is deficient but his hearing is acute, and if unaccompanied by a friendly bird called Kala (Crotophagi ani or Buphagi (beefeaters)) he is easily approached from under the wind. The bird by flapping with its wings and screaming gives him warning of the approach of danger. As his flesh is usually loaded with fat, and a single bullet behind the shoulder is sufficient to kill it stone dead, it soon becomes extinct after the introduction of fire arms into a country. His skin is from an inch to an inch and a half in thickness.[9]

On 1 March 1854 Livingstone and his party at last reached the edge of the wet, marshy and forested country south of the Kololo kingdom. This was welcome after the desert but the new country was plagued by the tsetse fly and malaria. Soon everyone, except Livingstone and a young African, Kebopetswe, was laid low with malaria, Fleming included. Two fit men were barely capable of getting two wagons through forest country. As Livingstone wrote:

I was employed the whole day in felling trees for the waggon to pass. Heavy rain commenced at 1 o'clock. Passed on all wet to the skin. Every stroke of the axe brought down a thick shower on me.[10]

It is strange that he does not appear to have used his anti-malaria preparation of quinine combined with other drugs. He had tried this successfully on his own children and others on his and Oswell's previous visit to the region. This procedure he was to use later on this trek and on the Zambesi expedition, giving the latter a much better health record than any previous British expedition into tropical Africa.

The nearer the caravan approached the Chobe River, the southern frontier of the Kololo kingdom, the wetter the ground became and the thicker the forest. Where there was not dense forest there were marshes lined with natural barriers created by masses of inch thick reeds that had grown together with tangles of convolvulus. Livingstone at that point abandoned the wagons and went ahead with one companion, Konate, a wagon-driver from Kuruman. They took with them a pontoon which the English travellers, W. F. Webb and W. Codrington, had presented to Livingstone.[11] The two men endured an exhausting struggle as Livingstone described in his *Travels and Researches*:

> Next morning, by climbing the highest tree, we could see a fine sheet of clear water, but surrounded on all sides by the same impenetrable belt of reeds. This is the broad part of the river Chobe, and is called Zabesa. Two tree-covered islands seemed to be much nearer to the water than the shore on which we were, so we made an attempt to get to them first. It was not the reeds alone we had to pass through; a peculiar serrated grass, which at certain angles cut the hands like a razor, was mingled with the reed, and the climbing convolvulus, with stalks that felt as strong as whipcord, bound the mass together. We felt like pygmies in it, and often the only way we could get on was by both of us leaning against a part and bending it down till we could stand upon it. The perspiration streamed off our bodies, and as the sun rose high, there being no ventilation among the reeds, the heat was stifling, and the water, which was up to our knees, felt agreeably refreshing. After some hours toil we reached one of the islands. Here we met an old friend, the bramble-bush. My strong moleskins were quite worn through at the knees, and the leather trousers of my companion were torn and his legs bleeding. We were still forty or fifty yards from the clear water, but now we were opposed by great masses of papyrus, which are like palms in miniature, eight or ten feet high, and an inch and a half in diameter. These were laced together by twining convolvulus, so strongly that the weight of both of us could not make way into clear water.[12]

At last finding some hippo tracks through the otherwise impenetrable banks of reeds, the two men were finally able to launch their pontoon onto clear water and sailed down the Chobe. Their arrival at the first Kololo village they encountered astonished the chief, who believed the reeds formed a secure barrier between the Kololo and any possibility of approach from the south. The reed barrier was seen as protecting the Kololo against Ndebele raids in particular. Kololo gossip later transformed the arrival of Livingstone and Konate on a pontoon into the legend of their arrival on the back of a hippo.

The new chief of the Kololo, Sekeletu, sent men and canoes to help Livingstone and his party reach his capital. By dint of a massive effort, using canoes bound together to form huge rafts, the wagons and the draught oxen were got across the River Chobe at a point much further to the east than where Livingstone had left them.

On Sunday 15 May Livingstone preached, as he had been doing each Sunday on the way, but this time in the land of the Kololo and to a congregation of about sixty Kololo. He could do this readily since they understood his Tswana. Indeed many of his congregation had helped in the famous transport of the wagons across the river and had created a song to celebrate the event. This song Livingstone recorded in his journal.[13] Then, after a week's trek, keeping the Sabbath rest on 22 May as was his wont, on Monday 23 May 1853, Livingstone rode his wagon into the Kololo capital at Linyanti.

Linyanti was a thousand miles, as the crow flies, from Loanda, eight hundred miles from Quilimane and twelve hundred miles from Cape Town; it was the very heart of the 'Dark Continent'. Yet when he brought his Kololo there and set up their domination of the Lozi valley and the Batoka highlands, Sebitwane was still in touch with his old friend, Moshweshwe, the creator of the kingdom of Lesotho a thousand miles to the south, as well as with Sechele, Livingstone's friend. He was also constantly aware of a threat to his people from other southern newcomers to central Africa, the Ndebele of Mzilikazi.

Sebitwane had brought the outside world into the Lozi flood plain just as other forces from outside were about to enter it. Before his death he had already made contact with the Portuguese of Angola. Soon after his death Swahili traders from the Zanzibar sultanate arrived to treat with his successor. Already at the time of Livingstone's first visit, European trade goods were in demand, at least by the local elite, and were paid for by selling people into slavery.

Even if the leaders of the various communities in central Africa had not seen a European, they had usually heard of them. Livingstone's face, hands and arms were so tanned that in the Zambesi area he was almost always taken initially to be Portuguese. This was not always an advantage and placed him in danger until he proved he was not Portuguese. It was only if some other part of Livingstone's body was revealed that his appearance occasioned astonishment and curiosity. Also, because of his praying and the medical care he offered, the people were able place Livingstone readily in a role that fitted into their world view, that of *nganga* or *sing'anga*, the traditional healer. The traditional healer, who is always in touch with the beyond, God and the ancestors, is known from the Cape to Lake Tanganyika by one or other variation of this word, *nganga*.

The new chief Sekeletu, Sebitwane's son, for whose benefit Sebitwane's chosen successor, his daughter, MmaMotsiasane, had abdicated, welcomed Livingstone warmly. The garden set aside for Livingstone by Sebitwane had been fruitful and the produce was available to supply the needs of Livingstone and his party. The annually flooded Barotseland plain produced food in abundance, the like of which Livingstone had not seen in Africa hitherto. Of this garden Livingstone wrote:

> The Makololo had made a garden and planted maize for me, that, as they remarked, when I was parting with them to proceed to the Cape, I might have food to eat when I returned, as well as other people. The maize was now pounded by the women into fine meal. This they do in large wooden mortars, the exact counterpart of which may be seen depicted on the Egyptian monuments. Sekeletu added to this good supply of meal ten or twelve jars of honey, each of which contained some two gallons. Liberal supplies of ground nuts were also furnished every time the tributary tribes brought their dues to Linyanti, and an ox was given for slaughter every week or two. Sekeletu also appropriated two cows to be milked for us every morning and evening. This was in accordance with the acknowledged rule throughout this country, that the chief should feed all strangers who come on special business to him, and take up their abode in his *kotla*. A present is usually given in return for the hospitality, but, except in cases where their aboriginal customs have been modified, nothing would be asked. Europeans spoil the feeling that hospitality is the sacred duty of the chiefs, by what in other circumstances is laudable conduct. No sooner do they arrive than they offer to purchase food, and, instead of waiting till a meal is prepared for them in the evening, cook for themselves, and then often decline even to partake of that which is made ready for their use.[14]

Richly fruitful Barotseland was also a land of swamps where malaria was ever present. The land around Sekeletu's capital, Linyanti, was not a suitable base for a missionary and trading base among the Kololo. Sekeletu, who became very attached to Livingstone and insisted that in him he had found a father again, was eager to help him find a base for a future mission. He was aiming to fulfil his father Sebitwane's plan. Moshweshwe had made known, to both Sebitwane and Sechele, his relations with the missionaries of the Paris mission as an example of the advantage a chief could gain through a missionary alliance. Sebitwane had seen Livingstone as his missionary and ally. A mission also promised more trade for a people who already had a taste for European goods brought to them by the Mambari slavers.[15] More important was that, when Livingstone returned to stay with his wife and children, the Ndebele, the most dangerous enemy of the Kololo, would not attack a people who were host to Moffat's daughter. The Kololo leadership was well aware that the Ndebele leader, Mzilikazi, had built up a very close friendship with Robert Moffat.

Sekeletu set out to cement his relationship with Livingstone. The chief, with a retinue of over a hundred followers, took Livingstone on a royal progress by canoe to the northern capital of the kingdom at Naliele. This large town, two hundred miles from Linyanti, was built on an artificial mound in the middle of the Barotse flood plain. Livingstone on the way saw no sign of the high ground he sought, high ground necessary as a healthy site for European missionaries and traders. He could find none because there were none.

Sekeletu then lent Livingstone an official herald, a group of servants and canoes to enable him to travel up the Zambesi a further hundred miles to continue his search. This journey took Livingstone into an area where the indigenous Lozi people were not yet completely absorbed into the Kololo *morafe* as their brothers and sisters to the south had been.[16] On this trip Livingstone acted out the alliance between missionary and royal house which Sebitwane had intended. The Kololo were using Livingstone as Moshweshwe of the Sotho had used the French Protestant mission to help reinforce his authority, while also helping the acceptance of the mission through his royal patronage. At each village as Livingstone entered his herald went before him who

> whenever we approached a village began to roar out at the top of his voice, 'Do we not see a great Lord? Here comes a Lord. Let everyone come and salute the father of Sekeletu. Whoever has corn or milk let him bring it'.[17]

What is typical of Livingstone is that there then follows in his journal a detailed study of the many different roles within Kololo society played by these heralds and an explanation of how they were paid. In that region the indigenous language Lozi still flourished and it was very different from the version of Tswana spoken by the Kololo. Livingstone immediately started to make up a word list and also attempted to see if Lozi syntax varied from that of the Tswana/Sotho family of languages. He was also aware that he was acting the role of an *nduna* of Sekeletu's and reinforcing the chief's claim to authority in the region, even as he sought a good site for a mission station.[18]

Whatever this trek did for Sekeletu's authority, it confirmed Livingstone's fears that there was no dry, highland, malaria free site in the Kololo kingdom. His long stay (he was there for over three months) also confirmed that the Kololo kingdom was involved in the trade in slaves and ivory. This appeared to have been started some decades earlier by the Mambari servants of the Portuguese but was being taken up by Portuguese themselves. A Portuguese, da Silva Porto, was already in the kingdom when Livingstone arrived. In addition, Swahili traders from the East Coast sultanate of Zanzibar had also reached Sekeletu's frontiers, though as yet there was no trade in that direction.

Livingstone felt all the more pressure now to find a readily accessible route from either the west or east coasts to bring legitimate trade into the region and, by undercutting the slave trade, to destroy it. Ivory, for which there was an enormous and increasing demand in the United States and Europe, would have to be, initially at least, the staple of this trade. But how was it to be transported to the coast? Livingstone knew that it had hitherto been transported by slaves who were captured or acquired inland, many of whom were also sold abroad at the end of the journey.[19] He saw the future as lying with the chiefs using their own domestic slaves and other servants to do that work, carrying the ivory to the coast and bringing the trade goods back. It was the international trade in slaves, and the slave raiding that took people out of Africa and was the source of the great violence and social disruption, that he wished to end. Traditional African domestic slavery he accepted as part of African culture which would eventually be changed as the African societies developed, but it was not something that warranted immediate interference.

How was he now to proceed to find this accessible route from the coast? He first considered going to the east. If Portuguese slavers could make the journey, surely missionaries and legitimate traders could. Da Silva Porto offered to guide him to Benguela, which was Porto's base, but Livingstone refused. This was the slavers' route and the slavers' base, so Livingstone felt it was contaminated. Rather he decided he should try to find a route to Loanda, the Angolan capital, where, according to the Mambari, there were British contacts. It was also, though he did not know it, a port where ships of the Royal Navy called and where a British Commissioner for the Suppression of the Slave Trade, Edmund Gabriel, was stationed.

A problem that pressed on Livingstone at the end of August 1853 was that he had no resources left. He had paid off the few men who had accompanied him from Kuruman. He had, in any case, found them to be unsatisfactory. How was he to make the trip to Loanda? It was here that his close relationship with Sekeletu came into its own. Livingstone had already acted as the chief's emissary in his journey among the northern Lozi. That relationship had

4. A coffle of slaves.

been put onto a new personal footing soon after his return from the north. Sekeletu went to visit Mpepe, a sub chief who was the chief's full cousin; indeed Mpepe thought that he would inherit the chieftaincy when Sebitwane died. Mpepe had become very close to the Portuguese and had received guns from them as well as, reputedly, a small cannon. Sekeletu wanted to investigate what Mpepe was up to and he took Livingstone with him as part of his court on a visit. Livingstone described what happened at the meeting. On arrival Livingstone had been disturbed to see many of Mpepe's people carrying arms in the *kgotla* or meeting place:

> Mpepe had a small battle axe, with which he had arranged with his people to hamstring Sekeletu as he rose in the *kgotla*. Had Sekeletu stood as he was, alone nearly, he would have attempted assassination in that way. A little circumstance knocked all on the head. When we sat down in the *kgotla* I sat down between Sekeletu and Mpepe. After sitting a little I asked Sekeletu, 'Where are we to sleep?' He replied, 'Come, I will shew you'. When he rose I did the same, and my body covered his. (All afterwards wondered why he (M.) did not cut me down too rather than fail.) In the evening Mpepe's confidential friends came to Sekeletu and revealed all. 'If what you say you believe to be true, take him off immediately.' He was immediately led forth by his own people and killed. Asleep in a hut close by I knew nothing about it till next day.[20]

Livingstone, the saviour, however unintentionally, of the chief's life, had discussed his plans on a number of occasions with Sekeletu, who saw the advantage to himself of a new route for trade from the coast and one pioneered by his own people. He now offered to give Livingstone men to go with him who would carry Sekeletu's ivory both for trade and to finance the journey. Sekeletu provided a riding ox for Livingstone, named 'Sinbad' by the latter. Sekeletu also gave several other oxen to the party; they were to be slaughtered for food on the journey. Livingstone's own equipment consisted of little more than a small tent, his scientific instruments, his magic lantern and slides to go with it, and two boxes, one of clothes and one of papers. Livingstone was unsure what might transpire, so he left his journal and some other papers with Sekeletu to be taken south by any traveller who visited the chief.

All of this took time to be organised and agreed. It was not until the beginning of November 1853 that everything was ready for this adventure. It was an adventure jointly undertaken by Livingstone and the Kololo, on whose subsidies and support he was completely dependent and for which he gave the Kololo full credit in his *Missionary Travels*.[21] The Kololo would not have attempted it without him but neither could he have done it without them. Only two of this party of twenty-seven men were 'Kololo' strictly speaking, the rest being of local stock but nevertheless representative of the Kololo chieftaincy.

Livingstone, by this time, had only six months left of the two years paid leave that the LMS had given him. While it was uncertain that he was going to be able to get the task done in time, it was clear that he knew that he was not going to go back to settled mission station type service. Would, however, the LMS continue to pay him as a pioneer opening up south central Africa to Christianity and commerce? He certainly did not see himself simply as an explorer. If he had done so he would surely have gone to see Mosi oa tunya, the Victoria Falls, as he would later name them during his time at Linyanti, as they were no more than two days distant. After all, he had known about them since his previous visit with Oswell. Clearly he continued to see his future as being a pioneer for Christianity and commerce who would always preach the gospel wherever he went. The problem remained of who would pay him to do this. He was also aware that some had come to see him as a mere traveller. It appeared that Mrs Moffat feared that this was what he had become. She had castigated his 'wanderings' and had written him several letters containing what he considered unasked for advice. He wrote to his old friend Sir Thomas Steele (one of the Indian service officers who had visited the Livingstones at Mabotsa and after whom the Livingstones had named their second son) on 24 September 1853:

> This is meant to be a confidential gossip about matters which I do not feel at liberty to communicate to anyone save yourself ... I was never in more need of your assistance than at present, and that which I most want is just what many people are amazingly fond of giving unasked, I mean advice.
>
> You are already acquainted with the circumstances which led me to the people in this quarter and of the discoveries which make me appear to many as more of a traveller than missionary. I have had but one object in view in all that I have done viz. the amelioration of the condition of the inhabitants of this unhappy country. For this I wish to live and in pursuit of it I hope to die ... but I fear that some grumblings on the part of ignorant constituents of our Society indicate that my researches must soon come to a close.[22]

He believed some spot might still be found for a base for European mission-aries, but the work of evangelism in this area would have to be done primarily by local people. They had a greater degree of immunity to malaria and the intermittent fever that Livingstone had come, rightly, to attribute to the bite of the Tampan tick. The work of opening up the area and building good relations with the people in preparation for these future developments had to go on and he could do it. He looked then to Steele, who might be able to open the way for some kind of unspecified governmental support, and at the end of the letter asked 'If you are acquainted with the sentiments of the Government and think I might make an offer of service I should be glad if you should act for me'.

Not knowing what the future was to hold for them, the expedition of the Kololo *morafe* set off, led by a leader authorised by Sekeletu, who also happened to be a European missionary. Livingstone was quite clear what his relationship with these men was; it was that of the chief's *nduna*. This he made explicit in his journal when describing how one morning the men were deeply disturbed and did not want to go on because of a dream one of them had had during the night.

> When I came out of my little tent in the morning, they were sitting the pictures of abject sorrow. I asked if we were to be guided by dreams or by the authority I derived from Sekeletu? [23]

Livingstone travelled by canoe, but progress was slow. This was, first, because they could only go as fast as those on the shore who were driving the oxen. Secondly, it was because at each village Pitsane, his senior companion, insisted on stopping until all the tribute of food due to a representative of Sekeletu had been delivered to Livingstone. Livingstone consoled himself by insisting, 'We have by these delays more time with the people, who receive instruction very favourably'. As ever Livingstone made copious notes about the wild life he encountered.

> When quite beyond the inhabited parts, we found the country abounding in animal life of every form. There are upwards of thirty species of birds on the river itself. Hundreds of the *Ibis religiosa* come down the Leeambye with the rising water, as they do on the Nile; then large white pelicans, in flocks of three hundred at a time, following each other in long extending line, rising and falling as they fly, so regularly along, as to look like an extended coil of birds; clouds of black shell-eating birds, called linongolo (*Anastomus lamelligerus*); also plovers, snipes, curlews, and herons, without number.
>
> There are, besides the more common, some strange varieties. The pretty white *ardetta* is seen in flocks, settling on the backs of large herds of buffaloes, and following them on the wing when they run; while the kala (*textor erythrorhynchus*) is a better horseman, for it sits on the withers when the animal is at full speed.
>
> Then those strange birds with the scissor-bills, with snow-white breast, jet black coat, and red beak, sitting by day on the sandbanks, the very picture of comfort and repose. Their nests are only little hollows made on these same sandbanks, without any attempt at concealment; they watch them closely, and frighten away the marabou and crows from their eggs by feigned attacks at their heads. When man approaches their nests, they change their tactics, and, like the lapwing and ostrich, let one wing drop and make one leg limp, as if lame. The upper mandible being so much shorter than the lower, the young are more helpless than the stork

in the fable with the flat dishes, and must have everything conveyed into the mouth by the parents, till they are able to provide for themselves. The lower mandible, as thin as a paper-knife, is put into the water while the bird skims along the surface, and scoops up any little insect it meets. It has great length of wing, and can continue its flight with perfect ease, the wings acting, though kept above the level of the body. The wonder is, how this ploughing of the surface of the water can be so well performed as to yield a meal, for it is usually done in the dark. Like most aquatic feeders, they work by night, when insects and fishes rise to the surface.[24]

Once beyond Sekeletu's dominions they were still received with friendship by the Lunda chiefs. By this time they were travelling in daily downpours of heavy rain as it was by then well into the rainy season. When one Lunda chief, Manenko, a woman and the niece of the paramount chief, Shinde, insisted that they stayed where they were until she came to visit, Livingstone pressed on after what he called 'four days of rain and diplomacy'. They were then stopped by Nyamaona's people. Nyamaona was the mother of Manenko. She told Livingstone that cataracts would soon stop his progress by canoe. Moreover, he ought to visit Shinde since it was through his territory he was passing. Livingstone was unhappy about this but matters were taken in hand by Manenko, who arrived and took charge. She stopped the Kololo from loading the canoes and simply led them off towards Shinde's court. Livingstone also succumbed to the authority of this striking young woman, naked apart from her ornaments and a tiny leather strip to cover her genitals. As he said:

> My men succumbed sooner to this petticoat government than I felt inclined to do, and left me no power; and, being unwilling to encounter her tongue, I was moving off to the canoes when she gave me a kind explanation and, with her hand on my shoulder, put on a motherly look, saying, 'Now my little man, just do as the rest have done.' My feelings of annoyance of course vanished.[25]

In his journal Livingstone records his feelings about Manenko and Lunda women in general. He wrote:

> Some of them might be good looking, but one cannot help feeling all is spoiled by their state of nudity ... The same feeling exists among my people. They say, 'The girls would be pretty were they not stark naked and always using their hands to cover themselves'.[26]

This frankness in his private journals does not appear in *Missionary Travels*, where there is simply one reference to Manenko's 'frightful nudity'. Although well received by Shinde, Livingstone had been travelling for weeks through incessant rain and was suffering from recurrent bouts of malaria. At Shinde's he was still almost exactly 800 miles from Loanda. He stayed at Shinde's for a fortnight, partly in order to conform to the traditional practice of politeness due towards a great chief and partly through his own weakness because of fever. He consoled himself by the fact that he was sowing the seeds of the gospel that would hopefully be cultivated and grow to be harvested later. Shinde's people were certainly keen to watch his lantern slides and listened politely to his explanatory talks on biblical truths based on them. Such a novelty was irresistible.

Livingstone was now in a type of region he had not encountered before, that of tropical forest, where in the rainy season paths tended to become obscured by rapidly growing creepers and progress was desperately slow. This was bad enough among the Lunda where Shinde extended the travellers his protection and provided them with food. Once Livingstone and his men crossed the Kasai river, however, they entered the territory of a people, the Chokwe, deeply involved in slave raiding and used to charging the Portuguese and Mambari a man or a woman as the price for passing a village. The usual African tradition of offering food to strangers had also disappeared in this area of the new slave trade. On a number of occasions Livingstone and the Kololo had to show very clearly that they were willing to fight, even though outnumbered, to be allowed to pass. They survived a dreadful three hundred miles of struggle through marsh and rainforest with very little food, con-stantly under threat from the Chokwe and subsequently the Shinje. They reached their lowest point of hopelessness when a chief on the banks of the Quango river challenged them with the usual demand for a tusk or a man to allow them to cross. They had nothing to give, since Livingstone and the men had given away all their clothes except what they stood up in and the Kololo had even given away their personal ornaments. All they had were a couple of riding oxen and Sekeletu's ivory, which they felt they could not give away.

At this point a Portuguese militia sergeant, Cypriano Abreu, appeared and got them across the river. At his post he fed them and sent them on their way to the Portuguese fort at Cassange. There, where they arrived after three days of cutting their way through six foot high wet grass, they cashed in their ivory to clothe themselves and to purchase cloth and beads, the currency with which to pay their way to Loanda. They left Cassange on 21 April and finally arrived at Loanda on the 31 May 1854. At the house of Edmund Gabriel, the Commissioner for the Suppression of the Slave Trade, Livingstone, ill with chronic dysentery and malaria, was put to bed and nursed back to health.

Livingstone and his Kololo were all well looked after by Gabriel, the men being housed and issued with fresh clothing. They showed initiative by starting a firewood business and later helped unload a coal ship at the princely rate of sixpence a day. Livingstone and his Kololo were also well received by the Portuguese authorities in the city, as they had been throughout their last three hundred miles trek from Cassange. The Bishop of Loanda, who was also Acting-Governor of Angola, received them at a formal levee. At this Livingstone and his followers were treated as an embassy from Sekeletu. Before they left to return to Linyanti the bishop, in his capacity as Governor, clothed all the party in blue and red uniforms and provided them with blankets. He also presented to them a horse, saddled and bridled, together with a colonel's uniform to be given to Sekeletu.

Soon after appearing to get well, Livingstone's health again broke down and it appeared as if he was about to die. He was saved by the attentions of the surgeon from one of the three British cruisers which were in the harbour. The *Philomel, Pluto* and *Polyphemus* were there to prevent slaves being exported to Brazil, one of the main exports of Loanda until the coming of the British blockade in the 1840s. The naval officers were most impressed with Livingstone's achievement; they did not see it as he himself saw it as a joint venture with the Kololo. They and Gabriel encouraged him, when he was well enough, to send reports of it to the LMS, also to Lord Clarendon, the Foreign Secretary, and to Sir Roderick Murchison, President of the Royal Geographic Society. Murchison was to become yet another of Livingstone's personal friends and supporters among the British elite.

Livingstone was clear that only human porterage could carry goods into the Zambesi valley from the west coast. This route could therefore hardly be seen as opening up central Africa to Christianity and commerce. Livingstone was offered a free passage home on a merchant ship, the *Forerunner,* but he refused, though he gave his notes, maps and a journal as well as letters to Lieutenant Bedingfeld of the Royal Navy to take back to Britain.[27] Livingstone had no alternative but to go back to Linyanti to try for the east coast. He also felt he was honour bound to his men in any case. When reported back in Britain, his loyalty to his men was blown up to become the principal reason for his return to Linyanti. Already his admirers were starting to create their own image of Livingstone, whether he liked it or not.

It was on 20 September 1854 that Livingstone and his men, arrayed in their Portuguese finery, set off on the return journey. This was six weeks after their arrival, during which time Livingstone had been given up for dead at least once. Partly because he was still not completely fit, but also because he wished to gain an accurate understanding of the state of the Portuguese colonial presence in Angola, the pace was leisurely and Livingstone indulged in a number of extended stays with various hospitable Portuguese officers along his route.

His Kololo were delighted with all that had happened to them on their great adventure. As Livingstone said of them:

> The roads, however, from Loanda to Golungo Alto were both hard and dry, and they suffered severely in consequence; yet they were composing songs to be sung when they should reach home. The Argonauts were nothing to them; and they remarked very impressively to me, 'It was well you came with the Makololo; for no tribe could have done what we have accomplished in coming to the white man's country: we are the true ancients, who can tell wonderful things'.[28]

Livingstone and the men were bound together by a shared experience that had not been without its difficult moments. It had been an African experience, not the experience of a European expedition with paid porters. Livingstone insisted that his authority came from Sekeletu. He was the leader of a Kololo expedition and, like any headman, he had to be willing to face down mutiny. We have seen the problem he faced by men having visions which called them to turn back. The worst moment for him came on 11 March 1854, when he was desperately ill with malaria and dysentery. Some of the men challenged his right to lead. He faced them down with a pistol in his hand. Within a few hours he fell into a coma, but loyalty prevailed: when he came to he found that the men, including the troublemakers, had ringed the camp with a stockade and were preparing to fight off a threatening party of Chokwe. After their return to Linyanti it was with many of these men, and others sent with him by Sekeletu, that Livingstone was going to march to the east coast of Africa.

After Livingstone's death, his biographer, Sir Harry Johnston, was to ask how was it that Livingstone 'managed his men' so well on this journey, while failing miserably with a number of different parties of paid porters in his journeying in east and central Africa after 1866. Johnston, like many since, in fact confused two very different situations. The expedition from Linyanti to Loanda, and back again and on to Mozambique, was Livingstone leading an African expedition, as an African leader under the authority of Sekeletu. In the years of wandering after 1866, his own personal followers like the Kololo stayed loyal, but Livingstone was a failure as an employer of paid porters. He was equally a failure, in the Zambesi expedition, as the leader of European employees.

After Livingstone and his men had gone past Cassange they again encountered the hostility of the Chokwe and the Shinje, but they survived to reach the territory of Shinde's Lunda, where, somewhat to their surprise, the spirited young woman chief Manenko did not come to meet them. They entered the densely forested wetlands, again at the worst time, the rainy season. Their progress, which had not been rapid, slowed down to about

seven miles per day, not only because of the terrain but also because of the
sickness which affected both Livingstone and the men. Weakened by dysentery and nearly deaf from his quinine therapy for malaria, and sleeping
night after night on the ground in waterlogged campsites, the last weeks
before breaking out onto the Zambesi flood plain and the welcoming villages
of the Kololo took on a nightmarish quality. In his journal covering this
period we find Livingstone writing, at least at times, as if he despaired of
Africa and Africans. Some of these words, if quoted as his considered views
of Africa and Africans, would be a travesty of the truth.

From the moment they reached the edge of the Kololo kingdom, Livingstone and his men were feted everywhere they went as heroes returned from
the dead. They so very nearly had not made it. Livingstone conducted two
services of thanksgiving on 23 July 1855 at the first home village they reached.

> The men decked themselves out in their best, for all had managed to preserve
> their suits of European clothing, which, with their white and red caps, gave them
> a rather dashing appearance. They tried to walk like soldiers. And called themselves
> 'my braves'. Having been saluted with salvoes from the women, we met the whole
> population, and having given an address on divine things, I told them we had
> come that day to thank God before them all for His mercy in preserving us from
> dangers, from strange tribes and sicknesses ... They gave us two fine oxen to
> slaughter, and the women have supplied us abundantly with milk and meal.[29]

In August Livingstone began talks with Sekeletu and the Kololo elders
about his intention of attempting to reach the east coast. At Sekeletu's capital
he had found a Swahili slave trader, Said bin Habib. Livingstone told the
Kololo leaders that he would go with Habib, if the Kololo did not want a
path opened to their land other than the west coast route he had already
explored.[30] He wrote:

> All expressed a desire that I should try to open the Zambesi to Quilimane, and
> so we could chose which was best. In the event of going with Rya Syde, I would
> have it in my power to discover Tanganyeta or Lake Nyassa, but down the Zambesi
> seems more in accordance with what I set before my mind as the path of duty,
> viz. 'open up paths to the East or Western Coasts from the Interior'. I wrote 'that
> having set this before me, I should either succeed or perish'. I have steadily kept
> my resolution, and now after much thought consider it will not be right to go
> with Rya Syde for the sake of the fame of discovering another lake, if the Makololo
> prefer my making the attempt to open a path by water to the East Coast.[31]

Through African and Swahili sources Livingstone had come to know about
a great lake which lay between Linyanti and the east coast. From what he
had heard he had been unable to distinguish between Lake Tanganyika and
Lake Malawi, the proper name for which he had heard of by the Swahili

name Nyassa – a stretch of water. Sekeletu and the Kololo elders agreed to
mount another expedition with Livingstone as leader, this time to seek a
route from the east coast for missionaries and traders. They understood that
Livingstone was going to return with his wife at the head of the new mission
if all went well. Livingstone was clear that the Swahili route, like that he
had just followed from Loanda, was only usable by porters. He was out to
prove that the way ahead was along the Zambesi. He felt sure that, beyond
the dramatic barrier of Mosi-oa-tunya, the Zambesi would prove to be the
Mississippi of Africa.

When he had arrived at Shesheke Livingstone received letters from the
south that had been waiting for him on an island in the Zambesi close to
the Falls for a year. His father-in-law had taken letters and various boxes
of dried fruit and maize meal on a visit to Mzilikazi, whose warriors had
then delivered them to their bitter enemies, the Kololo, who had stored
them in a specially built hut on the island. The food was now useless but
Livingstone was delighted by the letters, though somewhat nonplussed by
the absence of any letter from his wife. (She had written to him via South
Africa. Why none of her letters had reached Moffat in time for his journey
is unclear.)

He now took time to write a large number of letters which Said bin Habib
would take to Loanda. They included a very long, detailed report to the
LMS in London.[32] What is striking in this report is his insistence that the
policy of the widest possible diffusion of the Gospel was the way forward,
not intense concentration on individual conversions in a small area. He
wrote to Arthur Tidman, the LMS secretary:

> I do not undervalue the importance of the conversion and salvation of the most
> abject creature that breathes, it is of overwhelming worth to him personally; but
> viewing our work of wide sowing of the good seed relatively to the harvest which
> will be reaped when all our heads are low, there can, I think, be no comparison.[33]

In his letters and reports sent from Loanda, Livingstone again and again
remarked on the good work done by the Jesuits in Angola and of the tragic
consequences for Christianity in Angola when the Portuguese Crown had
expelled them from its territories. The Jesuits as missionaries clearly fascinated him and he referred to them on many occasions. In this letter to
Tidman, whether he was aware of it or not, Livingstone was arguing as
Matteo Ricci, the leader of the Jesuit mission in China, had done at the end
of the sixteenth century. It was that the widespread diffusion of the Christian
message laid the ground for long-term success on a large scale which
concentration on immediate individual conversions did not.[34]

As already noted, this interest in and admiration for the Jesuits was an extraordinary characteristic of Livingstone. At this time anti-Catholic feeling was strong in Britain, particularly in evangelical circles. The words 'Jesuit' or 'Jesuitical' were indeed taken as summing up all that was worst in that deplorable institution, the Roman Catholic Church.

In the same report Livingstone insisted that European missionaries could live healthily near Chief Shinde's and in the Kafue Hills, though not on the Lozi flood-plain itself. Despite the prevalence of malaria, he pointed out that he had brought all the men who started out for Loanda back to Shesheke and Linyanti. Malaria could be managed. After all, although he himself had had so many attacks, missionaries who came out would not be sleeping as he had done, night after night with only a blanket between him and the wet ground, after a day of walking sometimes knee-deep in a swamp. With regard to starting a mission station among the Kololo, he still had not found a healthy site. Livingstone informed Tidman that he and Mary would return there, but he could not risk bringing children unless a healthy site was found. With his letters written and his journal brought up to date, Livingstone was now ready to begin the new expedition.

On 3 November 1855 the second Kololo expedition led by David Livingstone set off from Linyanti, accompanied for a few days march by Chief Sekeletu himself. Sekeletu, who equipped the expedition with food and with ivory to trade, had appointed as Livingstone's second in command Sekwebu, a veteran of a number of journeys along both banks of the Zambesi. A wise elder of Nguni stock whose judgement Livingstone came to trust, Sekwebu also had the ability to make himself understood in several of the languages of the peoples they would encounter on the journey.

After the expedition left Shesheke, Livingstone decided to visit Mosi-oa-tunya which he was later to name, for European purposes, the Victoria Falls.[35] Even though the flow of the Zambesi was at its lowest point of the year, the Falls were still 'the most wonderful sight I had seen in Africa'.

The falls are bounded on three sides by ridges 300 or 400 feet in height, which are covered with forest, with red soil appearing among the trees. When about half a mile from the falls, I left the canoe by which we had come down thus far, and embarked on a lighter one, with men well acquainted with the rapids, who, by passing down the centre of the stream in the eddies and still places caused by many jutting rocks, brought me to an island situated in the middle of the river, and on the edge of the lip over which the water rolls. In coming hither, there was danger of being swept down by the streams which rushed along each side of the island; but the river was now low, and we sailed where it is totally impossible to go when the water is high. But though we had reached the island, and were within a few yards of the spot, a view from which would solve the whole problem, I believe that no one could perceive where the vast body of water went; it seemed to lose itself in the earth, the opposite lip of the fissure into which it disappeared, being only eighty feet distant. At least I did not comprehend it until, creeping with awe to the verge, I peered down into a vast rent which had been made from bank to bank of the broad Zambesi, and saw that a stream of a thousand yards broad, leaped down a hundred feet, and then became suddenly compressed into the space of fifteen or twenty yards. The entire falls are simply a crack made into a hard basaltic rock from the right to the left bank of the Zambesi, and then prolonged from the left bank away through thirty or forty miles of hills. If one imagines the Thames filled with low tree-covered hills immediately beyond the tunnel, extending as far as Gravesend; the bed of black basaltic rock instead of London mud; and fissure made therein from one end of the tunnel to the other, down through the keystones of the arch, and prolonged from the left end of the tunnel through thirty miles of hills; the pathway being a hundred feet down from the bed of the river instead of what it is, with the lips of the fissure from 80 to 100 feet apart; then fancy the Thames leaping bodily into the gulf; and forced there to change its direction, and flow from the right to the left bank; and then rush boiling and roaring through the hills, – he may have some idea of what takes place at this, the most wonderful sight I have witnessed in Africa. In looking down into the fissure on the right of the island, one sees nothing but a dense white cloud, which, at the time we visited the spot, had two bright rainbows on it. (The sun was on the meridian, and the declination about equal to the latitude of the place.) From the cloud rushed up a great jet of vapour exactly like steam, and it mounted 200 or 300 feet high; there condensing, it changed its hue to that of dark smoke, and came down in a constant shower, which soon wetted us to the skin. This shower falls chiefly on the opposite side of the fissure, and a few yards back from the lip, where stands a straight hedge of evergreen trees, whose leaves are always wet. From their roots a number of little rills run back into the gulf; but as they flow down the steep wall there, the column of vapour, in its ascent, licks them up clean off the rock, and away they mount again. They are constantly running down, but never reach the bottom.[36]

He then went on, as he always did, in the journal, to describe in detail all the local trees and the various edible fruits that could be found in the neighbourhood. He also described planting peach and apricot stones as well as coffee seeds on an island that received regular showers of spray from the Falls, hoping to start a plantation for his return.

At that time of the year the Zambesi valley is very hot, with temperatures of 100 degrees fahrenheit most days. Sekwebu wisely led them north east-wards along the escarpment above the valley, where it was cooler and the going was smoother. There, on the plateau which forms what is now the southern province of Zambia, Livingstone thought that he had at last found, on the edge of the Kaleya river valley, a healthy highland site for a mission within the lands of Sekeletu.

Once the column passed from the area of Sekeletu's authority, the people of the first independent Tonga village they approached were most suspicious of this Kololo troop led by a white man. Livingstone wrote in his journal how a menacing crowd of men approached them on the approach to the village:

> Then one came howling in the most hideous manner and at the top of his voice. His eyes were prominent, his lip covered with foam, and every muscle in his frame quivered. He came near me, and having a battle axe in his hand alarmed my men, but they were afraid to disobey my orders to offer no violence to any one. It seemed to me a case of extasy or prophetic frenzy voluntarily produced, as in the mysteries of the oracle priests of old. I felt a little afraid, but would not shew it before either before my people or strangers, and kept a sharp look out on the battle axe, for it seemed a sorry way to leave the world to get one's head chopped off by a mad savage, though it is perhaps preferable to hydrophobia, cancer, or *delirium tremens*. I at last beckoned to the civil headman to remove him, and he did so, taking him by the hand and drawing him aside. He pretended not to know what he was doing. I would fain have felt his pulse to see whether the violent trembling were not feigned, but the flow of perspiration shewed that it was real, though it continued fully half an hour and gradually ceased.[37]

They were then hospitably received and continued on their march.

Sekwebu continued to lead them in a north-easterly direction till they met the Kafue river. They then followed that river southwards till it joined the Zambesi. At that point the Zambesi is wide, placid and navigable in both directions for many miles, Livingstone's Mississippi of Africa. In following this route, a sensible one from the point of view of the health and comfort of the men, Livingstone had, however, missed the Kariba Gorge, which would have told him that the Zambesi was no Mississippi. Further downstream, near the end of this navigable stretch of the Zambesi, he was told there was another gorge, Mpata, but he skirted the area because there was an alternative road much easier for his hundred or so men to pass on foot. From what he was told he did not recognise Mpata as a bar to any kind of vessel navigating upstream.

As they marched on and approached the confluence of the Luangwa with the Zambesi, Livingstone and his men encountered the same kind of hostility, a breakdown of the African traditions of hospitality and courtesy, which he had encountered among the Chokwe on the journey to Loanda. The reason was the same. He had reached the outer fringes of the impact of Portuguese slave raiding. There, at the confluence of the Luangwa and the Zambesi, were the ruins of the Portuguese post of Zumbo. This was the furthest up the Zambesi the Portuguese had reached, but they had long since been forced to abandon the post in the face of African opposition. Mburuma, the chief of the district, halted the caravan in its tracks. Livingstone and Sekwebu had to use all their powers of diplomacy to persuade him that they had nothing to do with the Portuguese. The chief was eventually convinced and became a friend, an important matter if Livingstone was to come back up the river to found a mission among the Kololo as he intended. Just how serious the situation was before the successful negotiations can be gathered from the entry in Livingstone's journal as he and the Kololo waited on the banks of the Luangwa. He wrote on 14 January 1856:

> At the confluence of the Loango and Zambesi. Thank God for his mercies thus far. How soon I may be called to stand before him my righteous Judge, I know not. All hearts are in his hands, and merciful and gracious is the Lord our God. O Jesus, grant me resignation to thy will, and entire reliance on thy powerful hand. On thy work alone I lean. But wilt thou permit me to plead for Africa? The cause is thine. What impulse will be given to the idea that Africa is not open if I die now? [38]

He and his Kololo were to meet confrontation on approaching every new community between the confluence of the Zambesi with the Luangwa and the Portuguese post at Tete. Only by proving that they had nothing to do with the Portuguese and with slaving were they able to go on.

Mburuma sent men to see Livingstone and his men safely across the Luangwa. Livingstone was able to pay them with what was almost the last of the beads and cloth which Sekeletu had given them to pay for guides and to hire canoes. The chiefs along the northern bank of the Zambesi were the most friendly they were to meet on this last stage of their journey, as soon they knew Livingstone was not a slaver.

> Pangola visited us and presented us with food. In few other countries would 114 sturdy vagabonds be supported by the generosity of the headmen and villagers, and whatever they gave be presented with politeness. My men got pretty well supplied individually, for they went into the villages and commenced dancing. The young women were especially pleased with the new steps they had to show, though I suspect many of them were invented for the occasion ... At every fresh instance of liberality, Sekwebu said, 'Did I not tell you that these people had hearts while we were still at Linyanti?' [39]

By this time the party was travelling very slowly, as the last of the oxen were dying from the effect of tsetse bites received higher up the valley. Also Livingstone was physically exhausted, although writing jauntily enough in his journal, even more so in the published version in *Missionary Travels*. He described how he kept missing a hippo at close range because he could not hold his gun steady. Although he said this was a result of the weakness of the arm bitten by the lion, it clearly was not, as he had shot successfully for game earlier in the journey despite the old injury. The north bank of the Zambesi was hilly and covered with dense vegetation and in their weakened state progress was dreadfully slow. Temperatures were consistently high, Livingstone recorded 91 degrees in the shade at sunset as being common.[40]

He was very tired when he and his people reached the territory of Chief Mpende, the southernmost chief of the Maravi or Malawi peoples, these southern groups usually called themselves Amang'anja. Livingstone had learned, however, from the trip to Loanda: when a really heavy outburst of rain came, they did not attempt to trudge on, but built grass shelters and fires and waited till the rain passed over. His willingness to stop in this way was also an indication of his tiredness.

Mpende was bitterly opposed to the Portuguese and had sworn he would not let whites pass through his territories. His people met the Kololo party with fierce hostility. Livingstone's Kololo were ready to fight, some of them saying it was about time they caught some slaves to carry Sekeletu's ivory. Livingstone and Sekwebu's policy of diplomacy was, however, successful. Sekwebu obtained an interview with Mpende himself on the strength of an ox leg sent to the chief as tribute. The rest of the ox was eaten by the Kololo. As Livingstone wrote about his old friend who had led his people from Lesotho to the Zambesi, 'this is a means Sebitwane employed to instil courage'.[41]

Sekwebu's interview with Mpende was of long-term importance. The Amang'anja chief strongly advised them to give up following the river on the north bank but to cross it and strike directly across country to Tete: the going would be very much easier for Livingstone and his men and the distance shorter. Livingstone agreed. He had wanted to cross to the south bank anyway, as it appeared to provide easier going than the north, and the additional advice to cut across country to Tete rather than following the northwards swinging bend of the Zambesi seemed sensible to very tired men. When he arrived at Tete he was told that there were rapids south of Chicova that he had missed, but he did not take them seriously. This mistake was of momentous consequence when he returned to the Zambesi heading a government expedition. It is explained at least partly by an error in scientific procedure rare with Livingstone. All along the Zambesi he had been taking altitude readings by checking the boiling point of water by an accurate thermometer. At Tete he made an error in his readings and did not realise the extent of the drop in altitude between Mpende's village and Tete. Had his reading been accurate, he would have realised that the rapids called the Cabora Bassa simply could not be navigable. This rare error may be explicable by tiredness but it is also possible that an obsessed and exhausted man unconsciously did not want to hear any suggestion that his African Mississippi was no such thing. At Tete, had he been in a different state of mind, he might have made more thorough attempts to find out about the Cabora Basa, but he did not.

During the long march from Mpende's to Tete, Livingstone's journal is full of careful notes of the fauna and flora as well as the geology of the area and of the customs of the various groups through whose villages the march took him. Exhausted though he was, his passion to observe and record never left him. The slowness of his progress gave him time to gain insights into local cultures. He was able to describe some of the customs that mark out the matrilocal, matrilineal peoples he encountered, whose ways were so different from what he had known in southern Africa let alone Europe.[42]

By this stage in the journey he and his men had nothing left to offer in return for village hospitality, so they took to bypassing villages to avoid any kind of confrontation, thus facing an increased mileage to cover with little or no food. Things became so bad that on 2 March 1856, when he was within a day's easy walk from Tete, that Livingstone stopped and sent forward a message to the commandant there, asking for help. Major Sicard, the Portuguese commandant at Tete, responded by sending soldiers with food for Livingstone and his party. The soldiers then escorted them into Tete.

Through all these terrible trials, even when they had nothing of their own and little or no food, Livingstone and his Kololo had kept the ivory sent by Sekeletu safe. There was no way that he could take a hundred Africans back to Europe, so Livingstone got Sicard's agreement that the Kololo could settle on some land and await Livingstone's return there. Malaria then struck Livingstone down along with Sicard and his family. Livingstone had no quinine left, but he used the bark of a tree related to the *Chinchona* from which Quinine is extracted and made an infusion which appeared to work. He carefully sketched the leaves of this tree and sent the drawings to Kew Gardens for identification. He was delighted that his medical care had helped Sicard and had repaid this courteous man somewhat for all his kindness. Despite his weakness, Livingstone also found time to make a list of all the local plants used by Africans to produce medicine, the list taking up almost a page in his published *Travels*. He also made careful enquiries about the Shire river and the lake out of which it flowed.

On 22 April Livingstone, with Sekwebu and sixteen other Kololo paddlers, set off downstream in canoes accompanied by a Portuguese officer with letters affording Livingstone help from the Portuguese authorities whenever needed. They arrived at Sena after five days and found it, like so many Portuguese establishments, in a very run-down condition. There he fell ill again with intermittent fever, which he had already attributed to the bite of the Tampan tick. When he recovered, he and his men paddled on to Mazaro, where again he became very ill. A Portuguese friend of Sicard's lent him a launch and with Sekwebu and seven others of his Kololo he moved down the river at a much greater speed than before, arriving at Quilimane on 20 May 1856, almost exactly four years after leaving Cape Town.

Waiting for Livingstone was a large amount of mail that told him he was already a national hero in Britain on the strength of his Loanda journey alone. In addition Edmund Gabriel had informed Lord Clarendon of what he thought might be Livingstone's date of arrival at Quilemane. As a result Royal Navy ships had been calling there regularly in the hope of picking him up. He was deeply moved to hear that two officers and five ratings of HMS *Dart* had died attempting to cross the treacherous bar at Quilemane on one of these visits. He was also delighted to meet an old friend and companion, the ex-slave George Fleming, who had been sent by Thompson, the LMS agent at the Cape, to Quilemane to meet Livingstone with money and supplies. Fleming had been instructed to use these resources to mount a search expedition for Livingstone should he not appear, a small preview of many search expeditions mounted during the last years of Livingstone's life.

Sekwebu agreed to go with Livingstone to Britain while the other Kololo went back upstream to join their comrades at Tete. Tragically, while on HMS *Frolic*, which picked up Livingstone and Sekwebu, Sekwebu became profoundly upset by the storms on the ocean; in a frenzy he stabbed a sailor and then deliberately drowned himself.

The *Frolic* took Livingstone to Mauritius where he was to pick up a steamer for the journey home. He again became ill and spent several weeks as a guest of the Governor. He finally left on the steamship *Candida* which took him to Egypt. At Alexandria he took ship on the *England*, which suffered severe damage in the western Mediterranean and had to divert from its route and put in at Marseille. From there Livingstone went by train and ferry to London, only to find that Mary was waiting patiently at Southampton for him to arrive on the *England*. He therefore had to rush from London to Southampton to be at last reunited with Mary after four years and eight months of separation. She handed him a long emotional poem she had written for him. One verse read:

> A hundred thousand welcomes! How my heart is gushing o'er
> With love and joy and wonder thus to see you face once more.
> How did I live without you these long long years of woe?
> It seems as if 'twould kill me to be parted from you now.[43]

What was to be their future? She did not know it but he had received at

Quilemane a letter from the directors of the LMS that made it clear they would not back any new venture into the area he believed he had opened up to Christianity and civilisation. Livingstone had, however, promised the Kololo that he would go back, and he had promised Sekeletu he would return to begin a mission. He had written that he had dedicated his life to opening up those lands to Christianity and civilisation.

8

Years of Triumph

Before Livingstone's arrival in Britain, and his emotional reunion with Mary and her 'hundred thousand welcomes', he was already being built up as a hero in whom the British could take pride. There had been a steady growth of publicity about him ever since news of his arrival at Loanda had reached London in 1855.

This publicity reached a new and growing audience which had not existed in the past. The ending of stamp duty on newspapers in 1855 had seen the beginnings of a vast growth in the number of newspapers and of widespread newspaper readership in Britain. The reports from the Crimean War of 1854–56, with their accompanying photographs, exposed not only the horrors of war in general but also the gross mismanagement of the whole campaign. A significant part of this increasing public interest, to some extent a reaction to the gloom produced by the news from war, was a thirst for stories about heroes and heroines. In the midst of all the disasters and bungling, the public's attention was drawn to the heroism of the Light Brigade and to the cool courage of 'the thin red line' of the Argyll and Sutherland Highlanders, standing alone between the Russian army and the British base at Balaclava. The classic example of this new development was the uplifting and well-promoted story of Florence Nightingale and her devoted nurses, who organised the care of the men suffering because 'someone had blundered' and blundered again.

Sir Roderick Murchison, President of the Royal Geographical Society, exploited this newspaper reading public over the next two decades and helped create an enormous public interest in 'heroic' explorers of Africa. Sir Richard Burton, J. H. Speke and J. A. Grant, as well as Livingstone, all became famous as a result of Murchison's efforts. The many expeditions raised to 'find' Livingstone between 1869 and 1873 were a product of this public fascination with heroes of African exploration.

It was news of Livingstone's arrival in Loanda that allowed Murchison to begin the build up of interest in Livingstone that reached a climax on his return to London. It all began on 8 August 1854 when the *Times* reported that Sir Roderick Murchison had declared that Livingstone's journey from the Cape to Loanda was 'the greatest triumph of geographical research which has been effected in out times'. In December of that year, as a result of the initiative of his old teacher Professor Buchanan, Glasgow University awarded Livingstone the degree of LL.D. *in absentia*. At a well-publicised meeting in May 1855 the Royal Geographical Society awarded Livingstone the Patron's Gold Medal for the feat of 'exploring and mapping the land between Lake Ngami and the Portuguese settlements on the West Coast'. Much was made of Livingstone's self-sacrifice in returning with his men to Linyanti. Whether this was a deliberate or unintentional misunderstanding of Livingstone's words we cannot now tell, but it certainly suited Murchison's publicity campaign.

It was this drive for publicity by Murchison which decreed that Livingstone, even though Mary and he had not seen each other for nearly five years, had to make a public appearance in London only three days after they met at Southampton on 12 December. This was to attend the meeting of the RGS at which Livingstone's gold medal, awarded the year before, was to be presented to him. On the evening of 15 December the meeting rooms of the RGS were packed by an audience who stayed until midnight. They listened to speaker after speaker adding their praises of Livingstone's achievements to that of Murchison's formal address. In his address, Murchison emphasised Livingstone's courage and dedication, but, above all, he praised his accurate charting of the lands through which he had travelled. Perhaps it was Professor Richard Owen who made the most important speech of the evening, at least in terms of bringing Livingstone prestige in the scientific community. Owen was one of the most famous scientists of the day. Darwin had sent fossil bones to him for analysis from the *Beagle* and he was the recipient of awards from the scientific societies of most of the nations of Europe. Herman Melville's reference to him in the pages of *Moby Dick* is an indication of just how famous he had become. Owen praised Livingstone for his enormous accumulation of careful scientific observation of animal and plant life in the desert, savannah and rain forest areas through which he had passed. At a time which saw the beginning of the bitter nineteenth-century controversies between science and religion, one of the scientific luminaries of the age gave a ringing endorsement of the scientific abilities of the Reverend Dr Livingstone – as the *Times* referred to him.[1]

One thing that Livingstone emphasised in his reply was his belief in human equality. He had repeated the idea regularly in the journals that he kept on the Kololo expedition and it was central to all his thinking on the future of Africa. He expressed this belief in different ways in different parts of the journals. One of his favourite forms was, when lamenting the faults of a tribe or speculating about the future, to quote Burns's great song of human brotherhood:

For a' that, an' a' that,
It's comin yet for a' that,
That man to man the world o'er
Shall brithers be for a' that.

He clearly asserted this belief and all that followed from it in his speech at the meeting of the RGS:

As a Christian missionary I only did my duty in attempting to open up part of southern intertropical Africa to the sympathy of Christendom, and I am very much gratified by finding, in the interest which you and many others express, a pledge that the true negro family, whose country I have traversed, *will yet become part of the general community of nations*.[2]

That night, however, his fundamental belief in human equality was simply not heard. It was not mentioned in any report of the meeting in the press.[3] People hear what their background and outlook lead them to expect to hear. Another example of the way that what Livingstone said appeared to pass though a filter, as it were, before a British audience could understand it, is the way in which the journey across Africa was perceived. Livingstone pointed out explicitly, in his *Travels and Researches*, that this journey had been an effort by the Kololo people which he had led as a representative of Sekeletu. None of the thousands who bought the book paid any attention. From 1858 until well into the second half of the twentieth century the journey was consistently discussed as a magnificent European achievement.

The day after the meeting of the RGS, Mary and Livingstone were guests of honour at another large public gathering. This was arranged by the London Missionary Society and took place, after a formal dinner in the Livingstones' honour, in the Freemasons Hall. This further gathering of luminaries, with Murchison and others from the evening before in attendance, was presided over by the celebrated evangelical Lord Shaftesbury. The formal address was delivered by the secretary of the LMS, Arthur Tidman, who sang Livingstone's praises, despite the letter he had sent both to Loanda and Quilemane to make sure that Livingstone understood that the society would not support any more adventures. Tidman had been equally laudatory at the meeting of the RGS in May 1855 when he accepted the award of the gold medal on Livingstone's behalf. In the issues of the *Times* of 16 and 17 December these events were fully reported as the main piece of 'home' news in each edition. Murchison's campaign to bring Africa and African exploration to the public's attention was certainly succeeding.

Soon after all this excitement Livingstone heard that the citizens of Cape Town had beaten the RGS and the LMS in the race to honour him;

this was a city whose inhabitants Livingstone disliked and where he had been treated with great suspicion in the early 1840s. On 12 November, the Governor, Sir George Grey, had presided over a meeting in Cape Town at which Mr Rutherfoord, the LMS agent William Thompson and many others had spoken in praise of Livingstone. It was reserved to his old friend, the Astronomer Royal at the Cape, Thomas Maclear, to make the principal speech, which was another encomium of Livingstone as a scientific observer and cartographer.

Then on 5 January, the Lord Mayor of London presided over a meeting of leading figures in the city at the Mansion House to discuss the raising of a testimonial to Livingstone. This later led to Livingstone receiving £3000, together with the freedom of the City of London.

Livingstone, now a celebrity, went to Scotland in early January 1857 to visit his recently widowed mother and his sisters in Hamilton; he had received news of his father's death at Alexandria on his way home from Mauritius.[4] He travelled to Scotland by train, another essential element in the new era of rapid communication and dissemination of news. On the journey he wrote a letter to the *Times*, which was published in the issue of 29 December, where it occupied two full columns – a very unusual allocation of space to a letter at that time. In the letter he insisted that the future of 'southern intertropical' Africa lay in the production of cotton by free Africans, something of which they were capable despite all the denigration of their abilities then current. Africa would then provide an alternative source of cotton for British industry to the slave-produced cotton of the USA. He wrote the letter to challenge an editorial in the 18 December issue of the *Times*. The leader writer had praised Livingstone's achievement but with a patronising tone which suggested some scepticism over his claims about the virtues to be found in African societies. He had then gone on to assert that the African's only contribution to the world was his ability to work in the cotton fields in conditions which Europeans could not endure. The editorial accepted that in central Africa cotton production might overtake that in the United States but insisted that it still could only be produced by slave labour.

There is no record of what Livingstone and the family talked about on this visit to Scotland, which after sixteen years must have been an emotional one. Blaikie reports, without citing any source, that Livingstone wept on seeing his father's chair by the fire. It must also have been a difficult meeting in other regards. Mary Livingstone had been long estranged from the Livingstones in Scotland and indeed had cut them off from any contact with the children. As Livingstone's father, Neil, had written to the LMS on 24 June 1853:

I addressed a note to you yesterday enquiring after our grandchildren, having no other way of getting any word about them, as their mother was pleased to forbid all communication with us no less than three different times. We received a note from her this morning which I enclose, but owing to her remarkably strange conduct ever since we became acquainted with her, we have resolved to have no more intercourse with her until there is evidence she is a changed person.[5]

Neil Livingstone went on to say that he and his wife were willing to take the two boys, Robert and Thomas, and see to their upbringing and education, but oddly made no reference to Agnes.

Because Livingstone had received almost none of Mary's letters during the four years and eight months they were apart, he knew little or nothing of her unhappiness until they met again at Southampton. How much she told him in the short and very busy time between their meeting at Southampton and the visit to Scotland is not recorded. When Livingstone learnt of her misery, however, he came to blame the LMS directors for not having taken better care of his wife and children. He makes no mention of his father in this connection in the many references he made to the failure of the LMS to care properly for Mary. After the visit to Scotland, which appears to have been made by Livingstone alone, Mary and children seem to have developed better relations with Livingstone's mother and his sisters. It may be that a lack of sympathy between father-in-law and daughter-in-law was the root cause of the breakdown of relations with the Livingstone family which had made Mary's bad situation so much worse.

Quite apart from the failure to establish good relations with Neil Livingstone, Mary and the children underwent a massive culture shock on being transplanted from Botswana to Lanarkshire. Mary stayed there for less than six months and in that time had two different addresses in Hamilton, first number 6 and then number 46 Almada Street. She appears to have stayed only very briefly with the Livingstones in their new house in Burnbank Street. In addition to the cold, grim environment and the tension with Livingstone's parents, Mary simply could not cope on the money allowed her by the LMS.

In January 1853 she fled to Hackney, where she thought the large number of LMS sympathisers who lived there, including acquaintances of her parents, would look after her. In Hackney she was not far from the home of her sister Helen in Kent. Helen had married a prosperous silk merchant called Vavasour. Helen, however, appears to have done little or nothing for her sister; though, in Helen's defence, it has to be noted that she already had two of her younger sisters living with her. Mary and the children moved yet again, going to Manchester to her mother's relations, all the while seeking advances on her allowance from the LMS. In Manchester she again found that she could not cope with the cost of life in Britain. This competent woman, who had gained the admiration of men like Steele, Vardon and Oswell for her courage, calmness in danger and her domestic skills, was brought close to a total physical and mental breakdown.

A Quaker family, the Braithwaites of Kendal, came to Mary's rescue. Miss Braithwaite paid the fares for Mary and the children to come to Kendal. There they were clothed, fed and cared for by the Braithwaites. All this care came too late to prevent Mary becoming very ill for several months in the first half of 1854. When she got back to something like her old self, she planned to go out to Cape Town in August, expecting Livingstone to be there. This plan fell through, to Mary's utter dejection, when news of Livingstone's plans to follow the Zambesi to the east coast came to London. Her last change of address came late in 1854, when she moved to Epsom, where a Miss Eisdell cared for her and the younger children until Livingstone finally returned. Robert and Agnes stayed on at the Quaker school in Kendal, where Robert was happy for the first time since his arrival in Britain.

Mary's letters to the directors of the society, throughout this time, were mainly complaints about lack of money and requests for help. The secretariat of the society clearly did not know how to cope with the problem she presented. At that time missionaries went to their posts for life. There was no regular furlough provision and no furlough accommodation and allowances that were to become the norm later. On top of all these problems, Livingstone was supposed to be away for two years only, not nearly five. None the less, it is clear the directors of the society showed a lack of serious concern over the welfare of Mary and children. Steele and Oswell, who had done a great deal for the Livingstones in the past and were to do so again, were too deeply involved in the conflict in the Crimea to be of help.

What Mary thought of the plaudits and tributes she received, once Livingstone was back as man of the hour, is not recorded. One of Sir Richard Owen's letters, however, reveals a great deal about the Britain in which she had been so miserable; the same Britain her husband was going to try to persuade to help 'the true negro race' take its place 'in the general community of nations'. Owen wrote of taking Mary Livingstone to a soirée organised to view a photographic exhibition at King's College, London. Livingstone came to the soirée with a different party.

> Mrs L., with a straw bonnet of 1846 and attired to match, made a most singular exception to the brilliant costumes. Who could that odd woman be that Professor O. is taking round the room and paying so much attention? I caught sight of Will's countenance; he and Carry had gone with Dr Farre, before I arrived. Disgust and alarm most strongly portrayed. He could not conceive what badly dressed housemaid I had picked up to bring to such a place. Carry was equally mystified.

1. David Livingstone, photographed by Thomas Annan, one of the pioneers of photography in Scotland. (*David Livingstone National Memorial, Blantyre*)

5. Three Ngoni chiefs with their bodyguards. (*National Archives of Malawi*)

6. The Cabora Bassa Gorge, drawing by John Kirk. (*National Library of Scotland*)

7. The *Lady Nyassa*, the shallow-draught river boat in which Livingstone sailed to Bombay, being assembled beside the paddle-steamer, *Pioneer*. (*National Library of Scotland*)

8. Livingstone with his youngest child, Anna-Mary, on his last visit to Scotland. (*David Livingstone National Memorial, Blantyre*)

9. Robert Livingstone. (*David Livingstone National Memorial, Blantyre*)

10.   The last of Livingstone's Kololo, who settled in the Shire valley. (*Centre for the Study of Christianity in the Non-Western World, University of Edinburgh*)

11. Agnes (Nance) and Tom Livingstone, with Chuma, Susi and Horace Waller, at Newstead Abbey. (*David Livingstone National Memorial, Blantyre*)

The extraordinary scrutinies of many fine ladies as they shrank, at first, from contact as far as the crowd permitted! But when the rumour began to buzz abroad that it was Dr and Mrs Livingstone ... what a change came over the scene. It was which of the scornful dames could first get introduced to Mrs Livingstone and the photographs were comparatively deserted for the dusky strangers.[6]

Even before Livingstone had arrived back in Britain, Murchison had been pressing him to write a book based on his great journey. John Murray, one of the most successful publishers in Britain, was eager to publish it. As early as January 1856, before it was known whether Livingstone would emerge safely out of the bush at Quilemane, Murray had written offering him a generous publishing deal. Livingstone found the letter waiting for him when he arrived eventually at the Portuguese town. Murray offered to bear all the costs of publication himself, including the engraving of maps and drawings, and to give Livingstone two-thirds of the profits made by the book. This may, at first sight, appear to have been an extraordinary gamble, but Murray's publishing success over the years shows he was no gambler but in fact someone who knew the market for books exceptionally well. He was proved correct and Livingstone's *Missionary Travels and Researches in South Africa* was an outstanding publishing success. Twelve thousand people paid prepublication subscriptions for the first edition. A reprint of the same number of copies followed almost immediately and was sold out very quickly. Other reprints were to follow. As early as the spring of 1858, Livingstone was able to deposit with Coutts something over £9000 produced by royalties. Royalties on the book continued to come in and, together with the various testimonials presented to him, Livingstone gained an enviable degree of economic security. A significant sum was deposited with trustees in Britain for the education and welfare of the children. Most of the rest he was to spend on African projects, including giving his younger brother-in-law, John Smith Moffat, £500 for equipment and a salary of £150 a year for five years, to enable him to be a missionary to the Ndebele or the Kololo.

The book not only sold well, it also received good reviews. Perhaps the most significant was not strictly a review. Charles Dickens, whose scorn for missions and everything to do with Exeter Hall is clear in his support for Governor Eyre of Morant Bay Massacre fame, as well as in his grotesque character Mrs Jellaby in *Bleak House,* chose to discuss Livingstone's book in an editorial he wrote for *Household Words* of 23 January 1858.[7] The article was sympathetic to Livingstone and Dickens wrote admiringly 'I have been following a narrative of great dangers and trials, encountered in a good cause, by as honest and courageous a man as ever lived'.

We have, however, to note the emphases and omissions that Livingstone put into his book. He insisted on his rebel Highland ancestry but that admission consisted of two or three lines on pages 1 and 2 of a 600-page volume. He also told the story of the wreck of his mission by the Transvaal commando and criticised the voortrekkers for their treatment of Africans. He did not, however, repeat explicitly his insistence on the rights of Africans to defend their freedom from European rule by force of arms, nor his belief that their possession of firearms was their only hope for freedom. He was not being dishonest; he still defended the fundamental humanity of Africans and their right to join the general community of nations. However, in writing a book that aimed to interest the British public in investing significant commercial and capital resources in south central Africa, as well as sending missionaries, he would have been ill-advised to repeat anything of his bitter condemnation of British policy in South Africa and of the British settlers there. The rejection of his article on British policy in the Cape in 1852 had taught him a lesson about what the British were willing to hear. People hear and see what makes sense to them, not necessarily what is there. Already during this stay in Britain, when people appeared to hang on his every word, what people understood from what they heard and read was often different from what Livingstone said. Livingstone, in making his own views more palatable, had started down a slippery slope. By presenting his *Travels* in the way he did, Livingstone was increasing the distance between what he believed and what his audience understood him to mean. He was himself participating in a process, completed after his death by others, in which he, a defender of the rights of Africans to take up arms in defence of their freedom, was gradually transformed into an icon of liberal imperialism. This process enabled Livingstone's pleas for the intervention of outside powers to end the east African slave trade to be used to justify the Scramble for Africa as a series of moral actions for the benefit of Africans.

For the first few weeks after Livingstone's arrival in Britain, he and the family had stayed with his old teacher from medical school days, Dr J. Risdon Bennett. From 21 January 1857 he and the family took lodgings at 57 Sloane Street in Chelsea, where he began work on the book. For the next few months he avoided all public engagements. Murray had been generous but he was also insistent that the book must be published for Christmas, so Livingstone was writing against a strict deadline. Murray wanted the complete manuscript by the end of July. Livingstone had before him all the notebooks and journals that he had kept meticulously during the journey, except when very ill, but it was still a mammoth task. He was helped greatly by his younger brother, Charles. Charles had come to Britain from his pastorate in upper New York state to visit their widowed mother and then stayed on to act as his brother's secretary. His task was the laborious one of producing a fair copy of the fifteen hundred words Livingstone tried to produce each day for the printer. Livingstone met his deadline and Murray got the book out in late November 1857, in time for Christmas.

With the manuscript delivered to the publisher in early July, Livingstone embarked on a massive round of engagements. He was greatly in demand as a lecturer and he was also invited to the meetings of many institutions. In August, he addressed the meeting of the British Association at its meeting in Dublin. In September, he addressed the Manchester Chamber of Commerce and attempted to persuade them of the good prospects for trade now and for investment in the future in what has been called Zambesia (now Malawi, Zambia, Zimbabwe and parts of Mozambique).[8] Later in the month, he was in Glasgow to receive the LL.D. from Glasgow University, an Honorary Fellowship from the College of Surgeons and Physicians, and the freedom of the city of Glasgow with a testimonial gift of £2000. Hamilton also granted him the freedom of the burgh and, at the end of the month, the city of Edinburgh followed suit. On this trip to Scotland, he lectured at least once a day, arriving at Edinburgh close to exhaustion and with the first cold he had had in years. The round of visits, lectures and honours went on and on, Oxford University awarding him a DCL in November, a little before he delivered a set of lectures in Cambridge.

When he had first arrived in the United Kingdom, Livingstone had talked of returning to the Zambesi as soon as possible, no later than April 1857; although how this was to be financed had been by no means clear. He had been persuaded to stay on to write the book. Before leaving Africa, he had become sure that his chosen role was to be that of opening up what he called 'intertropical Africa'. Even before receiving Tidman's letter refusing to countenance any more 'adventures', Livingstone had sensed that the leadership of the LMS, which had allowed him independence for four years, would not continue on this course. This had led him to ask Steele about the possibility of some kind of government support for his work. It is difficult to know in what order various plans and ideas occurred to him in these months, once he had decided to stay on in Britain for the time being. One thing, however, is clear. He wanted to open up Zambesia to the outside world and he wanted assistance from Britain to make it happen. The British had to provide missionaries and traders to create the input of Christianity and commerce that would end the slave trade there, as well as encourage what, in the second half of the twentieth century, came to be called 'development'.

Despite Livingstone's letter to Steele asking him to sound out the possibility of some sort of government support, it was Sir Roderick Murchison who not only initiated but also managed the process that led to Livingstone's government appointment. Murchison had spoken at the Mansion House

MISSIONARY TRAVELS

AND

RESEARCHES IN SOUTH AFRICA;

INCLUDING A SKETCH OF

SIXTEEN YEARS' RESIDENCE IN THE INTERIOR OF AFRICA,

AND A JOURNEY FROM THE CAPE OF GOOD HOPE TO LOANDA ON THE WEST COAST; THENCE ACROSS THE CONTINENT, DOWN THE RIVER ZAMBESI, TO THE EASTERN OCEAN.

BY DAVID LIVINGSTONE, LL.D., D.C.L.,

FELLOW OF THE FACULTY OF PHYSICIANS AND SURGEONS, GLASGOW; CORRESPONDING MEMBER OF THE GEOGRAPHICAL AND STATISTICAL SOCIETY OF NEW YORK; GOLD MEDALLIST AND CORRESPONDING MEMBER OF THE ROYAL GEOGRAPHICAL SOCIETIES OF LONDON AND PARIS, F.S.A., ETC. ETC.

Tsetse Fly.—Magnified.—See p. 571

WITH PORTRAIT; MAPS BY ARROWSMITH; AND NUMEROUS ILLUSTRATIONS.

LONDON:
JOHN MURRAY, ALBEMARLE STREET.
1857.

The right of Translation is reserved

5. *Missionary Travels and Researches in South Africa* (1857), title page.

meeting on 5 January 1857. He had then written, almost immediately afterwards, to the Foreign Secretary, the Earl of Clarendon, urging him to make some use of 'this extraordinary man'. Murchison then urged Livingstone to write to Clarendon, outlining his hopes for the future of south central Africa. It was Murchison who then arranged for Livingstone to be received at the Foreign Office by Clarendon. The outcome of the meeting was that Livingstone was asked to submit to Lord Clarendon a formal statement of his aims and what he needed to achieve them. This Livingstone did in a letter written at the family lodgings, 57 Sloane Street.[9] In it he insisted that his chief immediate aim was to make the Zambesi a path for commerce and Christianity into the centre of Africa: 'Because I believe we can by legitimate commerce, in the course of a few years, put an entire stop to the traffic in slaves over a large extent of territory'. He went on to say the best agricultural land was in Angola, where the Portuguese were fully in control of a large area. In the east, however, the situation was very different. With regard to the Portuguese there, Livingstone insisted that there was 'scarcely a vestige of their ancient authority' remaining. He was correct, but his planned return there and all the publicity surrounding him helped change that. A new interest in Mozambique on the part of the authorities in Lisbon can be dated from this period. Livingstone went on to tell Clarendon that he thought the Portuguese would cooperate in opening up a vast tract of fertile territory from which, at the time, the Portuguese were gaining nothing. He added that Prince Albert had offered to help. Soon after his arrival, Livingstone had had a long conversation with the Prince Consort. Albert had offered to arrange Livingstone's reception by King Pedro in Lisbon to help him gain the king's support for the project. Livingstone asked the Foreign Secretary for what he saw as the necessary supplies for the expedition. These were extraordinarily simple: three cotton gins, two or three strong iron ploughs, two presses for crushing ground nuts, two small roller presses for sugar cane, and a large supply of cotton seed for distribution to the chiefs of the interior highlands. He made no mention at all of European staff to assist him.

In the flurry of letters written at this time to Murchison and others, Livingstone constantly reiterated his desire to get back to the Kololo. Meanwhile, the LMS had begun to plan an advance into the territory opened up by Livingstone. In the midst of the extraordinary public excitement surrounding Livingstone, they had little alternative. On 22 January 1857, the southern committee of the LMS agreed to set up a mission to Moffat's friend, Mzilikazi of the Ndebele, to be overseen by Robert Moffat himself. They also planned another among the Kololo of Sekeletu, with 'a missionary to be appointed to assist Dr Livingstone in preparing this venture'. The Directors of the LMS endorsed this plan on 26 January, the same day Livingstone wrote to Lord Clarendon. It is not surprising therefore, that, at the meeting of the directors of the LMS on 10 February, Livingstone insisted that he would assist with the organisation of the Kololo mission but not be part of it. He did not make clear to the society what his plans were. Indeed, other than the certainty that somehow or other he would go back to the Zambesi to open up the area to Christianity and commerce, and would never again be tied to service on a mission station, it appeared that he had no specific plans. He was hoping that, with Murchison's help, he would get some sort of government support to enable him to carry on the task. Clearly, he saw the presence of the two missions planned by the LMS as a first step in the coming of Christianity and commerce to the area. His task was to open the way for the beginning of the commercial development of the region. He still intended to return to Linyanti with his Kololo companions, who were waiting at Tete. He planned to introduce the new mission to the Kololo and so fulfil his promise to Sekeletu. It seems not to have occurred to him that Sekeletu might not be pleased to receive these new Europeans, even if introduced by Livingstone. It was Livingstone and his wife, not strangers, whom Sekeletu believed were coming to stay with him.

No letter of resignation from Livingstone is known, but, in a letter to Tidman of 30 April 1857, Livingstone wrote that he felt that he must withdraw from pecuniary dependence on the LMS, or any other missionary society. Many of his friends advised him not to make a public break with the society, as it might lead people to think he was giving up the missionary task. On their part, the LMS did not want a public break with Livingstone at the height of his popularity. As a result of this fudging of the issue by both parties, Livingstone's situation remained ambiguous. For example, he attended the annual general meeting of the LMS on 14 May 1857, though both he and Tidman knew that he would not be going back to Africa as an agent of the society.

Livingstone has been accused of deliberate dishonesty in his dealings with the society in this period but there is no doubt that Tidman, and other senior figures in the LMS, connived at his behaviour. Neither side wanted a public break. The directors of the society knew, however, that it was coming. Livingstone had written in his manuscript of the *Travels*, which he had given to Murray at the end of July, his explanation of why he had left the services of the LMS. At that point in the manuscript he went on to outline his plan for the future of the lands through which he had made his famous journey. After referring to his promise to return with his Kololo to Sekeletu and the Kololo homeland, he wrote:

This I said, though while waiting at Kilimane a letter came for the Directors of the London Missionary Society, stating that 'they were restricted in their power of aiding plans connected only remotely with the spread of the Gospel, and that the financial circumstances of the Society were not such as to afford any ground of hope that it would be in a position, within any definite period, to enter upon untried, remote, and difficult fields of labour'. This has been explained since as an effusion caused by temporary financial depression; but feeling perfect confidence in my Makololo friends, I was determined to return and *trust to their generosity.* The old love of independence which I had so strongly before joining the Society again returned. It was roused by a mistaken view of what this letter meant, for the Directors immediately on my reaching home, saw the great importance of the opening, and entered with enlightened zeal on the work of sending the Gospel into the new field ... a fresh source of income having been opened to me without my asking, I had no hesitation in accepting what would enable me to fulfil my duty to my aged parent as well as to the heathen.[10]

Despite all the accusations about his having made certain of government backing for his scheme before dumping the LMS, from the spring of 1857 the leadership of the society knew he was unlikely to continue in their service. Although he and Murchison had been in touch with government since April, it was not until November that the final government decision was made. Livingstone and the LMS officials collaborated at least tacitly in blurring the state of their relations in this period. As we have seen, Livingstone in his *Missionary Travels* covered up the real breakdown in his relations with Tidman and the directors provoked by the Quilemane letter and the society's treatment of Mary, about both of which he was exceedingly bitter in private letters.

The climax of Livingstone's lecture tour was his address in the Senate House of the University of Cambridge on 4 December 1857. The excited and enthusiastic audiences he had had all over Scotland and England were surpassed by the enthusiasm of the Cambridge students. Livingstone ended his speech abruptly. He suddenly looked up at the audience and shouted:

> I beg to direct your attention to Africa. I know that in a few years I shall be cut off in that country, which is now open; do not let it be shut again! I go back to Africa to try to make an open path for commerce and Christianity; do you carry out the work which I have begun. I leave it with you.[11]

The applause was prolonged and deafening, and the impact of the speech on senior figures in the university and the Church of England, as well as upon the students, was remarkable. This was not simply an emotional moment. From the excitement of that day in Cambridge there emerged the Oxford and Cambridge Mission, later renamed the Universities Mission to Central Africa when it gained the additional support of Trinity College,

Dublin and Durham University.[12] This was the first overseas mission of the Anglo-Catholic wing of the Church of England, but it came into being in response to that most independent of Independent Christians, David Livingstone.

His warm welcome for the new society is yet another indication of a view of Christianity that had become, in twentieth-century terms, ecumenical. There had been a strong tendency in the revivalist evangelical tradition, from which he came, to discount denomination as being a secondary matter; but in those circles, that openness encompassed Protestantism only. The evangelical tradition was intensely suspicious of the growth of Anglo-Catholicism within the Church of England and was bitterly hostile to Roman Catholicism itself. Livingstone's acceptance of Anglo-Catholic support was part of his developing views of the Christian mission. He had already admired the work the Jesuits had done in Angola before their expulsion, and, in his *Travels* and in a number of letters, he expressly endorsed the system of St Boniface's mission to Germany in the eighth century. Boniface's system was to plant monastic communities of men and women among the pagan Germans. Each of these communities proclaimed Christianity, created schools using Latin and initiated new forms of agriculture. The German peoples, as a result of this mission's work, were changed culturally and economically as well as religiously. Livingstone had already articulated views similar to those of the Jesuit mission in China in the sixteenth and seventeenth centuries, where the primary concern was to create the widest possible diffusion of Christian influence in the hope of reaping a large future harvest, rather than concentrating on individual conversions in the short term. His deliberate taking up of the missionary approach of the eighth-century mission to Germany was a further move in his developing understanding of the nature of the Christian mission. These developments were taking him far from much of the Protestant missionary thought of his day, which held individual conversion to be the primary missionary task.

To many devout readers of his *Travels*, these views were puzzling. Knowledge and appreciation of the pre-suppression Jesuit missions and of the techniques of Boniface in eighth-century Germany were not part of the intellectual armoury of nineteenth-century British Protestantism. As a result, Livingstone's views, with his concern for economic, social and cultural issues, appeared to many of his readers to be secular. When specifically challenged on this point, Livingstone gave his answer:

> My views of what is missionary duty are not so contracted as those whose ideal is a dumpy sort of man with a Bible under his arm. I have laboured in bricks and mortar, at the forge and at the carpenter's bench, as well as in preaching and in medical practice. I feel 'I am not my own'. I am serving Christ when shooting a

buffalo for my men, or taking an astronomical observation, or writing to one of His children who forget, during the little moment of penning a note, that charity which is eulogised as 'thinking no evil'; and after by His help got information, which I hope will lead to a more abundant blessing being bestowed on Africa than heretofore, am I to hide the light under a bushel, merely because some will consider it not sufficiently, or even at all, *missionary?* [13]

David Livingstone would remain a hero to Anglo-American Protestantism and particularly to its evangelical wing for the rest of the nineteenth century and into the twentieth century. Yet it is clear that he had moved intellectually and spiritually to a new position, sensed by those who accused him in late 1850s of not being sufficiently a missionary. These critics have much in common with some twentieth-century writers who have asserted that he ceased to be a missionary around 1858, despite his continuing to use pious language. These writers, together with the critics of the 1850s, share the same narrow understanding of what it was to be a missionary (most British twentieth-century agnostics were still very Protestant). The eighth-century mission in Germany, whose approach Livingstone had come to see by 1858 as the way ahead, was simply outside their ken. The interesting question is how David Livingstone came to know so much about it and about the Jesuit missions, since neither figured in the academic setting in which he was trained. He was always a voracious reader and had never, since the old quarrels with his father, allowed the range of his reading to be circumscribed. Presumably, it was in this way he had come across Boniface and his propagation across Germany of Christianity, Latin culture and the new agriculture – the eighth-century version of Christianity, commerce and civilisation. This expanded horizon of reading can be found in a letter he wrote to his friend Watt in January of 1847.[14]

Even as Livingstone spoke at Cambridge, his modest plan presented in April to Lord Clarendon and about which he had heard very little officially, was about to emerge as a plan for a large official British expedition to the Zambesi. Although he was able to modify substantially the suggested size of the expedition, this was something Livingstone had not asked for and something that cast him in a role for which he was not suited.

9

The Zambesi Expedition

On 11 December 1857 the Chancellor of the Exchequer, Sir George Cornewall Lewis, announced in the House of Commons that £5000 from the civil contingencies fund was to be spent in financing a government expedition to the Zambesi valley. He told the House that this was an area well fitted for the cultivation of cotton and it was hoped that the expedition would have significant commercial consequences.[1] Since Livingstone had been going on at great length about these consequences all over the country, it would be surprising if anyone in the House was puzzled as to what they were.

From his return home, although hoping for some kind of financial support from government, Livingstone had insisted that he was determined to return to the Zambesi whatever happened. In his *Missionary Travels* he suggested that, if the worst came to the worst, he would return to Africa and rely on the help of the Kololo again to sustain him.[2] Soon after his return to Britain, as we have seen, Prince Albert had discussed with him how to achieve Portuguese sympathy and support for his activities and offered to arrange for Livingstone to gain an audience with King Pedro, the Prince Consort's cousin. This delighted Livingstone who, at that time, was advocating co-operation between Portugal and Britain in support of his project. He argued, somewhat naively, that the ending of slave raiding and slave trading in the region and the entry of its peoples into partnership with the world economy would be for the benefit of both European nations.[3]

The letter to Clarendon in which Livingstone suggested this cooperation was the same letter of 19 March 1857 in which he asked for a financial subvention and a very modest supply of technical equipment to help in his attempt to stimulate agricultural development among the Kololo. In his next letter to Clarendon, that of 2 May, he reiterated that he wanted merely to make 'a small beginning'. Only after it was clear how things might develop would it be appropriate, Livingstone suggested, to have a more substantial government input into the project. By December 1857, however, everything had changed and his modest plans had been swept aside.

As late as 1 December 1857 Livingstone wrote to Clarendon about his plans, still on the modest scale of his previous letters. Writing to a friend,

H. E. Stephens, on the day the Chancellor made his announcement to the House, Livingstone was still not clear about what was to happen. He still believed he was going to Lisbon to gain Portuguese cooperation and appeared unclear about what exactly the government proposed to do. He wrote:

> I am glad to hear from you and particularly obliged by your kind invitation, but I hope to start for Portugal on the 17th and on my return I shall have very little time to spend in England ... I don't know about the next trip or rather sojourn – the affair has to be mentioned in the House of Commons and then the whole thing will be in the hands of the Admiralty. I only wish I were away back to my poor friends at Tete.[4]

Livingstone was correct about the Admiralty. Since his plan was based on the Zambesi being a waterway leading directly from the ocean into the heart of Africa, when British ministers had considered his ideas in the autumn, they had decided that the Royal Navy should be in charge of the technical and logistical details of the project. The Foreign Office, in November 1857, handed over the task of planning the expedition to Captain John Washington, the Board of Admiralty's chief hydrographer.[5] Late in December, Washington produced for Clarendon plans for a large expedition, to be led by Livingstone, of close to two hundred officers and ratings of the Royal Navy. Livingstone was appalled. He saw that a civilian heading a naval expedition promised problems enough without the additional challenge an expedition on such a scale would present to the government in Lisbon.

Meanwhile on 12 December the Livingstones attended a reception given by the Prime Minister, where Lords Palmerston and Shaftesbury assured him of their support in his attempt to end the slave trade in Zambesia and to open the area to Christianity and commerce. A few days later, Livingstone was told there was no need for him to go to Lisbon as the Foreign Office was dealing with the matter. He was also told by Shaftesbury that all he had to do was to go to the Foreign Office and ask for whatever he wanted. Livingstone took this opportunity to quash the idea of the massive naval expedition. He insisted that Washington's suggested plan was on too large a scale and, in a letter to Clarendon on 7 January 1858, put forward specific alternative proposals. His plan was an attempt to make the expedition of a size that made it appear serious and worthwhile in eyes of the politicians, while being still small enough for him to manage. The expedition envisaged by Livingstone would not present the same challenge to Portugal that Washington's naval expedition would have done. His plan called for a team of only six Europeans, each with specific responsibilities, and Livingstone went on to suggest candidates to fill four of these six posts.[6]

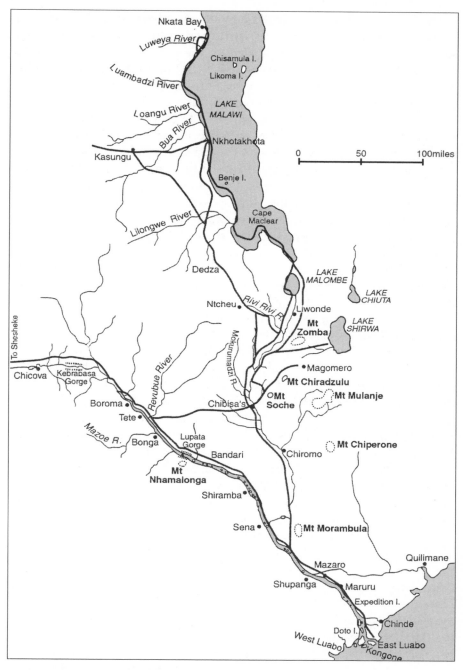

3. The Zambesi Expedition, 1858–64.

The Foreign Office, under Lord Clarendon, had been trying for some time to come to an agreement with the Portuguese authorities on what Livingstone's return to the Zambesi entailed for the formal relations between the two countries. The publicity generated by Livingstone and his ideas had reached such a wide audience across Europe, not simply in the United Kingdom, that alarm bells had begun to ring in Lisbon. The Portuguese authorities were aroused by what appeared to them to be a threat to their traditional claim to all the land lying between their Angolan possessions in the west and their scattered posts on the east coast. Officials began to search the archives for records that might substantiate these claims in the eyes of the international community. What they did immediately was to insist that they could not accept Livingstone's proposed appointment as British consul at Sena and Tete. They said that he could be appointed to Quilemane, since it was a port open to international trade. In response to Livingstone's complaints about this, Clarendon accredited him as consul to the chiefs beyond Tete and gave him a letter from the British government formally offering its friendship to Sekeletu and the Kololo people.[7] The Portuguese had no presence on the ground beyond Tete and so, according to the Foreign Office's understanding of international law, this left the British free to appoint a consul to deal with the chiefs directly.

Although Livingstone was satisfied with this, he was well aware that the free navigation of the Zambesi was an essential element in his hopes for the development of Zambesia. Meanwhile in Lisbon, the Portuguese Minister for the Colonies, Bandiera, was treading a delicate diplomatic line, not wanting to create bad relations with Britain, yet wanting to make sure that no permanent non-Portuguese European presence was established between Angola and the Portuguese east African settlements.[8]

Livingstone's letter to Clarendon of 7 January 1858 has often been seen as proof that Livingstone had had this plan and these names in mind for some time. Certainly, while still on his march across Africa, he had already determined that he would return in order to open up the Zambesi valley and the surrounding highlands to international commerce and Christianity. It is also equally clear, however, that, throughout most of 1857, what he hoped for was that the government would support him going back alone to the area. Once there he hoped to pick up his Kololo comrades at Tete and return to Linyanti. He would begin, in a small way, to introduce cash crops among the Kololo, whom he hoped also to persuade to move their capital to a healthy spot on the Batoka plateau. They would feel safe to do that, he hoped, because, by the time of his arrival, LMS missions would have arrived among the Ndebele at Bulawayo as well as among the Kololo themselves. He hoped these arrangements would guarantee peace between the two peoples. The

Kololo capital, out of its malaria-ridden position in the swamps of the Lozi flood plain and in its new situation on the Batoka plateau, would then be a healthy place for the newly arrived European missionaries to stay. Livingstone had already come to see that keeping the capital on the flood plain was in any case inimical to Kololo power, since the true Kololo lacked the comparative immunity of the local people to malaria.

As late as 6 December, in writing to Hudson Gurney, a member of Parliament and government supporter, thanking him for the £50 donation Gurney had sent to help Livingstone return to Africa, Livingstone was still writing in terms of a solo expedition. He wrote:

> On my return to Africa my chief efforts will be directed to making the river Zambesi an open pathway to the interior healthy highlands in order that a centre of civilisation and commerce will be formed. I shall visit all the chiefs along the banks and distribute cotton seeds – inviting the people to cultivate for our markets and I think if what I hope to begin is carried out that in the course of a dozen years Africa itself will have some material influence in diminishing the value of slave labour in America.[9]

When it was finally clear to him what the government planned, Livingstone rushed to cobble together the scheme he proposed in the letter of 7 January. He was, by then, desperate not to delay any longer and all the preparations for the expedition were done with extraordinary rapidity. Livingstone suggested the shape of the expedition on 7 January. On 10 March, only nine weeks later, the expedition sailed from Birkenhead with its full complement of six European officers. On board they had a river paddle steamer in transportable sections. This had only been commissioned on 12 December 1857, yet it was built in time for sea-trials on 5 February 1858. It was named the *Ma-Robert*, the Tswana name for Mary Livingstone.

On 7 January Livingstone had asked for a naval officer, a mining geologist, an economic botanist, an assistant and moral agent, an artist and storekeeper, and a ship's engineer. He clearly had relied heavily on the opinions of Sir Roderick Murchison and other scientists he had come to know, including the two Hookers, Sir Joseph and his son, in making his decisions about who might fill these posts.[10]

To fill the post of naval officer, Livingstone suggested the name of Commander Bedingfeld. He was one of the naval officers Livingstone had met at Loanda and who had been one of the survivors from the wreck of the *Forerunner*. Livingstone informed Clarendon that 'the fact of his volunteering to serve under me for a simple love of the enterprise in which we are to be engaged makes me entertain very sanguine anticipations of his efficiency'.[11] Livingstone later wrote to Maclear, Astronomer Royal at the Cape, confessing that Captain Washington had warned him against Bedingfeld because of his record of insubordination and somewhat irrational behaviour.[12] On the other hand, Bedingfeld was a senior naval officer volunteering to serve, one who was already known to Livingstone, and an officer praised publicly for his courage by both Palmerston and Clarendon. It is understandable why Livingstone, himself no lover of conformity, took a chance, despite Washington's warning.

In the case of the mining geologist, Sir Roderick Murchison warmly commended Richard Thornton. That was enough for Livingstone, despite Thornton's youth and utter lack of any experience. Dr James Kirk, appointed economic botanist and medical officer, was a well-supported and clearly well-qualified choice. Kirk was commended as a botanist by both the Hookers at Kew and by two prominent professors at Edinburgh University and was at that time being considered for the chair of botany at a Canadian university. He had also relevant medical experience from his service in the Crimean campaign. The appointment of Livingstone's younger brother, Charles, as general assistant and moral agent, appears simply to indicate that Livingstone wanted his brother with him than anything else.

The strangest appointment was one upon which Livingstone had not yet decided when he wrote to Clarendon. He had written:

> In respect of the person who is to combine the duties of artist and storekeeper, I have not yet fully made up my mind as to the best individual, though I am disposed to suggest the name of Mr T. Baines of the late North Australian Expedition.[13]

At that time Baines appeared to Livingstone to be a well-qualified candidate. Baines had recently returned from service with the North Australia Expedition where, apparently, he had ably fulfilled the requirements of the post of artist and storekeeper that Livingstone had set out in his memorandum. Both Sir Joseph and Dr Hooker, on whose judgement Livingstone laid great store, enthusiastically commended him, as did the committee of the Royal Geographical Society. By chance Livingstone had met Baines at a meeting of the RGS on 7 November at which Baines presented a paper on his Australian experience and displayed some of his paintings. Livingstone had been impressed and recommended Baines's paintings to Sir Morton Peto and the Duke of Argyll. Baines and Livingstone remained in contact after the encounter and Baines showed enthusiastic interest in the projected expedition. He drew plans for a boat, capable of being transported in three sections, with room for eight men and able to make progress in very shallow water. Captain Washington thought it a good plan but Livingstone turned it down as too expensive at £200, though later, on the Zambesi, Livingstone confessed that his decision had been a mistake.

Most commentators on Livingstone have been critical of his treatment of Baines. After all Baines, a Fellow of the RGS, was well qualified; and, after his dismissal from the expedition, he went on to have a distinguished career in African exploration. Baines was also held in high regard by many of the people whose opinions Livingstone usually respected. It has therefore been suggested that the responsibility for the breakdown of relations lay with Livingstone's irascibility and lack of managerial skills. What has never been mentioned by any of Livingstone's many biographers is the role Baines had played in the War of Mlanjeni, between the Cape Colony and the Xhosa people.[14] This was the war during which Livingstone wrote so extensively in support of the Xhosa people in 1852–53.

Baines had emigrated to South Africa in 1842 and had made a living by painting portraits and landscapes as and when commissioned. On the eve of the War of Mlanjeni he had been travelling on the Xhosa frontier. When the fighting began he attached himself to the 74th Highlanders and followed them through the campaign. He became a close friend of the regiment's colonel, Colonel Fordyce, who commissioned and bought paintings from him. Baines had no official status with the British army, not even as a member of one of the farmer commandos who served alongside the regulars from time to time. He had, however, in addition to his paints and easel, a high powered double-barrelled rifle. His proficiency with this weapon and his willingness to use it soon led to his being in demand as a marksman, able to bring down Xhosa warriors at long range.

> On a ridge seven or eight hundred yards away to the right of the path he was shown a fine looking Kaffir deriding the attempts of the Fingoes to reach him with their feeble muskets. Giving his horse to a private, Baines went forward and tried a conical bullet. It fell short but at the second barrel the native dropped. An officer told him afterwards that he was killed outright.

And again

> Once he had gone forward with the guns to support the 74th in a hut-burning expedition, Colonel Fordyce came up, and after watching him, commissioned a picture of the scene ... By then he and his rifle had won a reputation that often brought them into service to bring down some troublesome sniper.[15]

His biographer also recounted Baines's diatribes against 'the negrophilists and Exeter Hall' and quoted extensively Baines's reporting, as if fact, the Grahamstown gossip about the untrustworthiness of the so-called Hottentots. When Baines returned to Britain he found that Ackerman and Co., the Queen's lithographers, were publishing a volume of his war paintings. He tried but failed to have added to the volume a preface described as having ' digressed off into a refutation of the negrophilists'.[16] His biographer,

Wallis, recorded all this with evident approval of his hero's actions. Although he edited for publication a collection of Livingstone's notebooks and journals from the Zambesi expedition, Wallis appears to have been unaware that, in 1852, Livingstone had been a leading spokesman for the defence of the Xhosa and the 'Hottentots' by the 'Negrophilists and Exeter Hall'.

The wonder is not how such a well-qualified person so soon fell into Livingstone's bad books and was dismissed the expedition, but how did such a hater of Exeter Hall and killer of Xhosa warriors (whom Livingstone deemed as worthy of admiration as any Magyar hero in the fight for Hungarian freedom) was appointed to the expedition at all. One can only assume that Livingstone, in the hectic rush to get everything in place for a speedy departure, did not look beyond the Australian success of Baines and the enthusiastic endorsement he had received from the RGS and from friends like Sir Joseph Hooker.

A steady and experienced ship engineer was found in time to sail with the rest of the expedition. He was George Rae, a Glaswegian who had worked on the steamships plying the transatlantic crossing. Unfortunately, he was not appointed in time to take any part in the trials of the *Ma-Robert* on the Mersey, otherwise the inadequacy of this vessel might have been exposed and changes made.

The strangest members of the expedition who boarded the *Pearl* at Birkenhead were not on the list of six. They were Mary Livingstone and six-year-old Oswell Livingstone. The other members of the expedition were taken aback somewhat at Livingstone's decision to take Mary and Oswell along. Livingstone had, however, made clear on numerous occasions how important Mary's presence was to him, most notably at the farewell dinner given in his honour at the Freemasons Tavern in London on the evening of the 13 February. On the same day the Queen had granted him a private audience. In his speech at the dinner Livingstone insisted that Mary was 'the central spoke in his wheel' and would be of great help to the expedition as a true African veteran.[17]

The members of the expedition set sail from Birkenhead without having received formal instructions, contracts, or even what today we would call their job descriptions. It was only when the *Pearl* was off Tenerife and they had been at sea for eight days that Livingstone assembled the party and formally read to them the Foreign Office instructions which gave the expedition its legal status. He then gave them each a set of specific individual instructions on their two-year contracts. He had composed these instructions only after they had left port. Of this formal event John Kirk remarked casually:

Dr L. read the Foreign Office instructions to us all. They seem sensible but the most sensible part is that we are left much to our own discretion. The sum of them is, live at peace with the natives, obtain all the information we can, and try to begin civilisation among them by introducing arts and commerce as far as may seem proper.[18]

Each was told that they must put their hand to anything that needed doing until they could erect the prefabricated house at a healthy spot on the Batoka highlands. Then, with their base secured, each member of the expedition would be free to get on with their specific tasks as they saw fit. The orders presumed that the expedition would reach Tete quickly and then move rapidly on to the Batoka highlands. Each set of orders made clear that the members of the expedition were obliged to obey Livingstone's orders and that he had the power to dismiss them. One paragraph of the instructions common to all, though worded somewhat differently in each case, strikes a very modern note. It read:

> The Expedition is well supplied with arms and ammunition and it will be necessary at all times to use these in order to obtain supplies of food, as well as specimens of animals for the purposes of Natural History. In many parts of the country which we hope to traverse, the larger animals exist in great numbers and being comparatively tame may be easily secured. I would earnestly press on you the duty of a sacred regard of life and never to destroy it, unless some justifiable end is to be answered by its extinction ... The wanton waste of animal life I have witnessed from night hunting and from the precocious but child-like use of instruments of destruction, as well as the wish that the habits of certain races of animated creation which are evidently destined at no great distant date to extinction, should be calmly and philosophically observed while there remains the opportunity, make me anxious that none of my companions should be guilty of similar abominations.[19]

Two problems soon emerged. The first was that the seasickness that Mary had suffered along with the others turned out to be morning sickness. There was no alternative but to leave her and young Zouga, as Oswell was usually called, at the Cape. The second problem was that Commander Bedingfeld showed signs of an attitude of mind that did not bode well for the future. He was unable to hide his irritation with Captain Duncan of the *Pearl*, and he chafed at being on a ship captained by an officer of the merchant marine. He was particularly upset that this situation was to continue until the *Pearl* had taken them up the Zambesi to Tete. Bedingfeld's duties were to consist of chart and map making in the Zambesi delta and on the river itself in addition to being skipper of the *Ma-Robert*, once it was assembled. The crew of the paddle steamer, in addition to George Rae as engineer, was to consist of twelve experienced Kru seamen who were picked up when the *Pearl* stopped at Freetown en route to the Cape.

When the expedition finally arrived in Table Bay on 22 April, Livingstone found Robert and Mary Moffat waiting for them there. The Moffats had come to Cape Town to meet the Livingstones and were also hoping that the two mission parties the LMS were sending out, one for the Kololo, the other for the Ndebele, might also arrive during their stay in the city. It was arranged that Mary and Zouga would go with the Moffats to Kuruman. When Mary had recovered sufficiently after the birth of the new baby, it was agreed that she and the two children would then travel overland to the new mission that would, by then, have been planted among the Ndebele of Mzilikazi. From there it would be a short journey for Mary to meet up with Livingstone at the expedition's projected base on the Batoka plateau near to Mosi oa Tunya. That Mary's desire, so passionately expressed in her 'hundred thousand welcomes' poem, to remain with Livingstone always, should be frustrated by childbirth, is skirted round by most of his biographers.[20]

Cape Town had already celebrated Livingstone's journey across Africa in his absence; the arrival of the *Pearl* was seized as an opportunity to welcome him in person at a dinner presided over by the Governor, Sir George Grey. As a mark of their respect, the citizens of Cape Town presented Livingstone with a silver casket containing eight hundred guineas. The change in attitude of the ruling circles in Cape Town had not a little to do with the fact that Sir George Grey was a close friend of that extraordinary, rich and independent woman, Miss Angela Burdett-Coutts. She had come to admire and trust Livingstone, who wrote to her regularly. It was Miss Burdett-Coutts whose financial support had made possible the creation of the Anglican diocese of Cape Town, of which Robert Gray was the first bishop. In addition, the LMS was no longer seen in the city as a vehicle of negrophile agitation as it had been in Dr Philip's day.

A Royal Navy surveyor, Mr Skead, sailed with the expedition when the *Pearl* left Cape Town on the first of May. His task was to chart as much of the Zambesi delta as was possible in the short time the expedition expected to be there. He was then to return to the Cape. On the voyage up the coast, Bedingfeld began to find reasons to quarrel with Skead over matters of navigation and chart-making as well as continuing to bicker with Captain Duncan.

The *Pearl* reached the Zambesi delta on 14 May 1858. What was supposed to happen at that point, according to the plan approved by Lord Clarendon, was that the *Ma-Robert* should be assembled and should then pilot the *Pearl* though the delta and up the Zambesi to Tete. This journey had to be accomplished rapidly in order to get the expedition through the unhealthy area of the lower Zambesi as quickly as possible. At Tete the stores were to be unloaded and the *Pearl* would then return down river to the ocean and proceed on the rest of her scheduled voyage to Sri Lanka. The *Ma-Robert* would then ferry the stores, Livingstone's Kololo followers and the members of the expedition up the Zambesi to a suitable spot beyond its confluence with the Kafue and within the area of Sekeletu's authority. There on the Batoka plateau, the prefabricated house was to be erected as the centre of the new settlement.[21] The development and evangelical work of the expedition would then begin, with each of the members free to get on with their allotted tasks, while Livingstone went to Linyanti with the Kololo. He would ensure the new LMS mission was well received by Sekeletu and his people and would also help persuade Sekeletu move his capital to the highlands. If the projected Universities Mission came into being, it too could be found a place in one of the highland areas. At that point, with four centres of Christian and civilising influence in the area, the bringing of the people of Zambesia into 'the general community of nations' would be well and truly begun.

None of this happened. From the day the expedition arrived at the delta of the Zambesi it appeared as if almost everything that could go wrong did go wrong. One thing alone went right, though it was not in the plan submitted to Clarendon. This was Livingstone's institution of an effective prophylactic as well as therapeutic therapy for malaria. Soon after leaving the Cape everyone in the expedition began take a daily dose of quinine. Livingstone's insistence on this regime and his use of his quinine-based pills in treating those affected by the disease was an undoubted success. The expedition, including the thirty other Europeans who joined it later for longer or shorter periods, did not suffer the appalling death rate from malaria which had decimated all previous nineteenth-century European exploratory journeys in tropical Africa. All the members suffered from malaria at various times, but there were only two deaths from it.[22]

The first problem, which necessitated disastrous delay in the proposed timetable of the expedition, was that no one knew for sure which of the many branches of the delta led into the main channel of the Zambesi. Some of these openings were dead-ends, some were the mouths of separate small rivers which also fed into the delta. The *Ma-Robert* was assembled quickly and, with the help of the two whalers of the expedition, it carried out the slow and exhausting process of finding a navigable channel to the Zambesi. It was not until June 4 that the narrow Kongone mouth of the Zambesi was found and the *Ma-Robert* piloted the *Pearl* into the Zambesi proper. This could be called a success since no one before had found a clear channel through the delta to the Zambesi proper; the Portuguese certainly knew of none.[23] It was by then the middle of the dry season and the Zambesi was approaching its lowest flow. It was clear to everyone that the *Pearl* could not risk going any further upstream; indeed it was in constant danger of running aground where it was. On 16 June Livingstone held a council with Captain Duncan and the European staff and it was decided that the *Pearl* should go back down to the sea and continue on her voyage. The mass of stores which had filled the *Pearl*'s holds had to be unloaded four hundred miles from where the plan had specified they would be unloaded. They were put into the prefabricated house erected on an island in the river off which they were anchored. Livingstone named it Expedition Island. The island was only forty miles from the sea.

Livingstone was then left with the *Ma-Robert*, a small pinnace and two whaleboats to transport all their stores and the prefabricated house up the river to Tete. This was a daunting task made worse by the complete unsuitability of the *Ma-Robert* for the task in hand, an unsuitability matched only by that of her captain, Commander Bedingfeld. The *Ma-Robert* had been built in three sections of new, experimental thin steel to make her light and transportable. This thin skin of experimental steel was, however, very vulnerable to damage in negotiating the great number of shoals and sandbanks in the Zambesi at that time of the year. The vessel was also hopelessly underpowered for the work she had to do, so much so that she was passed easily by fully loaded canoes. What added to everyone's, but especially Livingstone's, misery was that it took an exhausting day of wood-cutting to produce just a few hours of steaming at no more than walking pace. A further reason for Livingstone's bitter cursing of the steamer was that the wood needed to keep her going took up so much room that the cargo had to be put into the whalers and towed behind. In the heat and humidity of the lower Zambesi, all the time and energy of the staff was absorbed, as the days turned into weeks, in the struggle up and down the river in the *Ma-Robert* and her little flotilla ferrying the mountain of supplies left by the *Pearl*. Instead of being able to carry out the duties detailed in their formal instructions, they were little more than Thames lightermen, as Bedingfeld declared.

Bedingfeld had already quarrelled with Captain Duncan and with the surveyor, Mr Skead. Then, when it was clear that the *Pearl* had to be got out of the Zambesi lest she became stuck there, he had had a shouting match with Livingstone. This was over Livingstone's decision to have the *Ma-Robert* pilot the *Pearl* back to the Kongone mouth and the sea. On this occasion Bedingfeld directly challenged Livingstone's authority as head of the expedition. What made the situation worse for Livingstone was that he was becoming aware that Bedingfeld could neither navigate competently nor could he make charts and maps, attributes basic to his job description.

Many commentators have discounted Livingstone's accusations that Bedingfeld's intention had been to make the expedition his own. The virulence of Livingstone's language about Bedingfeld and the makers of the *Ma-Robert*, together with the general state of frustrated anger which characterised Livingstone at that time, have been treated as evidence that his judgement was not to be trusted at this point. A reasonable case, however, can be made to support Livingstone's accusation. Why should a naval officer of some seniority who was unable to chart the river, and the surrounding countryside through which the expedition was to pass, go on an expedition simply to be the sailing master of a small river paddle-steamer? The question becomes even more pointed when it is recognised that he was not an efficient sailing master. Long before the crisis, John Kirk commented, when on an exploratory trip in the delta:

> I often wished to go on shore to do different things but unless under great temptation, could not think of wasting time, which was precious; and Bedingfeld, who was in command being no lover of science in any of its branches, it was not easy to persuade him that there was much good to get by it. I must say for him that he is a good skipper and manager of Krumen although no surveyor or navigator if he came to charts or sextants. Without Skead, there would have been no sketch of the river at all and he is hampered in every possible way.[24]

And the very next month Kirk noted again:

> I think Bedingfeld is tired of the service. He seems now to have expected to live the life of a Man of War Commander and *has no idea of being a subordinate*. He also feels he has done nothing but act sailing master of the launch; but I do not see much desire for scientific observations and of surveying.[25]

Livingstone should have marked this lack in Bedingfeld when preparations were still being made for the expedition. Livingstone had considered taking out a ready-built steamer called the *Bann* instead of having the *Ma-Robert* built. The *Bann* would have had to sail out to the Zambesi and Bedingfeld had insisted that to do so required a sailing master. Livingstone had turned this down as an unnecessary expense. Bedingfeld had then refused to sail her out himself and Livingstone had thought this was because of Bedingfeld's embarrassment over his susceptibility to seasickness. Bedingfeld refused, in fact, because he could not have sailed her out without a sailing master. He was one of an older style of naval officer who relied on class and patronage for promotion and sailing masters to navigate the ships. That class of officer did not bother to become competent navigators and readers of charts, let alone makers of charts. In addition, Bedingfeld's ostentatious piety, strict sabbatarianism and insistence on shooting birds for fun not food all contributed to the conflict between the two men. Livingstone refused one letter of resignation by Bedingfeld but then accepted his offer when, on 28 June 1858, Bedingfeld resigned again.[26]

Livingstone took over the navigation of the *Ma-Robert* himself, which he did competently enough. Progress was slow, not only because of the faults of the little steamer but because the Zambesi was so low that going aground on a hidden sandbank was a regular occurrence. Some of these banks stretched so far across the river that the ship could not be pulled off the shoal but had to be slowly winched across it, exhausting work in the heat which did damage to the already paper-thin hull. With all these problems it took the expedition months to get even some of the stores up to Shupanga, which they reached for the first time on 4 August and where Livingstone met again his two old friends Captain Nunes and Major Sicard. They provided a stone house for the use of the expedition near the river. This building, owned by the Portuguese government, became the new base to which the majority of the stores were to be brought up eventually from Expedition Island in the delta.[27] This friendly reception by his two old friends would not have been exceptional but for the fact that, in all these journeys up and down the river, Livingstone had been moving in and out of a war zone. Although the rebel leader, Mariano, was in prison, his people, led by his brother, were fighting the Portuguese all along the northern banks of the Zambesi. The rebels did not attack any of the expedition's boats or canoes and were friendly to Livingstone and his colleagues when they landed, as they had to from time to time, in areas which the rebels controlled. When this was reported to Lisbon, it was taken as a sign of an attempt by the British to set up an alliance with the rebels and it increased the suspicion of Livingstone's intentions. In the field, on the other hand, the Portuguese officers accepted, without demur, Livingstone's neutral role and continued to aid him when they could. After all, at Mazaro, while under heavy rebel fire Livingstone had personally rescued the Governor who was sick with malaria and having carried him to the *Ma-Robert* then attended him till he recovered.[28]

The expedition had arrived at the Zambesi delta on 15 May but it was not until 8 September that Livingstone finally reached Tete and met up with his Kololo comrades. Some members of the expedition and much of their stores were still stuck at various points along the river behind him. According to the original plan the expedition was supposed to have set up base on the Batoka plateau by September. Livingstone with his veterans from Tete should have already returned to Sekeletu at Linyanti.

To the inhabitants of Tete, 8 September was a red-letter day. The *Ma-Robert* was the first steamer ever to reach their town. To the Kololo, however, it was the day that their leader came back and they carried him ashore singing. Livingstone described the scene:

They grasped my hands all at once and some began to clasp me round the body, but one called out 'Don't do that! You'll soil his clothes'. It is not often I have shed a tear, but they came in spite of me, and I said, 'I am glad to meet you, but there is no Sekwebu'. Then they began to tell me how many they had lost, but the Portuguese invited me to go to the house of the Commandant, and we deferred our talk for an hour. They came on board and again expressed their joy at seeing me. 'Now our hearts will sleep. We have seen you.'

Thirty of them have died of smallpox ... Poor fellows, how sad I feel when I think on those who have departed from this scene, and I pray, 'Free me, O Lord, from blood-guiltiness'. The principal men are here. 'Grant Lord, that I be more faithful to them that remain.' [29]

Of the 114 men Livingstone had left on the Zambesi, thirty had died of smallpox and six had been killed by some of Mariano's rebels.

Almost immediately after this emotional reunion, Livingstone had to turn round again and head downstream to meet HMS *Lynx* at Kongone. The *Lynx* was bringing stores and mail for the expedition. The crew of the *Lynx*, having heard of Bedingfeld's departure, inundated Livingstone with offers of service. He refused three offers of service by officers of the warship; instead, he accepted two offers of service by petty officers, John Walker, a quartermaster and William Rowe, a leading stoker.

On 7 October the *Ma-Robert* left the Kongone mouth and started up river again for Tete. The trip was agonisingly slow. Livingstone stopped at Shupanga where some of their original stores were in order to load these onto a number of canoes to be taken up to Tete. Above Sena, the Zambesi was, by then, at its very lowest and they ran aground again and again. To progress entailed back-breaking work for the crew, numbers of whom had to get into the water and, with the aid of the winch, push off the 'Asthmatic', as Livingstone always called the steamer. They finally reached Tete on 3 November. As ever they found Major Sicard an excellent host. This was just as well since Thornton and Baines were both unwell, as they had been for most of their time on the Zambesi so far.

Livingstone was, by this time, becoming frantic because of all the delays and the sheer difficulty of travel on the Zambesi in the dry season when by no stretch of the imagination was it a river 'highway'. The base on the Batoka plateau should have been set up and the various members of the expedition ought to have been getting on with their individual tasks, and he was desperately aware he should have been at Linyanti with his Kololo veterans. Instead the expedition was still at Tete, some of their supplies and equipment had not yet been brought up from Sena and Livingstone did not even know if the *Ma-Robert* could get past the Cabora Bassa rapids. Although Livingstone always insisted that he had no previous information about the

6. The *Ma-Robert* in the Zambesi above Sena.

Cabora Bassa other than that there were some rapids there, he must have heard talk among Africans and Portuguese that alarmed him. Why else should he have told Kirk, on the way to Tete, that he was contemplating blasting his way through with dynamite, if that was needed, to ensure a waterway to the Kololo country.[30]

Livingstone set off to explore the Cabora Bassa on 8 November with Kirk, Rae, the Kru sailors and some of his Kololo volunteers. Charles Livingstone had asked to stay at Tete to do some photography, while Baines and Thornton were, yet again, too unwell to travel. The *Ma-Robert* steamed readily over smooth deep water for two days until she entered a gorge. After only four miles of struggling to steer between rocks as large as houses, Livingstone brought the steamer to the shore and they landed to assess what their next step should be. Kirk and Livingstone scrambled over the massive rocks for a mile or so to see what else lay in store for anyone who attempted to ascend the river further. They returned to the ship and, the next day, together with Rae and some Kololo volunteers, set off to see how far the rapids extended and how severe they were. The going was very rough and they passed at least two falls that Kirk thought would block the passage of any vessel except when the river was in flood. They then reached an even more dramatic stretch of rapids which broke the river up into four narrow torrents hurtling between massive rocks. Some commentators have described this as the worst moment in Livingstone's life. That is as may be, but certainly he was deeply shaken. He decided that a more thorough examination of the whole stretch of rapids had to be done as the river continued to rise, so the party returned to Tete to prepare for a new reconnaissance.

On 22 November 1858 the whole expedition headed back up river to the Cabora Bassa. They left the *Ma-Robert* outside the gorge and went ahead on foot. The early rains had swollen the river somewhat, which gave Livingstone some hope. As they marched up the left-hand shore it was clear that Baines, Thornton and Charles Livingstone could not cope with the appalling terrain and the pace at which Livingstone demanded they move. Finally Livingstone, angry and tense because the Cabora Bassa threatened all that he had planned and hoped for, said he would go on with some of the Kololo and the rest should return to the steamer. Kirk then had one of his few serious disagreements with Livingstone. He insisted that Livingstone's decision was an insult to the other Europeans on the expedition. Livingstone relented somewhat and said that, if he, Kirk, was volunteering, he could come along. The incident reveals Livingstone's underlying feeling that the rest of the European members of the expedition were a burden that he and his Kololo could do better without, Kirk excepted. During the months that Livingstone left them to stew in the sweltering, wet heat of Tete, his attitude must have become clear to them. Thornton's reaction was to be almost permanently laid up with an illness that Kirk was at a loss to diagnose or treat. Baines, in his turn, entered enthusiastically into the life of the local Portuguese community, many of whom commissioned him to do their portraits.

The next day, 1 December, Livingstone and Kirk set off with some Kololo. By the following evening all except Livingstone, Kirk and one of the Kololo were utterly exhausted. Leaving the others to recover, the three fit survivors tried to go on. Kirk described their situation:

> The men were thoroughly done up now. The heavy marches and the burning heat of these stones which was fearful, had blistered their feet. We accordingly left them to rest, for what else could be done. They were unable to proceed.
>
> The Doctor and I went on, accompanied by one of the Krumen and spent several hours in getting about a mile further on. Such climbing I have never seen. We had to find our way among these gigantic stones, every step as if we should slip and go down some great crack out of which it would be no easy thing to extricate oneself, even with all the bones entire.[31]

On 2 December a local chief gave them some guides, but after two more days scrambling over the searingly hot rocks, the guides and Livingstone's Kololo insisted they simply could not go on. Livingstone wrote:

> The Makololo declared that they had always believed I had a heart till now, that I had become insane surely, for they shewed me the broken blisters on their feet in vain, and if they could only speak so as to be understood by the other [Kirk], they would return with him and let me throw myself away.[32]

Livingstone had to accept defeat and the party returned to Tete. They arrived just in time to witness the Portuguese officials paying their annual tribute to the 'Landeens'. The Portuguese had defeated Mariano's rebels on the north bank but they were still paying annual tribute to the Nguni warriors of Gazankulu, whom Livingstone referred to as 'Landeens', in order to preserve their settlements at Tete and Sena. They could not have resisted an all out attack by the Gazankulu. These were yet another offshoot, like the Kololo themselves, of the *difaqane*: the mass movement of peoples in southern Africa provoked by the creation of the Zulu kingdom by Dingiswayo and Chaka.

Livingstone in his letters to officials and friends in Britain still insisted that a powerful steamer could pass the Cabora Basa cataracts when the river was at full flood. He sent his brother and Baines to look at the cataracts when the Zambesi was at its height in January 1859 and reported, somewhat misleadingly, that they agreed with his conclusion. However, his behaviour from the first days of December, when he was forced to return to Tete, showed that he knew that the Zambesi was not to be 'God's Highway'.

Having reached this conclusion, his response was to go back down the Zambesi to the mouth of the large river which entered Zambesi from the north, the Shire. He went with Kirk, Rowe, Walker and a team of Kololo and Kru seamen. They entered the Shire on 28 December, and, after visiting Mount Morambala and finding the mountaintop cool, healthy and well cultivated, pressed on up the river.

Livingstone and Kirk were impressed by the productivity of the land. Tobacco and cotton were grown in profusion and the people wove their own cloth. To the east Livingstone, to his delight, saw a large highland area. Was this the healthy area which could become the base for his settlement? This was a critical moment in his life. Could the expedition now fulfil its purpose, not on the Batoka plateau beyond the Kafue river but in the Shire Highlands? Livingstone was also excited by the insistence of the local Africans that the Shire came from the great lake he sometimes referred to as Nyenyesi, 'the Lake of Stars', of which he had heard on the march from Linyanti to Quilemane. When the cataracts he was later to name after his benefactor, Murchison, held up the progress of the *Ma-Robert*, he did not despair. He understood from local people that there was a good path that bypassed the rapids and once beyond them it was plain sailing on the Shire into Nyenyesi. He decided then to return to Tete and prepare for a more thorough exploration of the new region.

Meanwhile, the other Europeans of the expedition, Rae, Baines, Thornton and Charles Livingstone, left to their own devices at Tete, had not been getting on well. This is hardly surprising, as they had no real work to do. The expedition's base had not been set up on the Batoka highlands where they were to have had the freedom to conduct the tasks prescribed in their instructions. Instead they either worked as labourers helping to get the boat off sandbanks, loading and unloading stores, or they were left with little or nothing to do in one of the hottest spots in Zambesia while Livingstone, Kirk and the Kololo went off exploring.

Livingstone noted in his journal after his return that Thornton has been doing nothing at all and remarked that he had to speak sharply to Baines about carelessness, to put it no worse, with the stores. What is clear is that he was not much concerned about them. They were an annoying distraction; all he was concerned about was to get back to the Shire to see if the apparent failure of the expedition could turned into a triumph.

His obsessive concentration on this task drove from his mind all concerns about going to Linyanti with those Kololo who wished to go home to make sure of a good reception there for the LMS mission when it arrived. He was reminded of his promise to the Kololo by the Kololo themselves and dismissed it briefly in his journal.

Makololo propose returning. I agreed to their request to give Mr C. L. to lead a party of them, but they afterwards thought that it might be construed as disobedience, *for Sekeletu had given them orders to return with me.*[33]

His careless dismissal of the issue boded ill for the new mission, but all he could think of were the Shire highlands and the lake.

Together with Kirk, the two naval petty officers and a crew of Kololo and Krumen, Livingstone set of for the Shire again. Charles Livingstone, Rae, Baines and Thornton were left yet again at Tete to suffer in that unhealthy spot with little to do and a deepening sense of being disregarded. A short distance before the first of the cataracts on the Shire was the village of Chibisa, a chief who had influence over a wide area.[34] The expedition halted there and Livingstone spent time getting to know the chief. The two struck up a friendship of sorts, one that was not without affection but also based on the realisation that cooperation was to their mutual advantage. Livingstone then moved on from Chibisa's and left the paddleboat at the foot of the cataracts in charge of Walker, Rowe and the Krumen, while he moved off on foot with Kirk and the Kololo.

They did not follow the Shire but struck out across the rolling plain, dotted with sharp conical mountains like Chiradzulu and Soche, which lies between the two great massifs of Zomba and Mulanje. On the march Livingstone became more and more excited. Here was ample water, fertile soil, no tsetse fly and many highland locations, any one of which could provide a healthy spot for the planned settlement. They reached Lake Shirwa on 18 April. Since no stream flowed from this lake its waters were brackish but they were drinkable and the local Mang'anja assured the visitors that the great lake was very near. Livingstone and his companions were, by then, very tired and their supplies were nearly exhausted, so Livingstone decided to return to the ship. Disappointment at not having seen the fabled Nyenyesi was tempered by the comforting thought that they could, however, report another 'discovery', that of Lake Shirwa, to add to the European mapping of Africa. Livingstone was determined that they would return to confirm three things: first, the existence of Nyenyesi; second that the Shire flowed from it; and third the navigability of the Shire from the cataracts into the lake.

Everything appeared to be falling into place. One worry, however, was that the shadow of slave raiding and slave trading was beginning to appear over this peaceful and prosperous land. From the Mang'anja people near Shirwa, Livingstone learned of a recent outbreak of raiding for slaves. A few days later Kirk and Livingstone met some Yao, a people who, at that time, were moving into the area from the north east, and a number of whose chiefs participated in the Zanzibar slave trade.

Livingstone was now in a state of high excitement. The utter frustration created by his much-vaunted 'Mississippi of Africa' being shown to be no such thing was swept away. The apparent set-back, he believed, had been used by God to turn him toward the place where his dream would be fulfilled. The Shire highlands would provide an even better site than the Batoka plateau for the missionary and economic colony which would begin the process of ending the slave trade and initiate the developments whereby the peoples of central Africa would take their place in the family of nations.

From Chibisa's, Livingstone sailed down the Shire to the Zambesi and on to the delta, where he hoped to meet a Royal Navy vessel on one of the navy's routine visits to the Kongone mouth of the river. After waiting a week and no man of war having appeared, Livingstone steered the 'Asthmatic' back up the river towards Tete, where they arrived at the end of June. While returning to Chibisa's from Lake Shirwa, Livingstone had suffered from severe intestinal bleeding due to typhoid, a condition made worse by bleeding haemorrhoids. His bad health compounded the desperate state of excitement and tension that gripped him on this journey. The Cabora Bassa had dashed his hopes only for them to be revived again by the Shire. He feared they were to be dashed yet again when, while waiting at the Kongone mouth, he saw the Portuguese beginning to erect a customs post. If the Portuguese were to block the free entry of non-Portuguese ships and goods to the Zambesi and the Shire, his plans for the economic development of the Shire highlands and the Lake Malawi area by British missions and commerce would be still-born. He had been feverishly writing letters and reports for the government and to many influential friends about the Shire. He was hoping the government would extend the life of the expedition for another two years and provide him with a more useful vessel than the *Ma-Robert*. He became desperate to hear what had been decided. It was in a mood of apprehension and frustration that he returned back up river. It was from this period that Livingstone began to condemn the Portuguese presence on the Zambesi as a blight on the land. Despite his continued good relations with individual Portuguese officers, their government's intention of closing the Zambesi and the dramatic and clearly apparent increase in Portuguese slaving activities meant that, far from his dream of 'new day dawning for Africa' being achieved with Portuguese cooperation, it was clear that it now had to be achieved despite the Portuguese.

While Livingstone was in this bad state of health and desperately anxious about the future, he returned to Tete. There he met the other members of the expedition who had been waiting at Tete all this time, detached from all the excitement and promise of the Shire. Livingstone is cryptic in his comments on them in his journal. Kirk, in his journal, gives a fuller account of the situation. He reported:

> Poor Baines has had many touches and his head seems often to have been quite out of equilibrium. He has done many things, which, without this excuse, would have been quite difficult of explanation. Thornton has no doubt been sick but he is now in excellent health and, although he often complains, yet I could not venture to prescribe for his mostly anomalous symptoms, many of which are only expressions of one giving in to the feeling of lassitude which all have felt and which if once yielded to become daily more difficult to overcome. His geological work has been very limited indeed and he can say very little, even in respect of the coal fields which it was his special work to examine minutely. Mr Rae has been very busy at a hundred little jobs. He has had many touches of his old fever. Mr L. has had the same. He has made a good collection of birds of which I am right glad, as Botany keeps me well occupied. He has here an unenviable post and being on no good terms otherwise with some of the officers, it has been doubly so. I am very glad I was not tried in his position.[35]

Livingstone, even when in better shape mentally and physically than he was at the end of June 1859, could not put up with 'slacking'. Often in his journal he deplores his own failings, bitterly and without excuse, if he 'gives in' to sickness or tiredness. Kirk summed it up succinctly, 'sickness is a thing with which the Doctor has no patience either in himself or any one else'.[36] It was almost inevitable that Livingstone turned on Thornton and, despite the young man being protégé of Murchison, summarily dismissed him.[37] Thornton did not seek to return to Britain but struck off on his own, going to explore the Luangwa river. Livingstone then read the riot act to Baines, telling him in effect to 'shape up or ship out'. Baines appeared to accept the legitimacy of this severe reprimand and returned to work. His response at that time, and Kirk's comments on him, have to be noted because commentators, both contemporary and since, have gone out of their way to present him as entirely innocent of all wrongdoing. He has been portrayed as the subject of irrational prejudice on the part of Livingstone, or of Charles Livingstone who then poisoned his brother's mind against Baines.[38]

On 11 July Livingstone set off again to the delta on the 'Asthmatic'. On the way, Livingstone wrote a letter to Baines, whom he had earlier put on probation, dismissing him forthwith and instructing him to put the expeditions stores into the care of Major Sicard. The letter did not reach Baines till September and he was justifiably incensed at the form of his dismissal. Livingstone insisted that he did this because of further evidence of bad conduct on Baines's part had been presented to him by Rae. Be that as it may, this was a singularly unfeeling way to treat Baines and Baines's feelings were not helped by Livingstone's very harsh interview with him at the Kongone mouth at the end of November before Baines left for South Africa.

The journey to the delta was made in the hope of meeting a man of war bringing mail and supplies from Britain. Livingstone took with him, on the *Ma-Robert*, his brother Charles, Kirk and the Kru sailors who were returning to Sierra Leone – Livingstone wanted to replace them with his Kololo. Walker was also on board as he was ending his engagement with the expedition. At Kongone they met HMS *Persian* and received two large sacks of mail and a new naval petty officer to replace Walker, John Hutchins.

Although there was much mail, there was still no news of whether the British government would extend the life of the expedition and send him out a new and efficient river steamer. Livingstone was in a fever of excitement. He felt he had to produce news that would reawaken the excitement of influential people in Britain about the project. If he could 'discover' and begin to chart the much-talked of great lake, and show that the Shire was navigable from the cataracts into the lake, that might do the trick. On steaming back up the Zambesi, he did not therefore aim for Tete but pushed the *Ma-Robert* back up the Shire. Livingstone was desperately tense and upset, something shown by his taking a piece of wood and beating a Kololo stoker who had broken part of the boiler of the steamer through carelessness. He also shocked Kirk by saying he would break people's heads if need be to get things done. Livingstone confessed all this in his journal and admitted that it filled him with shame.[39]

The 'Asthmatic', by this time dangerously leaky and having to be pumped clear of water constantly, reached Chibisa's at the end of August. It was left there in the charge of the naval petty officers while Livingstone, Kirk, Charles Livingstone, Rae and thirty Kololo set off through the Shire highlands towards where they were told the great lake lay. On the 16 September the party skirted round the little Lake Malombe, through which the Shire flowed from Lake Nyasa itself, as Livingstone had by then decided to call the lake. Then, on 17 September 1859, the five Scots and their Kololo allies stood on a beach near Mangoche, admiring the startlingly clear waters of Lake Nyasa, fringed by high wooded mountains to the east and west, which stretched before them all the way to the horizon.

Now Livingstone entered upon an extraordinary period of writing; long letters and reports flowed from his pen of which there are still over seventy examples extant. He was anxious to convince the British government that the original intentions of the Zambesi expedition could still be carried out, not on the Batoka plateau but in the Shire highlands. The Mang'anja country was indeed a better site both because it was healthier and agriculturally more productive and because the southern end of Lake Nyasa was the focus for the slavers coming from the west to the coast. A vast caravan coming from Kazembe's, which he and his companions had encountered at Mangoche, could have been seen as representing a severe threat to achieving the purposes of the expedition. Instead, Livingstone turned this encounter into a further reason for government to extend its support. The increasing devastation caused by the slave trade could be stopped only as economic and spiritual change were brought about in the region by the expedition. As he wrote to Lord Malmesbury on 15 October 1859:

> It is highly probable that a small steamer on the Shire and Lake Nyassa would, through the influence of the English name, prevent slave parties from passing the fords and, should our merchants not be obliged to pay dues for entering upon English discoveries for trade by a part of the Zambesi unused by the Portuguese, goods could be furnished to the native traders at Lake Nyassa as cheap as they can get them on the East coast which involves a month's journey further ... The capability of the country for the production of cotton cannot be exaggerated.[40]

If this was to happen, the Portuguese had to be persuaded to allow the free navigation of the Zambesi. After all, Livingstone had found the Kongone mouth of the Zambesi, not they. The increasing slave trade was a serious threat to Livingstone's dream but, with the aid of a new steamer, one main route of the slave trade could be broken, a blow against the slave trade would be struck and the wished for development could begin. In order to accomplish this, the life of the expedition had to be extended. Eager to find out if the required government support was forthcoming, Livingstone wished to hurry down to the delta to await the British mails.

Before leaving he sent Kirk and Rae overland to Tete to convey Baines down to the Kongone. The two had a terrible journey because it was at the end of the dry season and both water and provisions were scarce. At Tete they received a very cool reception from the Portuguese, who sympathised with Baines, by then a popular and valued member of their community. The Portuguese were also annoyed by some highly critical remarks of Kirk's about certain prominent local Portuguese which had become public.[41] Eventually Kirk and Rae were able to get away with Baines in rented canoes and made their way down the Zambesi to meet the others at Kongone.

Livingstone decided that Rae should go back to Britain to show the government the design of a vessel specifically adapted for the Shire and Nyasa. If the government was not willing to build it, Livingstone instructed the trustees of his money in Scotland to make the money available for it to be built privately. When the 'Asthmatic' finally arrived at the Kongone mouth on 3 December 1859, they had to wait some time for HMS *Lynx*. Tragically all of their supplies and most of their mail were lost when a boat from the *Lynx* capsized in the surf. Some packets of letters were later recovered and sent up to Tete.

What was Livingstone to do now? The expedition's formal authorisation was about to come to an end and there would be no further mail for some months. Baines went off on the *Lynx* but Rae asked to stay on, as their future had become so unclear – Kirk somewhat unkindly suggested Rae stayed because of his hopes of an affair with a planter's wife at Sena. The members of the expedition struggled disconsolately up river to Tete where Livingstone decided they simply could not sit around and wait for further instructions. It was time to go back to Sekeletu, with as many Kololo as wished to return, nearly two years later than had been intended. First, however, they all went down river again to drop off Rae at Mazaro, whence he could go across to Quilemane to board ship for Britain. The 'Asthmatic' and the steam pinnace both leaked badly and, as ever, the 'Asthmatic' needed an abundance of wood cut to steam even a short distance, so the journey took from early January till late April. Back in Tete they began to prepare for the march along the north bank of the Zambesi to Sekeletu's. Charles simply did not want to go and was appalled at the prospect of this gruelling journey; even Kirk was not sure it was worth doing. Livingstone, his spirits buoyed at the prospect of the march, refused to take no for an answer and estimated the return journey of fourteen hundred miles would take about six months, as it did. On 16 May 1860, Livingstone, Charles Livingstone, James Kirk and sixty Kololo set off. They took with them a group of locally recruited carriers who carried many presents to Sekeletu, including the formal letter offering Britain's friendship to the chief and his people that had been all this time in store at Tete waiting to be delivered.

10

Linyanti

Before Livingstone set off for Linyanti he received two letters from Robert Gray, the bishop of Cape Town, telling him of the creation of the Oxford and Cambridge Mission.[1] Although he was about to visit the Kololo lands, Livingstone, in response to Gray's request for guidance as to the best location for the mission, directed the attention of the mission to the Shire highlands. The Batoka highlands were no longer the site for Livingstone's planned missionary and commercial colony. This new Anglican mission, it appeared to Livingstone, could become the core round which the colony might develop in the Shire highlands and so initiate the spread of the Gospel, check the slave trade and begin the economic development of the region. Indeed, on first hearing the news, Livingstone wrote in his journal: 'Answered the Bishop of Cape Town's letter of 31 March 1859, informing me of the Universities sending a mission similar to that of old. It rejoices my heart to hear of it.'[2]

His words 'similar to that of old' would appear to refer to Boniface's monastic settlements in eighth-century Germany, which he saw as the model for the future in the Shire highlands. Apart from this good news, Livingstone's spirits had begun to lift in any case at the prospect of the long hard tramp along the banks of the Zambesi with his Kololo veterans. He was delighted at the prospect of being free from the backbreaking burden of cutting wood for the 'Asthmatic', of dragging her over sandbanks, and of the constant patching needed to keep her afloat.

The six months trek from Tete to Linyanti and back was a strange episode in the story of the Zambesi expedition, full of dramatic events and conflicts which provoked bitter attacks on Livingstone in missionary circles in Britain and also raised serious questions about the character of Charles Livingstone. In the book which David wrote in the early months of 1865, *Narrative of an Expedition to the Zambesi*, this journey, which took up only an eighth of the expedition's existence, occupied fully one third of the pages.[3] Despite this disproportionate concentration on the journey, Charles's strange behaviour during the journey went unmentioned and the tragic end of the LMS Linyanti mission, together with the question of Livingstone's responsibility for the tragedy, were dealt with briskly and briefly.

The writing in that section of the *Narrative* is the liveliest in an otherwise rather pedestrian volume and reflects how much this trek, for all its hardships and problems, was one that Livingstone enjoyed. Enjoyment of the people and the fauna and flora was what he conveyed in these pages of the *Narrative*. Details of plants, of animal behaviour, of tribal custom and culture, measurements of the Victoria Falls, these were the things he wrote about with both zest and great attention to detail.

When Livingstone, with his brother, Kirk and the thirty odd Kololo who finally decided they did want to go back, set off from Tete leaving the *Ma-Robert* in the care of the two Royal Navy petty officers, Rowe and Hutchins, they marched along the north side of the Zambesi.[4] They took care to skirt well clear of the barren and precipitous hills that surrounded the Cabora Bassa and which had cost so much suffering in the past. They reached Zumbo at the junction of the Luangwa with the Zambesi on 26 June. En route Livingstone met with a number of old friends, including Chief Mpende, who, on the journey from Shesheke to Quilemane, had fatefully told Livingstone to cross to the south bank of the river and head directly for Tete thus bypassing the Cabora Bassa. At Zumbo Livingstone took time to meditate in the ruins of an old church built by the Jesuits. In describing this he did not hesitate to express again his admiration for the Society of Jesus. Livingstone referred to the Jesuits as 'those ancient and honourable men who dared so much for Christianity' when fellow Protestants saw them as less than Christian at best. He then went on to speculate that perhaps it was their tolerance of Portuguese slavery that led to their failure in the Zambesi.

He was saddened, however, to hear that Chief Mburuma had been murdered. It had been among his people on the highlands to the west of the Luangwa that originally Livingstone had intended originally to site the centre of the expedition's activities. The news of the murder was doubly distressing since the Portuguese elephant hunters who had committed the murder had been led by a nephew of his friend, Nunes, whom Livingstone always addressed in letters as 'My Dear Jose'. Despite the murder of their chief by whites, Mburuma's people received Livingstone cordially and hospitably. The crossing of the river itself was an example of Livingstone's ability to improvise and of the trust the Kololo put in him. There were ferrymen at that part of the river but they were on the other side and, while making merry with a pot of beer, paid no attention to the shouts from the members of the expedition. Remembering the inflatable raft he had used on the Chobe years before, Livingstone improvised one from skins and a waterproof cape. One of the Kololo then paddled across the wide mouth of the Luangwa on this improvised inflatable raft and gained the attention of the ferrymen.

NARRATIVE

OF AN

EXPEDITION TO THE ZAMBESI

AND ITS TRIBUTARIES;

AND OF THE DISCOVERY OF THE LAKES SHIRWA AND NYASSA.

1858—1864.

By DAVID AND CHARLES LIVINGSTONE.

WITH MAP AND ILLUSTRATIONS.

LONDON:
MURRAY, ALBEMARLE STREET.
1865.

The right of Translation is reserved.

7. *Narrative of the Expedition to the Zambesi and its Tributaries* (1865), title page.

Once across the river Livingstone had to call a halt because Kirk had fallen
seriously ill. Livingstone was alarmed by Kirk's condition, which had been
brought about in part by the latter's experiments with alternative therapies
for the treatment of malaria. Livingstone treated him with his usual quinine-
based pills. After three days Kirk could ride (they had two mules) and on
the sixth day he could walk. A very typical Livingstone remark follows in
the *Narrative*, 'Moving the patient from place to place is most conducive
to the cure ... the more pluck a man has, the less likely he is to die'.[5]

The expedition then reached the first villages under the authority of
Sekeletu. Here their march became a triumphal return but also one darkened
by the news that the LMS missionary party had reached Linyanti in February
but that many had died of fever and the rest had withdrawn. At this point
Livingstone had no detailed information about what had occurred. The party
marched on till they reached the Victoria Falls on 8 August. There they
found that Livingstone's plants on Garden Island had been destroyed by
hippos. Undeterred Livingstone replanted the garden and surrounded it with
a brush stockade. Livingstone and Kirk were astonished to find a European
traveller from Natal at the Falls; some have called him the Zambesi's first
tourist. He was a Mr Baldwin from Natal who had set off, with no companions save hired carriers, to see this astonishing sight that Livingstone
had recorded in his *Missionary Travels*.

The party continued on their trek and found Sekeletu at Shesheke. The
chief was delighted to see them, particularly as he had been sick for some
time with a disease which he and his traditional healers had thought was
leprosy. So serious had his situation been that the services of the witch-
finders had been called on and a number of suspected sorcerers had been
put to death.[6] Before examining Sekeletu, Livingstone sought and obtained
the agreement of the old female *ngaka* who had been attending him. Courtesy
to traditional healers was a fundamental element in Livingstone's approach
to African culture, in which he found many things that were acceptable as
well as things he wished to reject. There, at Shesheke, he put into practice
the principle he had forcefully expressed in his formal instructions to Kirk
in the latter's capacity as medical officer. Livingstone had written:

> They possess medical men among themselves who are generally the most observant
> people to be met with; it is desirable at all times to be on good terms with them.
> In order to do this, slight complaints, except among the very poor, ought to
> be referred to their care, and severe cases, before being undertaken, should be
> enquired with the doctor himself and no disparaging remark ever made on the
> previous treatment in the presence of the patient.[7]

On examining the chief, Livingstone and Kirk found that the disease was not leprosy but another skin disease, almost certainly *forgo selvagem*, a disease whose outcome, before twentieth-century medical developments, was always fatal, as it proved in Sekeletu's case. The treatment given by Livingstone and Kirk dealt with the chief's many severe skin sores with some success, however, and Sekeletu's condition dramatically improved and he seemed to be on the mend. Livingstone, as a result, felt free to borrow the horse he had brought to Sekeletu from Loanda years before, astonishingly still alive in that tsetse-plagued area, and rode to Linyanti, the other capital of the Kololo *morafe*. There he found his wagon standing where he had left it, with its contents untouched; contents that included his medicine chest, his books and his magic lantern. He also found the graves of those of the LMS party who had died there only a few months before. The bitter irony was that these poor people, British and Tswana, had died from malaria for which they had no effective medicine, while a supply of Livingstone's famous quinine pills was there in the wagon. Livingstone was accused in missionary and other circles of being responsible for their deaths, a judgement with which some of his biographers have concurred. A hard look at the evidence that is available indicates that Livingstone was not primarily responsible. But if he did not let down the LMS mission party, he did let down the Kololo [8]

The LMS had agreed somewhat reluctantly, before the Zambesi expedition had set out, to send two new missions to Africa, one to the Ndebele and one to the Kololo. The hope was that the existence of the two missions, both under Moffat's patronage, would bring peace between the Kololo and the Ndebele. The Ndebele would not do anything that would endanger Mzilikazi's close relations with Moffat. The Kololo leadership, free from the threat of Ndebele raids, would then feel safe enough to move their capital to the Batoka highlands. On the highlands European missionaries could live reasonably comfortably away from the malarial swamps surrounding Linyanti.

The LMS was slow in sending these missions, so much so that Robert Moffat's son, John, began the mission to the Ndebele on his own initiative. John's salary and expenses were provided by a direct grant from Livingstone. However, after much delay, the directors of the LMS recruited staff for both missions and sent them out together to Cape Town. The missionary families, it was decided in London, would travel together to Kuruman, where they would part company; two families would go to Bulawayo, the other three to Linyanti.

The new missionaries were William Sykes and Morgan Thomas, who were, along with their wives, to serve with the younger Moffats among the Ndebele, while Holloway Helmore, with his wife and four young children, and Roger

Price, with his wife and baby daughter, and John Mackenzie and his wife were to go Linyanti. The party arrived at Cape Town in July 1858 where they were met by Robert Moffat, who introduced them to Livingstone's friend, Thomas Maclear. Maclear was somewhat taken aback by them, especially their intention of taking the children to an area that few Europeans had ever seen and which presented so many health risks. Moffat was also alarmed and wrote to Tidman expressing his grave concerns. The most experienced LMS missionary in Africa wrote:

> Glad as I am of the arrival of so many of our liberal recruits to fill up the thinned ranks of the mission band, I have my fears and feel my mind beset with difficulties connected with the mission to the Makololo which I cannot overcome ... The Governor informs me that Dr Livingstone had sent a message to the effect that he intended to be down at the mouth of the Zambesi on Christmas Day. Now before that time he may or may not have surveyed the country between the Kafue and the Zambesi, the supposed sanatorium of that part of the country.
>
> The same may be said with respect to his reaching Linyanti to prepare the Makololo for the probable arrival of the missionaries. Without there be a considerable degree of certainty of their removing to a more healthy situation, the inhabitants of Linyanti will not feel willing to leave their swamps and rivers, especially till they have been assured that they will not be molested by the Matebele [Ndebele].
>
> This they will require to know through a source upon which they can place the fullest reliance – i.e. either from Livingstone or myself. That they will break up their town and remove some hundred miles immediately on the arrival of the missionaries without some such assurance, we can hardly expect.
>
> Now all this makes it rather a serious matter to recommend three missionaries and their wives to proceed at once to Linyanti. In summer this might prove fatal to some, if not all.[9]

Moffat went on to recommend that the missionaries wait at his station, Kuruman, until matters were clearer.

Moffat, in this letter, had already made the case for Livingstone's defence against the charge of betraying the mission before the missionaries had even set out for Linyanti. Arthur Tidman, secretary of the LMS, had made no attempt to send any word to Livingstone about a schedule of approximate dates for the movements of the missionaries. This he could have done with the aid of the Governor of Cape Colony, whom the Royal Navy managed to keep in regular, if infrequent, contact with Livingstone. How did Tidman expect Livingstone to know when the missionaries were to arrive at Linyanti? After all Livingstone had informed the directors of the LMS very clearly that he could only help their mission if his duties took him to Linyanti at the time of their arrival.[10] Yet Tidman and the directors allowed the missionaries to persist in the belief that Livingstone would certainly be waiting for them when they reached Linyanti.[11] What was worse was that the directors and the missionaries disregarded Moffat's warning and his sensible suggestions, suggestions that would not have cancelled the setting up of the mission but only delayed it until a rendezvous with Livingstone was certain. Moffat also provided another alternative plan. This was that both the Kololo and Ndebele parties should go to Bulawayo and then that the Kololo party should only move on to the Zambesi when they knew Livingstone was at Linyanti. This plan also had the additional advantage that the Kololo party would thereby avoid the terrible problems of the direct route to Linyanti which demanded the crossing first of the Kalahari and then of the malarial swamps around the Chobe. Moffat thought that this peaceful expedition coming from the lands of the Ndebele with his blessing might have convinced Sekeletu that the promised peace between the two peoples had come into being.

This suggestion was also disregarded and the Helmore and Price families together with some Christian Tswana from Kuruman set off along Livingstone's old route with its barriers of desert, rainforest and swamp between Kuruman and Linyanti. John Mackenzie stayed behind because his wife was ill. The party had no doctor and no quinine; these were scarcely believable omissions considering the country into which they were entering. It might be argued that, since they thought they were going to be in the care of Livingstone when they reached their destination, these omissions can be excused. To argue thus, however, is to ignore the fact that they would enter a malarial area at least two weeks before they could reach Linyanti. Indeed some were ill with malaria before they reached Linyanti. There is no doubt they believed Livingstone would be waiting for them. They had it on the authority of the directors in London and continued to believe it, though Moffat pointed out that, without liaison with Livingstone to arrange the timing of a rendezvous, this could not be guaranteed.

On 11 February 1860, men and canoes sent by Sekeletu ferried the mission party across the Chobe River into Kololo lands. The chief welcomed them to Linyanti with gift of an ox. The missionaries were surprised that there was no Livingstone waiting for them and, in turn, Sekeletu was profoundly disappointed that Livingstone and Mrs Livingstone were not with them. As far as he was concerned Livingstone and Mrs Livingstone were supposed to return, their presence being the guarantee of peace with the Ndebele that would enable him to move the capital from Linyanti to a new site on the Batoka plateau. The presence of LMS missionaries sent by 'Mosheti' (Moffat) with Mzilikazi and his Ndebele, when combined with the presence of Moffat's daughter with the Kololo in the new capital, was to guarantee the end of the Ndebele threat to the Kololo. Sekeletu also expected that he and his people would then benefit from the new trade route to the outside world that Livingstone had promised would emerge along the Zambesi. That was why, after all, he had subsidised both of Livingstone's journeys with men, supplies and ivory. He had been paying Livingstone as an *nduna* and diplomat, a role that Livingstone had been well aware he was performing.

Sekeletu could see no particular advantage to his people in cooperating with these newly arrived Europeans. They brought him nothing, not even news about peace with the Ndebele. He refused to set in motion the move to the highlands, which was, in his eyes, dependent on the presence of Mrs Livingstone or some other proof that the Moffat connection was in place to guarantee peace with the Ndebele. Whether he prevented the missionaries from going themselves to the Batoka plateau, as has been asserted by some, is not clear.

What is clear is that both the Tswana and European members of the party soon became seriously ill with malaria. Two of the principal African helpers, then one of the Helmore children and the Price baby died, to be followed by Helmore's daughter, Selina, and another Tswana helper. Then Mrs Helmore died. When Helmore himself died on 21 April, Price decided to withdraw the mission. He started off to return south with his wife, the two surviving Helmore children and the surviving Tswana missionaries. Sekeletu allowed Price to take only his wagon, confiscating the Helmore wagon since the adult Helmores were dead. He did send guides with the Price party to lead them south and then, after demanding payment in goods, authorised the building of the canoe-based raft necessary for Price's wagon to cross the Chobe. Mrs Price, already very ill, soon died and the sick survivors were only saved by the arrival of John Mackenzie, who led them safely back to Kuruman.

Price insisted that Sekeletu had deliberately poisoned them all in order to obtain their wagon and goods. The directors accepted this version of events. With the widespread but mistaken understanding that Livingstone had promised to be waiting for the missionaries at Linyanti, many in Britain believed that the tragedy was fundamentally Livingstone's fault. Livingstone had broken his promise to the missionaries and had callously left them to their fate among his much-vaunted Kololo, who turned out to be murderous savages. Various commentators on this topic, however, including experts in tropical medicine, have agreed that the evidence supports Sekeletu's innocence on the charge of poisoning the party. The African and European members of the party almost certainly died of malaria or the complication of malaria known as blackwater fever.[12]

There is no doubt that Sekeletu was unhelpful and unsympathetic but he cannot be blamed for the missionaries falling ill with malaria. From his perspective, Sekeletu saw these missionaries as uninvited strangers who were in his capital under false pretences. He treated them badly but his behaviour was a piece of opportunism by a sick and disappointed man, not the culmination of a poison plot. After all Sekeletu's help, which was essential for Price to get his wagon across the Chobe, was given, though Price had to pay for it. The language that has continued to be used by late twentieth-century biographers of Livingstone about the roles played by Sekeletu and the Kololo in this tragedy still resonates with the implication that they were criminally responsible.[13] Insisting that Livingstone was guilty of the utmost credulity in believing anything that Sekeletu told him about the affair is a modern version of Tidman's furious condemnation of Livingstone for listening to 'natives' and for Livingstone's suggesting there was a side to the story other than that told by Price.

There is no doubt that Livingstone's harsh condemnation of Price and Helmore for the disaster was heartless. It was utterly unacceptable to people whose imaginations were filled with the images of the deaths of European women and little children in the hostile environment of the Dark Continent. (The deaths of the Tswana members of the mission play no part in the recriminations directed at Livingstone then or since.) Livingstone did not help his case by his continued unsympathetic references to Price for years after the event. These have been seen as another example of a bitter, unforgiving side to Livingstone's character. Livingstone did bear grudges, there is no doubt, but his continued anger with Price was not without reason. After all Price had insisted that the Kololo had deliberately poisoned the missionaries, which was simply not true. In addition, Price's much-reported version of events, in confirming the popular image of Africans as unpredictable and irrational savages, supplied ammunition for the growing literature of the scientific race movement. Ultimately the question that was asked by Maclear has to be asked again. Why did the directors insist on the mission party going ahead as if Livingstone was waiting for them, when he was not and they knew it? Why did they let the party go without a doctor and with no effective medicine for malaria despite Livingstone having already publicised the effectiveness of his quinine-based medication? Equally puzzling is the refusal of both the missionaries and the directors of the LMS to listen to Moffat, who accurately forecast disaster should they follow their intended plan.

Livingstone did not let the missionaries down, nor did he break a promise to them. Where Livingstone was very seriously at fault was that he broke his promises to Sekeletu and the Kololo who, nevertheless, continued to be supportive of him. Livingstone had promised Sekeletu to return as soon as possible with Mrs Livingstone. When they returned, Sekeletu was to receive payment for all he had done for Livingstone. His repayment was to come in the form of peace with the Ndebele, a new, comparatively malaria-free, capital on the highlands beyond Mosi-oa-tunya, and the profits from the new trade route Livingstone was to have opened up.

After the Cabora Bassa rapids had made clear that the Zambesi was not God's Highway into the centre of the continent, and, when he had found that the River Shire led to a much better setting than the Batoka highlands for the missionary and commercial colony upon which he had pinned all his hopes for the future, Sekeletu and his people ceased to have any kind of priority in Livingstone's thinking. The only obligation to Sekeletu that he continued to recognise was to go back to Linyanti, at a time convenient to him, with those of the Kololo, placed at his disposal by Sekeletu, who wished to return. Sekeletu waited patiently for seven years for this new day that was to dawn for the Kololo *morafe*, a patience and trust symbolised by his care of the loaded wagon Livingstone had left with him. Yet all Sekeletu belatedly received was medical treatment that eased the pain but could not cure the disease that was killing him – nothing else. (In 1864 Sekeletu died and the next year the rule of the ever-dwindling band of Kololo was overthrown and the old Lozi dynasty regained its authority in the area.) Sekeletu stayed loyal to Livingstone to the last. Despite his disappointments, he sent sixteen Kololo men to help Livingstone on his way back down the Zambesi. Fourteen were to remain with Livingstone to aid him in any way he deemed necessary and two were to return from Tete with more medication for the chief.[14]

On the return journey Livingstone decided to make a more accurate survey of the Victoria Falls, where his party arrived on 27 September 1869, having left Shesheke ten days before. Livingstone measured the breadth of the falls as 1860 yards and then lay on a rock projecting out over the edge of the falls and reeled out a weighted line with a white rag on the end. This line caught on a rock about fifty feet above the water having been played out for 350 feet. This event was remembered by the local people who later told Arnot about it when he visited there twenty years later. Their version of the event reflected the way in which Livingstone had come to be part of their history and had been fitted into a role that made sense in their culture. They said that the *ngaka* (significantly they did not use the common word for European of him) had dropped a line into the falls and from it pulled a white fluttering bird together with some pearls.

Livingstone was determined to follow the line of the Zambesi exactly so as not miss any feature of the river on this occasion. This forced the expedition to trek through very rough country indeed, which exhausted Scot, Kololo and Tete carrier alike. Eventually at Moemba's village they were able to hire enough canoes to carry everyone on the river. In the canoes they shot the rapids in the Kariba Gorge. Thus emboldened, Livingstone then tried to shoot the rapids in the Mpata Gorge. This was another example of Livingstone's stubborn refusal to accept defeat and his horror of giving in to anything that could be called weakness. It was only the bravery and initiative of their Kololo escort that saved the party from disaster in a headlong dash through rocks, rapids and whirlpools. Instead of taking this experience as a warning, Livingstone took it as encouragement to attempt to shoot the Cabora Bassa rapids, despite the appeals of Charles Livingstone and Kirk not to do so.

The canoes of Livingstone and of Charles Livingstone got through the first set of rapids but Kirk's canoe overturned. He clung to a rock and, although the Kololo managed to save the canoe, all of Kirk's notes and journals as well as his rifle and clothes were swept away. Even Livingstone had then to accept defeat and agreed that enough was enough. All the canoes were now beached and the party continued on foot, though the Kololo and the carriers would have preferred to attempt a portage of the canoes to the placid waters beyond Cabora Basa. Given the exceptionally rugged terrain on either side of the gorge, which stretched for thirty miles, it is doubtful if such a portage was possible without a massive detour. On foot, without carrying these large and heavy Zambesi canoes, the party only managed to get through the precipitous hills with their scattered boulders 'as big as houses' with great difficulty. Once clear of these obstacles, the last stage of the journey to Tete was covered more easily, though they arrived hungry, exhausted and in rags.

Throughout most of this trek of 1600 miles, Charles Livingstone behaved strangely. The Kololo thought he was mad, and perhaps they were correct; his behaviour does appear to indicate that he was suffering a nervous breakdown. Most biographers of Livingstone have followed Kirk in judging Charles's behaviour on this journey as simply an exaggerated version of his usual unpleasant and untrustworthy character. That Charles Livingstone was his brother's evil genius has been so often asserted as to be almost taken for granted in the story of the Zambesi expedition.[15] Whatever the outcome of the argument about the role played by Charles Livingstone on the Zambesi expedition, it cannot be denied that before and after the expedition he appears to have been a gentle and pleasant man. It also cannot be denied that on the long march to and from Sesheke his behaviour was bizarre on numerous occasions. Kirk, who did not like Charles, reported these episodes, but they are also recorded with dismay and, at times, furious anger, by Livingstone. Charles's strange behaviour took the form, in the main, of blazing rows with Livingstone, often about small matters but always ending with a general verbal attack on all Livingstone's actions. Livingstone, in the entry in his journal for 11 June 1860, recorded a somewhat cryptic summary of one of these attacks:

> Manners of a cotton spinner – of Boers – didn't know how to treat men – an old filthy pillow that I got in benefit of it – that I cursed him – that I set the devil into him and asked if it was not his work to take time for me – and repeated again and again that I had cursed him. What part of Botany is Sunday cursing – seemed intent on a row – would be but a short time in the Expedition regretted that he was on this journey would rejoice when he would leave it – so for my brother Charles.[16]

Kirk records a number of these furious encounters, one of which this entry in Livingstone's notebook appears to report. According to Kirk, Charles, on at least two occasions, attacked David physically. The most critical moment for Charles in all these outburst of anger came at Sinamane's village on the way back to Tete. There Charles attacked not Livingstone but Livusi, Sekeletu's *nduna* sent to command the thirteen man escort the chief had provided. Livusi was not one of the paid Tete carriers, used to the Portuguese lash and who would have accepted a blow from an employer, but a proud warrior. Immediately he raised his spear, as did others among the Kololo. It was only Livingstone's swift intervention and his status among the Kololo that saved Charles from death. Charles's response, only minutes later, was to indulge in another outpouring of verbal abuse which culminated in his hurling himself against Livingstone in such a violent attack that it left Kirk still somewhat incoherent in the notes he wrote in his journal that evening.[17] Charles appears to have returned to a more normal pattern of behaviour after that, as neither Kirk nor Livingstone subsequently record any other similar episode.

When the ragged band of Scots, their Kololo escorts and their Tete carriers struggled back into Tete on 23 November 1860, Livingstone's spirits were immediately revived. First he found that the *Ma-Robert* had been brought into better shape than for some time by the hard work of the two petty officers, Rowe and Hutchins. It is worth noting that Livingstone has often been accused of not being able to get on with European colleagues, unless perhaps they were Scots like Kirk and Rae, but his relations with Rowe and Hutchins were consistently good throughout their service with him, as they had been with Walker.

Second and much more important was the news contained in the long-awaited despatch from the new Foreign Secretary, Lord John Russell. Russell congratulated Livingstone on the 'discovery' of Lake Nyasa, informed him that a new vessel, the *Pioneer*, was already on its way out to him, and told him of the new mission under a bishop, Charles F. Mackenzie, which was on its way to the Shire highlands. Russell warned, however, that Livingstone should curb his criticism of the Portuguese, an instruction which Livingstone ignored. The Foreign Secretary also commended Livingstone's suggestion that an alternative route to Lake Nyasa might be investigated by exploring the Rovuma river, which was outside any kind of Portuguese claim to sovereignty. If the Rovuma gave ready access to Lake Nyasa then the government would escape the apparently hopeless task of trying to persuade the Portuguese to accept the Zambesi as an international waterway, at least as far as its junction with the Shire.

Livingstone was delighted. After failure and frustration, here was a new beginning. He went about things with renewed vigour, from time to time humming 'Scots wha ha'e', a sure sign, according to Kirk, that he was contemplating 'some grand design'.

11

Failure and Defeat

Lord John Russell, in the despatch renewing the life of the expedition for a further two years, had had to warn Livingstone to moderate his criticisms of the Portuguese in East Africa. Livingstone had changed from praise of the Portuguese policy of racial equality in Angola to consistently attacking the Portuguese and all their works in his letters and reports from the Zambesi. The change was provoked by a number of things. One was simply the massive difference between the organised colonial structure, racial tolerance and economic development that was Angola and the scattering of small forts and villages that made up the Portuguese presence in the east. The second was Livingstone's horror at discovering Portuguese slave raiding was increasing rapidly in the Zambesi valley. His anger knew no bounds when he discovered that these traders were expanding their activity into the Shire valley, where they had not operated before his exploration of the Shire. Was he opening the way for slavers and the destruction of African society, not its development? The third cause of his anti-Portuguese stance was Livingstone's alarm at the new vigour that Lisbon evinced in asserting Portuguese sovereignty over more and more territory, and the Portuguese insistence that the Zambesi was not an international waterway.

If the Zambesi was not recognised as an international waterway, any hope of the development of international trade with the peoples of what is now Malawi via the Shire and Zambesi was doomed. He was furious about the Portuguese assertions of sovereignty because he knew that, as late as 1858, the Portuguese had struggled to maintain any sort of foothold on the Zambesi in face of the power of the rebel forces of Mariano. Even after the defeat of Mariano, it was only because they paid regular tribute to the Gazankulu Nguni in the south that allowed the Portuguese to hold onto Tete and Sena.[1]

A further Portuguese threat to Livingstone's hopes emerged at this time. The authorities in Lisbon began a campaign in academic journals to show that they knew of everything that Livingstone had 'discovered', though they granted he might have charted his 'finds' with much greater accuracy than their Portuguese 'discoverers' had.[2] There is no doubt that in the late seventeenth and through the eighteenth century Portuguese travellers had visited much of the Zambesi valley, though they had missed the Mosi oa Tunya (the Victoria Falls), and at least one had seen Lake Maravi, as they named it, Livingstone's Nyassa, the modern Lake Malawi.[3] That they had done so did not in any way change the fact that the Portuguese presence in east Africa was a marginal one, though, to Livingstone's chagrin, his work appeared to be stirring them into such activity as had not been seen for a century. This new activity on the ground in east Africa was worrying, but the diplomatic activity between London and Lisbon was the serious problem. What Livingstone feared was that the assertion of Bandiera, that Livingstone was simply mapping accurately Portuguese territory which they had not yet managed to do themselves, would be accepted by the British government and the international community. Were this to happen, his hopes for a 'new day' in Africa were gone, and the old day of Portuguese corruption and slaving would continue.

He responded to the threat in two ways. One was to attempt to deny the Portuguese claims about the achievements of their early explorers. These attempts by Livingstone in a series of letters and reports were foolish and misplaced. They were foolish because they made him appear petty and small-minded in his desperate attempts to make the Portuguese reports appear to be the work of 'armchair geographers', which most of them were not. His efforts were misguided because an effective line of attack would have been to point out that the experiences of these travellers of previous centuries had little or nothing to do with the reality of the Portuguese presence in East Africa in 1860. In his defence, however, it has to be said that in Lisbon and London these ancient Portuguese adventures did appear to carry weight and give the Portuguese a new status in east Africa. Livingstone felt that he had to demolish these claims; otherwise the dead hand of the Portuguese slave economy would crush all his hopes for Africa. His pride was not his primary concern in this campaign, as has been sometimes asserted, but his hopes and dreams for Africa and her peoples. His pride was involved (how could it not be, after all he was a human being?), but it was not the fundamental source of his anger and despair.

His second strategy in response to the Portuguese initiatives was to attempt to find an alternative route into the Lake Malawi region. The River Rovuma, he had been told, flowed from or, perhaps, rose near to the lake. By reason of an earlier international treaty, its southern bank was the northern boundary of the Portuguese sphere of influence. By definition, it was not in Portuguese territory and so might be the key to solving Livingstone's problem. He had suggested to London earlier that it should be explored and now Lord John Russell, in his despatch, agreed and instructed Livingstone to survey the river.

From the Portuguese perspective, if Livingstone were to establish his missionary and commercial colony in the region, they feared any hope of connecting their east and west African possessions would be over. So anxious were they to frustrate Livingstone that, in 1862, the Portuguese government sent representatives to negotiate with the Sultan of Zanzibar over the possibility of closing the Rovuma to any but Portuguese and subjects of the Sultan – an effort which failed.

A variety of interpretations of what Livingstone meant when he declared that he sought to plant a 'colony' in the region, whether on the Batoka or Shire highlands, have been put forward. Some have insisted that what he hoped for was something like Rhodes's Southern Rhodesia. The grounds they have for this assertion are a number of references in his letters in which he envisaged significant numbers of the 'honest poor' coming to the Zambesi to escape the misery of life in British industrial cities. None of those who support this 'Rhodesian' understanding of Livingstone's plans have attempted to relate this view to Livingstone's virulent condemnation of the British settlers in the Cape Colony, nor to his passionate defence of the Xhosa in the War of Mlanjeni, and his insistence on seeing them in the same category as the Magyar rebels of 1848 against Austrian rule. There is no doubt that in some letters the language he used does indicate that he toyed with the idea of large-scale white immigration into central Africa. This was in order to bring hope of a good life to the honest poor, many of whom had, he believed, no hope of a good life in Britain.[4] All these references, however, are in letters in which he was thinking aloud on paper and are limited to a short period of time some months of 1857 when he was in Britain. Whenever we find him writing about a definite plan, what he wanted was clearly not large-scale white migration. His colony was a missionary and commercial settlement, whose members would begin spreading of the Gospel and also initiate the legitimate trade that would drive out slave raiding and trading. The only precise suggestion about the 'honest poor' in any firm detail that he made was in a letter to Sir Roderick Murchison on 5 October 1859. In that letter what he envisaged was clearly a settlement of Scots set down as one community among the indigenous communities with the agreement of the latter, not a white settler take-over of the area. He said:

> I give all credit to missionary societies and would not say a word to disparage, but I think twenty or thirty good Scotch families with their minister and elders would produce an impression in ten years that would rejoice the hearts of all lovers of our race ... So far from being considered an intrusion I feel certain it would be esteemed a benefit to have a community ready to trade with them.[5]

Another statement of this view of the 'colony' as one community set down

among the indigenous communities appears in a letter to Miss Burdett-
Coutts:

> I am becoming more and more convinced that a small English colony in the
> highlands of Africa is indispensable to working out her civilisation, and producing
> a sensible effect on American slavery, and I lately ventured to tell Lord Malmesbury
> so. Should my wish ever be realised, I meant and would apply to you for a
> Clergyman. I did not soar so high as a Bishop, but I still believed in you the length
> of a Clergyman. I would have the church to be the first building.[6]

Again, in a letter to Palmerston written at Kongone while waiting for
the arrival of the *Pioneer*, Livingstone wrote as if the UMCA mission might
itself act as such a 'colony', initiating agricultural development and trade.[7]
Perhaps the clearest statement of what he envisaged appeared in another
letter to Palmerston, written soon after he had seen Lake Malawi for the
first time and had encountered a large caravan of slaves carrying ivory
from Kazembe's country on their way to the east coast.[8] He suggested to
Palmerston that if the British set up a small trading colony in the Shire
highlands then the traders would rather cash in their ivory there, rather
than struggle on for another month of hard marching to the coast. The
'colony' would also harvest the produce of what he called 'a vast cotton
producing region of unknown extent'. This would only work, however, he
insisted to the Foreign Secretary, if there were no Portuguese export dues
levied at the mouth of the Zambesi.[9] From these and other references it
appears that what Livingstone wanted was something resembling the settlements set up among the German tribes by St Boniface in the eighth
century whose work Livingstone had praised in earlier writing. In practice
this was what, in honour of Livingstone's memory, the Free Church of
Scotland and the Church of Scotland did in the 1870s with the establishment
of the Livingstonia and Blantyre missions. Both these industrial missions,
whose very existence depended on the good will of local chiefs, worked in
cooperation with the African Lakes Trading Company and attempted to
fulfil precisely the role within African society that Livingstone had envisaged
for his 'colony'.[10]

Having absorbed the good news in Russell's dispatch, Livingstone prepared
to go down to the Kongone mouth of the Zambesi to meet his new steamer,
the *Pioneer*, and the first contingent of the UMCA mission. Despite the hard
work of Hutchens and Rowe, it was not clear how long the 'Asthmatic'
would last, but Livingstone decided they should start off in her and take
her as far as she was able to stay afloat.

On 3 December 1860 the expedition started off from Tete. Livingstone
never visited the town again. Nine days later Kirk recorded in his diary that

they were struggling to keep the steamer afloat, as they plugged one hole in the thin hull after another. On the fifteenth, Kirk reported 'steam on in a sea-worthy state, only one compartment full up to the water level'. Finally on 21 December the *Ma-Robert* ran aground on a Zambesi sand bar for the last time. Kirk reported:

> The water began to rush into the cabin and soon it was evident that she was gone. We got the things out but mostly quite wet as boxes floated about in the cabin and I was working for couple of hours up to the middle, getting all I could out. Soon the whole vessel went down, shewing only the gunwale masts and funnel and uppermost part of the house above water ... camped on a sandbank but water rising fast.[11]

Canoes were obtained from one of Livingstone's Portuguese friends, H. L. Ferrao of Sena.[12] He entertained them at his house at Sena before the expedition moved on to the delta, where they arrived at the Kongone mouth on 4 January 1861. Somewhat incongruously, they then stayed in the house built by the Portuguese officer who had come to the Kongone to raise the Portuguese flag and build a customs post there. Livingstone and his comrades had a long wait in this spot, where they were particularly vulnerable to malaria. Livingstone's quinine therapy, however, saw them through.

On 31 January the *Pioneer* arrived escorted by HMS *Sidon*. On board the *Sidon* were the first UMCA missionaries, who were followed by a bishop, Charles Frederick Mackenzie, and the rest of the advance party on board HMS *Lyra*. Mackenzie had been consecrated in the Anglican cathedral at Cape Town, the month before, as 'bishop of the mission to the tribes dwelling in the neighbourhood of Lake Nyasa and the River Shire'. The situation at that point was, as Owen Chadwick put it: 'The Bishop, then, landed at the Kongone intending to take his mission up the Zambesi and Shire. Livingstone sailed down the Zambesi to the Kongone intending to take himself and the mission to the Rovuma.'[13] On 9 February and for the subsequent three days Livingstone and Kirk argued with the bishop and his staff as to what they were going to do. At one point Mackenzie drafted a formal letter refusing to go to the Rovuma. Interestingly, despite the seriousness of the disagreement and the insistence by so many writers that Livingstone could not get on with anyone who opposed him, Livingstone and Mackenzie became and remained friends. Livingstone had been instructed by Russell to investigate the Rovuma as a possible route to Lake Malawi. He was officially instructed also to give what help he could to the mission. His primary consideration, however, was his official instruction to investigate the Rovuma. Mackenzie finally agreed to this arrangement.

The *Pioneer* then set off north, accompanied by the *Sidon* and the *Lyra*, as far as Anjoan in the Comoro Islands where there was a British consul, Mr Sunley, and where the British antislavery naval patrols called regularly.[14] The other missionaries and the stores were unloaded there while the bishop and H. H. Rowley of the UMCA went with Livingstone and his colleagues on the *Pioneer* to try the Rovuma. After taking some time to find the true mouth of the river, they entered it on 11 March and steamed about sixteen miles up river on the first two days. They then ran into difficulties because the *Pioneer* was drawing five feet, not the three feet that Livingstone had requested for a river steamer. This was due to the large amount of ballast that had been needed to allow her to steam safely from Britain to the Zambesi. It rapidly became clear to Livingstone that, if they did not get back to the sea immediately, they might be trapped in the river until its levels arose again with the next rainy season. Livingstone was frustrated because, had he been on his own with African associates, he could have pressed on by canoe and on foot to see where the river went, but he could not hold up the new mission in that way.

When the *Pioneer* emerged again at the mouth of the Rovuma, Mackenzie, Rowley and all but four of the seventeen man crew of the *Pioneer* were ill with malaria. Livingstone, a jack of all trades, took on a new responsibility: he navigated the *Pioneer* across open sea to the Comoros, where, at Anjoan, the mission party was reunited.

The *Pioneer* then sailed back to the Kongone, arriving on 1 May 1861. The party proceeded up the Zambesi and the Shire to Chibisa's. Livingstone had hoped that the journey would take about twenty days; instead it took ten weeks. The *Pioneer*, drawing five feet not three, went aground again and again in the Shire. Livingstone described the frustrations of the journey in his *Narrative*:

> It caused us a great deal of hard and vexatious work, in laying out anchors, and toiling at the capstan to get her off sandbanks ... Once we were a fortnight on a bank of soft, yielding sand ... In handling the *Pioneer* over the shallow places, the Bishop, with Horace Waller and Mr Scudamore, were ever ready and anxious to lend a hand, and worked as hard as anyone on board.[15]

There could be no higher praise from Livingstone.

The journey was not all frustration and struggle. The missionaries and the members of the expedition spent evenings in long discussions on theology, on Africa, and on the new developments in science; the bishop had a copy of Darwin's newly published *Origin of Species* with him. During these discussions Rowley would propound extremely high church views on many topics with a conviction that became, at times, very aggressive. He was already out of favour with Livingstone and this 'blethering' made things worse. Livingstone had already been upset by Rowley's constant scribbling, as he described it. He was angry with him for sitting in the cabin writing while his bishop worked at the capstan with the rest.

The *Pioneer* finally arrived at the foot of the cataracts on 15 July. The communities of the Shire valley and highlands were no longer the well fed, prosperous, cotton growing people that Livingstone had first encountered. Groups of Yao, whom he had first encountered in 1859 on the fringe of the area, had now penetrated deep into the highlands, while Portuguese slave trading was stimulating 'man-stealing' by the indigenous Mang'anja themselves as well as by the invading Yao. The latter also had contacts with the Zanzibar slavers. A bad situation had been made worse by crop failures as a result of the poor rains of the 1860–61 wet season; hunger was a sharp stimulus to slave trading. It was this situation facing the newcomers that led Rowley to report that Livingstone had misled them about the Shire and the Shire highlands and to question Livingstone's integrity.[16]

Leaving the *Pioneer* to be looked after by her crew, Livingstone, his brother Charles, Kirk and their Kololo escort started to recruit porters from among the local people to carry the missions goods up into the highlands. Livingstone and the bishop then led the caravan up the escarpment to seek a suitable base for the mission.[17] Mackenzie wrote:

> You would like to see our picturesque appearance on the march. Livingstone in his jacket and trousers of blue serge and his blue cloth cap. His brother, a taller man, in something of the same dress. I with trousers of Oxford grey and a coat like a shooting coat, a broad-brimmed wide-awake with a white cover, which Livingstone laughs at, but which all the same keeps the sun off. He is a Salamander.[18]

While the members of the caravan were resting at Mbame's village – Livingstone was unwell which always annoyed and upset him – slave traders with a coffle of slaves entered the village on their way to Tete. Kirk described what happened in his journal:

> About 1 pm while we were in the huts, a gang of eighty-four slaves was marched into the village with a few drivers. On being spoken to, the latter ran off, not before four guns had been taken and all the gear they carried with them. The bulk however of their goods being carried by the slaves remained safe also. One of them was Katura a slave of Sr Tito [Major Sicard] who served as our cook and steward at Tette ... The slaves were, most of them, tied by the neck with ropes, in gangs, some refractory ones had beams of wood as thick as a man's thigh and six feet long with a fork at one extremity in which the neck was secured by an iron pin.[19]

The majority of the slaves were women and children; although a few had been bought, most had been captured in raids. The fact that a significant number of the slaves were Yao should have warned Mackenzie that the issue in the Shire highlands was not simply one of the Yao as slave raiders and Mang'anja as victims. Livingstone already knew that the Mang'anja themselves had been unable to resist the temptation offered by the Portuguese traders and had become involved in the trade. He failed, however, to communicate this effectively to Mackenzie and his mission colleagues.

Most of the slaves freed on the sixteenth chose to stay with the bishop, who thus gained a ready-made constituency for his mission. This new community was added to over the next few days by smaller groups of slaves, also on their way to Tete, who were freed without the use of force. After some discussion, in which Mackenzie appeared to prefer a spot nearer the escarpment above the Shire, it was decided to site the mission at Magomero. The site was a little to the north east of Chiradzulo mountain beyond the Namadzi stream, with the Zomba massif to the north and Lake Shirwa to the north east. It was also the centre of a dense Mang'anja population. Before any kind of building could commence there was another incident with slavers, but this one had much more serious consequences than that at Mbame's.

Livingstone had hoped to visit some of the Yao chiefs to attempt to establish good relations with them on behalf of the mission. On 22 July he and the bishop, with Livingstone's Kololo escort, set off towards Zomba mountain. A large number of Mang'anja followed behind. The Mang'anja presence led to a disaster. As Livingstone's party moved towards Zomba they passed through deserted Mang'anja villages with crops unharvested in the fields. Then, as they approached the first Yao settlement, they saw a group of armed Yao entering their village with a large number of captives. Livingstone went forward to establish a dialogue with the leaders, as he had so often done in the past and would do again on many occasions equally fraught. He went forward entirely unarmed, not expecting trouble. Why should he when these tactics had worked again and again in the past? Behind him on this occasion, however, there was not simply a group of his own Kololo, or other personal followers, but a crowd of very excited and upset Mang'anja people. They shouted and yelled challenges at the Yao, making it clear they had come with the Europeans to attack and punish their adversaries. Livingstone's lone advance was ignored by the Yao and, in response to the screamed threats of the Mang'anja, they fired their muskets at the newcomers together with, what was much more dangerous than their ancient firearms, a mass of arrows. Livingstone was astonished and utterly disconcerted. For the first and only occasion he had failed to make a good contact with an African community to which he was making an approach.

On being attacked, Livingstone's Kololo and his European companions immediately opened fire with their rifles, whose range and accuracy convinced the Yao to retire. They moved off, with their women and children and most of their captives, while the Mang'anja fired the encampment. Livingstone always believed in being willing to fight if pushed but, throughout almost all his life in Africa, he nearly always managed to talk his way through potential conflicts, though sometimes he was only successful in this by making clear that he would fight if he had to. On this occasion he was never in charge of the situation. The result of this encounter, in which at least six Yao were killed by the first rifle volley, was that from then on the Mang'anja saw Mackenzie and his mission as an important military ally, and the Yao saw the mission as their enemy. Before this understanding became permanent Livingstone warned Mackenzie very firmly not to get involved in a Yao-Mang'anja war, insisting that a negotiated understanding with the Yao might still be achieved. Mackenzie, however, after Livingstone's departure became involved in a series of what he called 'wars' on the side of the Mang'anja against the Yao.[20]

Critics of Livingstone in the 1860s as well as modern writers have laid the blame for this involvement squarely on Livingstone's shoulders. Yet to do so is to treat Mackenzie somewhat patronisingly, implying that he was not adult enough to make decisions for himself. It is also to ignore Livingstone's advice to Mackenzie and his insistence that the first clash with the Yao did not necessarily mean an irreparable breakdown in relations. Face to face negotiations might still have brought about some sort of modus vivendi with the Yao chiefs, but it was Mackenzie's judgement that this was not possible and he believed he had no alternative but to side with the Mang'anja.

Livingstone, after leaving Magomero, went off to get on with his primary responsibility. He left the *Pioneer*, its crew and the rest of the expedition at Chibisa's and set of to explore the lake in a gig with Kirk, his brother Charles and an Ulsterman, John Neil, a bluejacket from the *Pioneer*. Livingstone's Kololo and some Sena porters also came along as a shore support party. The shore party carried the gig, four-oared with a sail, past the Murchison Cataracts. From there the Europeans sailed in the gig while the African escort followed along the riverbank then along the west coast of the lake. It is a puzzle, to which neither Livingstone's journal and letters nor those of Kirk give any answer, why Livingstone went up the west coast when one of his principal aims was to find if the Rovuma on the east started from the lake or somewhere close to it.

Between the rapids and Lake Malawi they passed thousands of people fleeing from the slavers, an ominous sign of the disastrous changes that were happening in the region. The explorers arrived on the lake at the stormiest time of the year and only Neil's fine seamanship saved them from disaster on many occasions. Livingstone, so often said to be unable to brook any apparent threat to his leadership, accepted Neil's judgement on the water throughout the whole trip. The most important aspects of the journey were twofold. The first was enormously exciting for Livingstone; he had never before seen such a densely populated region in Africa. The second was not encouraging but depressing: it was that the area was suffering from two massive and disturbing alien inroads. The first was by Zanzibari slave traders whose dhows and canoes were carrying slaves across the lake in much larger numbers than either Livingstone or Kirk had dreamt.[21] The second was the presence of the Ngoni of Mbelwa, who were establishing hegemony over the highlands to the west of the lake north of Nkhotakhota.

On reaching the fringe of the Ngoni area, the Kololo on the shore would go no further. Here was another version of their old enemy the Ndebele of Mzilikazi; indeed Kirk referred to the Ngoni, not wholly inaccurately, as Ndebele.[22] Livingstone went ashore and, encouraged by his presence, the shore party moved northwards again. Livingstone then had an encounter with a small party of Ngoni warriors; they must have been a patrol sent out by an *impi* of Mbelwa. Livingstone went to meet them with Maloka, a Kololo who could speak Ndebele. At one point the warriors drummed on their shields with the butts of their short stabbing spears, the usual prelude to a charge. Maloka took them aback by insisting they sit and talk – since 'it was not the first time we have heard shields rattled'. After some talk, during which Livingstone refused to give them a present, the young warriors left as Livingstone began to question them about how many people they had killed. In his *Narrative* Livingstone wrote that on leaving 'they sped away up the hills like frightened deer'.[23] This was a mistaken perception. Livingstone, who had never dealt with Nguni people, failed to recognise the remarkable jogging pace Ngoni, Ndebele and Zulu warriors used, allowing them to cover ground at a speed that confounded their adversaries – it had nothing to do with being frightened.

Somewhere between Nkata Bay and Usisya, Livingstone and the shore party made contact again with those in the gig – they had been out of touch for four days and those in the boat had feared the worst. At this point they had almost no supplies left, much of their clothing and equipment had been stolen and the lake shore had been stripped of resources by Ngoni raids, so reluctantly Livingstone decided they had to turn back. On the journey they had heard from local people many different versions of the relationship of the Rovuma and the lake, but the consensus appeared to be that the river rose about fifty miles from the lake, which was what two Zanzibari travellers they met also told them. Livingstone still hoped that the travellers were wrong.

At the point where they decided to go back, Livingstone and the others thought that they had come close to the north end of the lake. The mountains on each shore appeared to come together not very far ahead, so they believed that they had come within sight of the north end. Kirk drew a map of the lake which he sent to the Royal Geographical Society showing the lake ending somewhere near Usisya.[24] This was an illusion, as the lake stretches on for another hundred miles.

As they began to retrace their route south along the western shore, Kirk constantly complained about the Kololo shore party holding them back. By the time they reached Mangoche, where the lake ends and the Shire begins, relations had become so bad between the boat and shore parties that the Kololo refused to return to the *Pioneer* and went off elephant hunting. Local people helped the four Europeans and the Sena porters past the rapids and they got back to the *Pioneer* on 8 November 1861.

It was it this point that a number of events came together, with disastrous consequences for the expedition and for the UMCA mission, and at least one which had long-term importance in the creation of what is now the republic of Malawi. This last was the decision of Livingstone's sixteen Kololo, rejected by their old leader because of their desertion to go elephant hunting at Mangoche, to stay on in the Shire valley. They insisted for the rest of their lives, however, that they were still the men of Dotoro Livisto. Because of the widespread unrest Chibisa had fled to a village near Tete, and into this power gap stepped the Kololo. They took over the leadership of Chibisa's people and the other Mang'anja groups of what is now Chikwawa district. They provided very quickly a stabilising influence in the Shire valley below the cataracts. They attacked Yao and Portuguese slave parties, freeing the slaves and, after reserving some of the girls for themselves, sending the others to the missionaries at Magomero for shelter. In the long term these Kololo, led by Ramakukane and Moloka, who were true Sotho, and Kanyou, a Lozi, energised the Mang'anja peoples of the valley and their survival as a people has been attributed to this Kololo leadership by a leading historian of the Mang'anja.[25] The Kololo chiefs also played an important role in the 1880s, resisting the Portuguese advance up the Shire. This contributed to the crisis resolved by the declaration of the British Protectorate over what is now Malawi in 1891.

Back on the *Pioneer*, Livingstone found that a number of the crew had become sick and had gone up to Magomero for convalescence. The river was rising rapidly and he wanted to get away as quickly as possible, as the five-foot draught of the *Pioneer* was a problem except when the river was in full spate. He therefore sent to Magomero for the sailors. While waiting for them he received exciting news brought by the Reverend Henry de Wint Burrup, a new recruit for the UMCA who had come up river by canoe. The news was that a warship and a civilian vessel were expected at the mouth of the Zambesi very soon. They were bringing not only supplies but also the bishop's sister, Miss Mackenzie, accompanied by her housekeeper Jeannie Lennox, and a maid.[26] The ship was also bringing Mrs Livingstone, a new missionary for the UMCA, Dr James Stewart of the Free Church of Scotland, and Livingstone's colleague Rae along with the *Lady Nyassa*, the steamer Livingstone had paid to be built under Rae's supervision in Scotland. To Livingstone's chagrin he learned that the *Lady Nyassa* was in parts and would have to be assembled. Livingstone had wanted it to be towed out by a man of war so that it could of use immediately. James Stewart was coming out to survey the possibility of setting up an industrial mission of the Free Church of Scotland in the region; 'a small Scotch colony' as Livingstone put it.

Speed was of the essence. He had to get down to the delta as soon as possible so as to get everyone back up to the Shire highlands while the rivers were still being fed by the rains. He told the bishop to meet him at the confluence of the Ruo and Shire at the beginning of January. He would bring the UMCA people there and then he would turn back to the Zambesi to go up to Tete to recover the stores of the expedition which were still there. He would then go back up the Shire and begin the task of getting the *Lady Nyassa* past the cataracts and onto the lake This was a very tight timetable for a vessel notoriously unsuited for the Shire and Zambesi river system.

Disaster struck almost immediately. The *Pioneer* left Chibisa's on 15 November 1861, the start having been delayed so as to get members of the crew back from Magomero. Thirty-six hours later she was aground on a sandbank that had changed position since their last visit. They were stuck there with little forward movement until 22 December, more than a month. Robert Fayers, the ship's carpenter, died from malaria. He was the first European under Livingstone's care who did so. Both Livingstone and Kirk were unhappy at that time about the quality of quinine and other drugs with which they had been supplied by the navy.[27] As a result of this death, Livingstone restarted quinine prophylactic measures on board ship as well as treating those who came down with the disease with his special quinine pills.

What of the bishop now the timetable was so disastrously awry? Livingstone hoped to pick him up at the mouth of the Ruo, since now the *Pioneer* would reach there on the way down at the time they had hoped to be there on the way up. When the *Pioneer* finally reached the junction of the two rivers there was no sign of Mackenzie. What had happened was that two missionaries the bishop had sent to reconnoitre a route from Magomero to the Ruo-Shire confluence had been held up and only narrowly escaped death at the hands of a chief near the headwaters of the Ruo. The bishop then led a punitive expedition against that chief which, but for the warlike ability of some of the Kololo who went with Mackenzie, might have been a disaster. Only after this adventure did Mackenzie set off with Burrup and three Kololo for the rendezvous, reaching it on 11 January 1862, three days after Livingstone had passed going down river. Mackenzie's canoe had overturned several days before and, though the Kololo had rescued the two missionaries and the canoe, the medicine kit was lost. Waiting on a mosquito-infested island in the Shire without quinine or any other medicine, Mackenzie died of malaria on 31 January 1862.[28] The Kololo buried him on the mainland and then took Burrup back to Magomero, carrying him for the last part of the trip on a litter. He died a few days later.

On 23 January 1862, the *Pioneer* reached the Luabo mouth of the Zambesi which Livingstone had come to prefer to Kongone. They had to wait until the last day of the month before HMS *Gorgon* appeared towing a brig, the *Hetty Ellen*. Despite Livingstone's delight on being reunited with Mary, the months that followed were among the most frustrating and unhappy of his life. Even as the passengers began to disembark, their number, the amount of goods that they had brought, and the fact that the *Lady Nyassa* was in forty pieces in the hold of the *Hetty Ellen*, presented Livingstone with logistical problems that were beyond his abilities to deal with.[29] The sheer weight of people and goods, even if their handling had been well organised and had proceeded according to a clear plan, were far too much for the *Pioneer* to manage except by many slow relays of journeys up and down the Shire and Zambesi system.

Another and very personal problem for Livingstone was the gossip that the UMCA ladies brought with them. James Stewart had travelled to Cape Town with Mrs Livingstone of whom he had taken great care and to whom he had paid anxious attention when she had bouts of depression and occasionally drank too much. Stewart's arrival with her at Cape Town, en route to explore the possibility of setting up a Free Kirk industrial mission in the Lake Malawi area, had, however, provoked hostility in the circles there that supported the UMCA. Miss Mackenzie and her entourage were particularly hostile. It was only on the firm insistence of Mrs Livingstone that Stewart was allowed to accompany them on the *Hetty Ellen*. During the wait in South Africa, an ugly rumour had started of an illicit relationship between Stewart and Mrs Livingstone; these rumours were believed and repeated by Miss Mackenzie and her circle. When Rae arrived to join the company going to the Zambesi, he had contributed to the whispering campaign. Livingstone was made aware of these stories and dismissed them out of hand; however, they hurt Mary terribly.[30]

Eventually the *Pioneer* set off with ninety people crammed into it while stores as well as the pieces of the *Lady Nyassa* were left behind to be picked up again. Captain Wilson of the *Gorgon* and some of his crew contributed to the overcrowding on board. When, on 17 February, it was clear how slow their rate of progress was, Wilson decided to take the mission women upstream to the rendezvous in a whaler manned by his ratings. It was agreed that Dr Kirk would go along as guide and interpreter. So Miss Anne Mackenzie, Miss Lennox, the maid and Mrs Burrup set off not knowing the men they were going to meet were already dead. At the mouth of the Ruo they were told nothing by the local people and did not realise they had anchored so close to Mackenzie's grave. Finally, on 4 March, they reached Chibisa's to hear the terrible news. Kirk and Wilson were also informed that the missionaries at Magomero were in desperate straits from lack of food. In response to the news of their distress, Kirk and Wilson then set off with the bluejackets for Magomero, about which adventure Kirk wrote bitterly:

> Nothing but what seemed an absolute necessity would have induced me to go off thus without medicines, proper food, sufficient supply of cloth during the wet season and with a large body of untried Englishmen. But it was an act of humanity from doing which there was no escape. The letters from the Mission represented their state as one of frustration from disease and famine. Had we known that some of them were healthy and strong and possessed not only of goats but of preserved meats coffee and tea, I should have remained quietly waiting their appearance and sent off a messenger immediately.[31]

They met a party from the mission at Mbame's, and were astonished and angry to find them well fed and supplied (though delighted to share those supplies). Kirk, Wilson and the sailors then staggered back, weak and ill, to Chibisa's. They gathered the distraught ladies and their luggage and started back for Shupanga, reaching the *Pioneer* on March 14. The next day Living-stone set off with the mission ladies down to the Luabo mouth in the *Pioneer* to see them safely on their way back to Cape Town.

During these weeks at Shupanga, Livingstone and Mary were very close and she appeared to be in a happy frame of mind despite the ugly rumours. Many of the company were taken with her but Kirk showed the snobbishness that characterised so many of his judgements when he referred to her as 'a coarse vulgar woman'. Mary and Livingstone's period of happiness did not last long. She fell seriously ill with malaria on 21 April and they quickly moved her off the ship into the expedition's house at Shupanga. Livingstone was with her every moment, and Kirk gave her his best care, but on Sunday evening 27 April she fell into a coma and died. Livingstone was utterly devastated and wept uncontrollably, while his companions took over. Kirk saw to the grave and Rae built a coffin. The Portuguese offered a military escort to fire a salute, which Livingstone, though touched, declined. James Stewart conducted the funeral service the next day under the great baobab tree on the river's edge at Shupanga.

For a time Livingstone appeared paralysed by grief; then he turned to incessant activity, so often his solution to unhappiness and loss. He wrote an enormous number of letters, to the Moffats, his children, friends and colleagues. There are two very touching themes he picked up in his journal and in some of the letters, his love for Mary and, what must surprise those who only know of the couple's years of separation, the fun that was in their relationship.

> It is the first heartstroke I have suffered, and quite takes away my strength. I wept over her who well deserved many tears. I loved her when I married her, and the longer I lived with her I loved her the more.[32]

And again:

> In our intercourse in private there was more than would be thought by some a decorous amount of merriment and play. I said to her a few days before her fatal illness 'We old bodies ought to be more sober and not play so much.' 'O no,' said she, ' you must be just as playful as you have always been. I would not like you to be so grave as some folks I have seen.' [33]

As ever work was his solace and Livingstone flung himself into getting the *Lady Nyassa* ready. It had taken three months to transport the twenty-two sections and two watertight compartments to Shupanga and two more months were spent putting them together. It was then that Livingstone and Rae had their first angry confrontation. Rae refused to assemble the engine and put it in place, since at Chibisa's the ship would have to be dismantled to be carried past the cataracts; waiting until then to put in the engines would save labour. Livingstone gave in, partly, at least, because other things were on his mind.

He was deeply troubled by the declaration of the local Portuguese authorities that slave hunting and slavery were not illegal in Portuguese territory. Next the UMCA mission had decided that their position at Magomero was not only unhealthy but also untenable in the face of increased Yao activity.[34] As a result, the missionaries and their flock retreated to Chibisa's on 6 May, where they were dependent, whether they liked it or not (and they did not), on the protection of the Kololo. On top of all of this, another unusually dry rainy season had not only caused the Shire to be at its lowest ebb for a generation but had also resulted in widespread famine. When people are hungry and afraid they do not cultivate cotton.

The expedition was now nearing the end of its allotted time and nothing appeared to have been achieved. Livingstone decided on one last attempt to fulfil Russell's instructions and seek a route to the lake free of Portuguese interference via the Rovuma. It would have been months before they could have moved up stream in any case. He asked Kirk, Rae and his brother Charles to go with him to Anjoan to obtain supplies from the British consul there. They would also buy oxen which were to be used to draw the carts to transport the parts of the *Lady Nyassa* along the projected road past the cataracts on the Shire. He appears not to have told Kirk and the others about the Rovuma part of the journey, so that Kirk reported, and many writers since have accepted his report, that going to the Rovuma was a sudden and irrational decision taken while at Anjoan.[35]

At Anjoan, Mr Sunley, the consul, was welcoming and arranged for their supplies and the oxen to be ready for them when they returned after attempting the Rovuma. Livingstone was given the help of a warship to tow the *Pioneer* to the mouth of the Rovuma. The little steamer anchored there in the bay while Livingstone with Kirk and his brother set off in four small boats crewed by naval ratings and some African crewmen from the *Pioneer*; Livingstone called the latter his 'Mazaro men'.[36] The trip was a constant struggle up a river where they had to drag the boats across sandbanks and where many of the local people were hostile. On one occasion this hostility was expressed by a flight of arrows fired at the boats. In reply two local people were shot dead, one by Kirk and the other by his naval coxswain. Livingstone did not mention these deaths in anything he wrote and was deeply unhappy about Kirk's decision to fire. Despite all the difficulties, they pushed on for 114 miles as the crow flies before Livingstone gave up. Kirk entered in his journal almost daily condemnations of Livingstone's insistence on moving forward despite all obstacles. His most bitter comment was also a gross misrepresentation of Livingstone's motives:

> At noon reach a wide part of the river, very shallow. Still Dr L. means to drag over it. The infatuation which blinds him, I cannot comprehend, getting the boats jammed up the river where they cannot float and where it will soon be impossible to return. It seems madness and to follow a man running such risks for the empty glory of geographical discovery is more than I would consent to ... I can come to no other conclusion than that Dr L. is out of his mind.[37]

Returning to Anjoan to collect the stores and livestock, the *Pioneer* then made its way down the coast, calling in at Quilemane and Kongone, and finally reaching Shupanga on 17 December 1862. At Quilemane some Portuguese reported that Livingstone 'slunk in like a dog with his tail between his legs', a description seized on with relish by his critics in Britain when it was reported to them.

Spending Christmas beside Mary's grave did not do much to lift Livingstone's spirits and most of the staff of the expedition was also deeply unhappy. Kirk had only been persuaded to stay on with great reluctance, Charles Livingstone was always unwell and Rae's behaviour had become insubordinate. The last's persistent refusal to put the engines in the *Lady Nyassa* meant that the *Pioneer* had to tow her. When that did not work well, the two ships were tied side by side like a crude catamaran.

This strange and cumbersome contraption entered the Shire late in January and on 25 January stuck on a sandbar where it stayed for three weeks. That was bad enough but what they now saw sent their spirits plummeting to a new low. The Shire had become what Rowley of the UMCA called 'a river of death'. The once very prosperous valley was a disaster area; bad rains had meant that crops had failed for a second year and slaving had become more widespread than ever. Corpses floated past the ship every day they were on the river. Charles Livingstone recorded that he was told that a trader had taken 450 women away after massacring their men and boys. In the middle of March, while the ships were still stuck on the lower Shire, Livingstone and Kirk went up stream in a canoe to Chibisa's in response to a call from help from the mission. The mission's only doctor had died and others of the staff were sick.

Livingstone was appalled that the missionaries had spent so long on the Shire at Mikorongo near Chibisa's. This was an unhealthy spot, the kind of place he had been insisting for years where it was impossible for Europeans to settle for any length of time.[38] He left Kirk to help the missionaries and went back to the *Pioneer*.

Livingstone managed to get ship on the move again and reached the foot of the Murchison Cataracts on 10 April 1863. There his spirits revived and he began planting a vegetable garden to supply food for the men who would help to cut the new road to bypass the rapids. Almost immediately he was cast down again. Richard Thornton, who, after adventures on the Luangwa and on Kilimanjaro, had rejoined the expedition again at Shupanga in July 1862, had recently come up to Mikorongo. Since July he had been pursuing, on Livingstone's orders, geological research. When he came up river in early February, he found the missionaries desperately short of fresh meat so he volunteered to go with Waller to Tete to buy goats at the Portuguese fort. This journey, one leg of which had led to the utter exhaustion of Kirk and Rae in 1860, left him physically broken down on his return. He died from a bout of malaria on 21 April. Whether Thornton's death was the last straw for Charles Livingstone or not, as his brother suggested, a few days later Charles asked Livingstone for permission to go home. Livingstone agreed and suggested to Kirk that, since he had wanted to leave for some time, he should also now leave the expedition. In his journal and letters at this time and for some time after his return to Britain, Kirk was highly critical of Livingstone and insisted that Livingstone had taken against him. In fact Livingstone wrote of Kirk at that time in highly complimentary terms and indeed a few months later named a mountain range in western Malawi after him, Kirk's Range. Kirk later learned of Livingstone's respect for him and the friendship was restored but it was then too late to stop his witness being added to that of Rowley as to Livingstone's incompetence and, more pointedly, Livingstone's dishonesty. The arrival back in Britain of James Stewart added to the bad publicity. He insisted that the Zambesi and Shire system was not a possible route for trade, but worse he insisted, like Rowley, that the Shire valley and highlands had been totally and deliberately misrepresented by Livingstone. Before leaving the Zambesi, Stewart had, in a melodramatic gesture, thrown his copy of Livingstone's *Missionary Researches* into the river, proclaiming:

> The volume was fragrant with odours of and memories of the earnestness with which I studied the book in days gone by. How different it appeared now! ... Thus I disliked the book and sent it to sink or swim into the vaunted Zambesi. So perish all that is false in myself and others.[39]

Yet only twelve years later in 1875, the pioneers of the Livingstonia mission, a mission organised by James Stewart, arrived in Malawi to be joined by the Blantyre Mission and the African Lakes Company to do what Livingstone had hoped to achieve and what Stewart had declared impossible.

Livingstone, even as he supervised the dismantling of the *Lady Nyassa*, knew that soon the expedition would be recalled. For a time he continued to have Rae and the crew of the *Pioneer* work at dismantling the *Lady Nyassa* to get her ready for transportation to the lake by means of the road that Livingstone still had men cutting over the rough hills beside the cataracts. It is not clear whether he hoped he might yet get a reprieve or whether he was just marking time.

On 26 June 1862, the new bishop of the UMCA mission, William George Tozer, arrived at Mikorongo, where his mission colleagues were profoundly disheartened by his decision to withdraw to the top of Mount Morambala, near the Shire and Zambesi confluence. They would have been more upset if they had known that he had already made up his mind to withdraw to somewhere safe on the coast, Zanzibar as it turned out. Since Tozer accepted all this territory was legally Portuguese, indeed in prayers at the mission he coupled the name of the King of Portugal with that of Queen Victoria, and that freeing slaves from Portuguese slavers was 'highway robbery', his position was entirely logical. The missionaries on the spot wanted to go back to the highlands, perhaps to Chief Mbame's, near where the Blantyre Mission of the Church of Scotland was to settle twelve years later.

Tozer also brought with him a despatch from Lord John Russell ending the expedition, a despatch which Tozer read before Livingstone did. Tozer and Livingstone met and had a polite but restrained conversation. Livingstone then became very angry when he learned from Waller that Tozer had decided to take only a few 'teachable boys' with the mission when they withdrew. Waller resigned from the mission in protest and later herded the men, women and children whom Tozer was abandoning down to the coast and eventually to the Cape.

Russell, in his despatch, made clear to Livingstone that salaries would be paid to the end of the year to enable him to get the *Pioneer* back down to the ocean, where it would come again under Royal Navy command. Livingstone had Rae and the men of the *Pioneer* reassemble the *Lady Nyassa*. He had just been informed in a letter from his friend 'Parrafin' Young that the trustees of his funds in Britain had refused to pay for the *Lady Nyassa* and Young had paid the costs from his own pocket. Livingstone had decided to try to get his little steamer away from the area because he did not want her to become an aid to Portuguese slaving. He also now needed to sell her.

There was, however, no way that the *Pioneer* and the *Lady Nyassa* could get down the river at that time of the year, August and September. So Livingstone decided to go off to the lake again with some Kololo and Mazaro men. He also took the steward of the *Pioneer*, Thomas Ward, who was anaemic. Livingstone thought the adventure would do him good, an utterly Livingstonian reaction to illness. They set off with a small boat which they carried past the cataracts. The overenthusiasm of some Mazaro men, who wanted to outshine the Kololo in Livingstone's eyes, led to the boat's loss as they tried to launch it beyond the cataracts. Livingstone decided to march on and clearly was enjoying himself.[40] Ward had to struggle hard to keep up but keep up he did. Livingstone led his men from Matope on the Shire across westwards to Ntcheu and to the mountains he named after Kirk. He then led his men due north to meet the lakeshore at Ntakataka. From there they followed the coast till the reached the Zanzibari slave depot of Nkhotakhota, where they received generous hospitality from the Jumbe's second in command, the Jumbe (the hereditary

ruler) being absent.[41] Livingstone found that the Zanzibari slave trade from
Kazembe's to Zanzibar was continuing to expand and was draining central
Africa of thousands of human beings annually. Nkhotakhota was a major
entrepot of this trade.

Livingstone then marched due west till he reached the Luangwa. He was
told of other lakes beyond the Luangwa and that a further river system
began about ten days march away. His old enemies, dysentery and haemorrhoids struck him down, however, and he felt he had to return. Twenty-nine
days after leaving the *Pioneer*, he and his men were back. Livingstone felt
much better and Ward was fitter than he had ever been, as were the Kololo
and Mazaro men (bar one who had died of malaria almost as soon as the
journey began). In addition to its therapeutic value, the trek taught Livingstone that the destructive impact of the slave trade was greater and covered
a larger geographical area than he had hitherto imagined.

The rains were late again that year and it was not until 19 January 1864
that the now unemployed Livingstone was able to set off downstream with
his two steamers. Off Morambala mountain, where Tozer had left those of
the freed slaves he had not taken with him to Zanzibar, the two ships
anchored and Livingstone took on board the thirteen women and children
and twenty-five young men whom Waller intended to take to the Cape. At
the mouth of the Zambesi they met up with two British cruisers en route
for Mozambique. The warships towed the two river steamers to Mozambique. There the *Pioneer* came again under the Royal Navy. She set off for
the Cape with Waller and the freed slaves on board, escorted by another
cruiser, HMS *Valorous*.

What was Livingstone to do now? He had to sell the *Lady Nyassa* to
recoup some money in order to repay 'Paraffin' Young. His 'Mazaro men'
were still with him as a crew, as was Rae, and three sailors who had not
gone off on any of the Royal Navy vessels, Stoker First Class John Pennell,
Quartermaster Charles Collyer and a civilian carpenter, John Reid.[42] They
had agreed to stay with him till he sold the vessel. While in Mozambique
he had the ship repainted and a host of minor repairs put right. There
were several Portuguese willing to buy the trim river steamer but, as he
knew they would use it for slaving purposes, he refused all the good offers
that were made. On 16 April 1864 Livingstone took the *Lady Nyassa* to sea
and set a course for Zanzibar, where he hoped a more suitable buyer might
be found.

At Zanzibar the frustration of Mozambique was repeated. Livingstone
then made a breathtaking decision: he decided to sail his little river steamer
across the Indian Ocean to Bombay. The African men, Amoda, Bachoro,
Bizenti, Chiko, Nyampinga, Safuri and Susi, agreed to go and Livingstone

also took with him two of the young freed slaves, Chuma and Wakatini, whom he hoped to put into a mission school in Bombay.[43] Then, on 28 April, Rae told Livingstone that he had decided to accept the offer of a business partnership in the Comoros. It was too late to engage another engineer because there was a limited window of opportunity available for a voyage to Bombay before the onset of the monsoon made it impossible. Livingstone now took on the roles of skipper, navigator and engineer, and the *Lady Nyassa* set out on her 2500 mile journey on 31 April 1864.

In 1912 John Kirk, by then Sir John, was interviewed about Livingstone for the *London Missionary Society Chronicle*. Referring to what he considered was Livingstone's most characteristic quality, Kirk said of Livingstone that 'His absolute lack of any sense of fear amounted almost to a weakness. He would go into the most perilous situations without a tremor or a touch of hesitation.'[44] At no other time did Livingstone show this characteristic more clearly than in embarking on this journey. The tiny *Lady Nyassa*, specifically designed for river work with only a three foot draught, could carry only enough coal for eight days steaming so they would have to rely on sail for a good deal of the journey.[45] In addition, two of his British sailors were ill for most of the voyage and the African crew were new to the sea. Although Livingstone knew how to navigate and had an unshakeable belief that God had a purpose for him, the journey was an extraordinary venture.

On 12 June 1864 the *Lady Nyassa* made landfall less than a day's sail south of Bombay, the climax of an astonishing feat of seamanship and leadership. Only two days later the monsoon broke. Livingstone recorded in his log for 13 June:

> Came to Bhoul rock at midday and latitude agreeing thereto pushed on by North and by West till we came to a Lightship. It was so hazy inland we could see nothing whatever – then took the direction by chart and steered right into Bombay most thankfully, and mention God's good providence over me and beg that He may accept my spared life for His service.
>
> A great many ships and ample space for them. No one came for a good while, but after we had anchored half an hour a pilot came and asked if we wished a pilot to take us further in. I replied in the negative.[46]

Although at first no one paid any attention to the newcomers, Livingstone was soon recognised and became the guest of Sir Bartle Frere, with whom Livingstone struck up a friendship. He left Chuma, Wakatini and some of the other crew members with Dr Wilson of the Free Church College, later Wilson College of Bombay University. For others in the crew he obtained employment in the Bombay docks. He did not, however, sell the *Lady Nyassa* but left it in the care of British officials for possible use later in Africa. On

24 June he and Reid left Bombay for Britain, having borrowed money for their fares. On 23 July 1864 Livingstone arrived in London without fanfare or fuss and booked into a room in the Tavistock Hotel, Covent Garden.

12

Home and Family

Next day, 24 July, Livingstone was whisked off by Sir Roderick Murchison to a reception hosted by the Prime Minister, Lord Palmerston. On the following evening, after dinner at Lord Dunmore's, Livingstone attended a reception given by the Duchess of Wellington. This appears to be an impressive enough welcome but it was not. It was a measure of the change that had come about in the public attitude to Livingstone. Murchison was able to arrange these invitations to private functions through personal connections and because Palmerston, unlike his Foreign Secretary, Lord John Russell, still had a measure of respect for Livingstone. These few private invitations were in marked contrast to Livingstone's reception in December 1856 with its massive public gatherings and an audience with Prince Albert. For some time before his return to Britain, Baines and James Stewart had been busy destroying Livingstone's reputation in Cape Town, where he had been so enthusiastically feted in 1858. In that city Livingstone's status as hero was only a brief interlude in his long-term status as villain, gun-runner and *kafir boetie* (nigger lover).

Public criticism of Livingstone in Britain had also become common some time before his return. The *Times* of 20 January 1863 was a marker which designated an important moment in the changing public perception of Livingstone. That morning the *Times* reprinted an anonymous attack on Livingstone, which had first been published in a much less significant newspaper, the *Examiner*. A short extract is enough to show its venom:

> We were promised cotton, sugar and indigo ... and, of course, we get none. We were promised trade; and there is no trade, though we have a Consul at £500 a year. We were promised converts to the Gospel, and not one has been made ... In a word, the thousands subscribed by the Universities, and the thousands contributed by the Government, have been productive only of the most fatal results. To say nothing of the great mistake of attempting to establish a mission and a colony among remote savages, the first great blunder was to attempt to plant them in the foreign territory of a European nation; for wherever Dr Livingstone attempted to set himself down he found he had been on what had been Portuguese territory almost from the time of Vasco da Gama.

No one attempted to rebut this devastating and pro-Portuguese diatribe which had been given such prominence in the newspaper.

What would have deeply saddened Livingstone, had he known, was that Kirk had also turned against him. When Kirk was leaving the Zambesi, Livingstone's brusqueness had convinced him that Livingstone was about to 'do a Baines' on him. In fact Livingstone was entirely oblivious to any change in what he saw as their close relationship. This is clear in the letter he sent after Kirk almost as soon as the latter had left the Zambesi. Unfortunately it, and several other letters Livingstone sent at the time, apparently did not reach him till some time after Kirk was back in Britain. Livingstone ended that first letter:

> I am sure I wish you every success in your future life. You were always a right hand to me and I never trusted you in vain. God bless and prosper you.
>
> If you see my boy Robert, say a kind word to him and advise him to work, for I fear he may turn out a 'Ne'er do weel'.
>
> I am yours with sincere affection,
> David Livingstone [1]

While still in Africa Livingstone continued to write to Kirk in this vein and wrote to him again from London during his first week back in Britain. When the two met again in Scotland a few weeks later, Kirk had, by then, realised his error and their friendship appeared unbroken as far as Livingstone was concerned.

Livingstone remained only a week in London before going up to Scotland to be reunited with his family. His arrival in Scotland began a period when he and the children were regularly together for the first time since Kuruman. After spending the sabbath with James Young and his family in Glasgow, on 2 August Livingstone went on to Hamilton and was reunited with his mother, his two sisters and Anna Mary, who really did not know who he was. She was confident enough child, however, to take his hand and go out walking with him. As he recorded in his journal:

> 2 August reached Hamilton. Mother did not know me at first. Anna Mary, a nice sprightly child, told me that she preferred Garibaldi buttons on her dress, as I walked down to Dr Loudon to thank him for kindness to my mother.[2]

The next day Agnes, Oswell and Thomas arrived. Only Robert, his first-born, was missing. Before leaving London, Livingstone had learned that Robert was serving in the Union Army in the Civil War.

After Livingstone left Britain with the Zambesi expedition, neither Mary Livingstone nor Livingstone's trustees had been able to form a good relationship with Robert. He refused to undertake higher education and was reported to have fallen into bad company in Edinburgh. After Mary left for the Zambesi, the trustees, except James Young who had wanted to accept Robert's suggestion, missed an opportunity to help Robert, refusing his request to be allowed to join the Royal Navy. As Livingstone wrote to Maclear on 8 August, 1863:

> Rae, who knows him better than I do, says he is clever but refused to go to College or do anything that the Trustees wanted him to do ... but the Trustees would not hear of it [joining the navy], on the plea that I would disapprove, and never said a word about it to me till all was over ... I would not have objected.[3]

Livingstone, soon after his wife's death, sent money to Robert to enable him to come to the Zambesi. The young man apparently spent the money on other things but, sometime later, 'Paraffin' Young gave him his fare to South Africa. It was because Livingstone knew that Robert was coming out to Africa that he sent letters to Kirk in South Africa asking Kirk to look out for the lad. Livingstone sent letters not only to Kirk, but also to the Mayor of Durban and to Maclear asking them to help Robert to get to the Zambesi; these all appear to have arrived too late or not at all.

Robert had landed penniless at Port Elizabeth and made his way to Isipingo in Natal where his uncle, Robert Moffat, had a store. He found that his uncle had died but his widow did what little she could to help. Robert, after leaving Isipingo, had gone to Cape Town and there had taken service as a sailor on a ship bound for the United States.

It is impossible to achieve certainty about what happened after that. Everyone is agreed that Robert left Cape Town for Boston as a working sailor and everyone is agreed that, by early 1864, Robert was a soldier in the Union Army. What is not clear is how he became a soldier fighting for a cause so dear to his father's heart. Whatever was at issue at the outbreak of the war, Lincoln's Second Inaugural Address made clear that it had become war about slavery. American slavery was always a deep concern of Livingstone's and was inextricably entwined with his concern for Africa and its peoples. One of his sharpest exchanges with his brother Charles took place long before the Zambesi expedition and was occasioned by an attempt by Charles in a letter to defend a moderate as opposed to an abolitionist position on American slavery.[4]

How far Robert was aware of this deep concern of his father's we cannot now be sure but it is difficult to imagine that he had no inkling of it. It is clear that, at the time of his South African trip, Robert was making some effort to sort himself out and regain his father's respect and affection. It is unclear whether Robert's effort to make amends was to embark on a career as a sailor or whether his boarding ship was simply a means of reaching the United States in order to join the Union army that was bringing the 'Day of

Jubilo' to the slaves in the southern states. A number of Livingstone's twentieth-century biographers have asserted that the letter Livingstone received from Robert in October 1864 resolves the issue. Some have been so sure of the kidnapping story that they have gone to embellish it with details of Robert being chloroformed in his bunk aboard ship. This letter, whatever else it says, reveals that the wild boy had developed into a mature young man.

My dear Sir, Hearing that you have returned to England I undertake to address a few lines to you, not with any hope that you will be interested in me but simply to explain the position. The agent of Mr McArthur of Port Natal said that he would write to him and inform him of my position and find me employment till I could find means to reach you. Mr Rutherfoord, Collector of HM Customs at Port Natal, interested himself in me for your sake and treated me with the greatest kindness. I believe I owe some obligation to Mr McArthur. All he heard of me was that I was to come out in a certain vessel. Concluding that I had run away he would have nothing to do with me. I should have been very badly off had it not been for the kindness of Mrs Robert Moffat to whom, besides £1, I owe a great deal, perhaps more than I shall ever be able to repay.

From Port Natal I went to Cape Town where your agent Mr Rutherfoord advised me to find employment on board a brig which brought me to Boston, America. Here I was kidnapped and one morning, after going to be on board ship, I found myself enlisted in the US army.

I have been in one battle and two skirmishes, and expect to be in another terrific battle before long. God in His mercy has spared me as yet. I have never hurt anyone knowingly in battle, have always fired high, and in that furious madness, which accompanies a bayonet charge and which seems to possess every soldier, I controlled my passion and took the man who surrendered prisoner.

The rebels are not likely to hold out much longer as we have nearly all their railroads. My craving for travelling is not yet satisfied, though if I had the chance that I threw away of being educated, I should think myself only too much blessed. I have changed my name, for I am convinced that to bear your name here would lead to further dishonour to it. I am at present in this hospital, exposure and fatigue having given me ague fever. Your quondam son, Robert.

Address: Rupert Vincent, New Hampshire Volunteers, 10th Army Corps, Virginia.[5]

On 2 June 1865, Livingstone was in Scotland at Hamilton when he was told that Robert had been wounded and taken prisoner at a skirmish at Laurel Hill, Virginia, and was in a prisoner of war camp hospital at Salisbury, North Carolina, where he later died. He was also informed that there was no certainty that Robert was still alive. W. G. S. Adams, retired Warden of All Souls, informed George Seaver that Livingstone told his father, John Adams, 'I am proud of the boy. If I had been there I should have gone to fight for the North myself'.[6] Although some have challenged this as a distortion of the memory of an eighty-five year old, what Livingstone wrote in a letter the week he received this news of Robert confirms Livingstone's identification with the Union cause. It is also consistent with Professor Adams's memory of Livingstone's reaction to the news about Robert. He reported Livingstone as saying:

> Robert we shall never hear of again in this world, I fear; but the Lord is merciful and just and right in all His ways. He would hear the cry for mercy in the hospital at Salisbury. I have lost my part in that gigantic struggle which the Highest guided to a consummation never contemplated by the southerners when they began; and many others have borne more numerous losses.[7]

Only Agnes, his sister, seems to have been close to Robert, and it was Agnes who began to draw particularly close to her father after they were all reunited at Hamilton in August. She soon became his constant companion and remained so until Livingstone returned to Africa.

Before leaving London, Livingstone had agreed to speak at the meeting of the British Association, which was to take place at Bath in September. His subject was to be the Portuguese slave trade, despite admonitions from Russell to stay clear of anything that might annoy the Portuguese. Before he settled down to prepare for this event Livingstone received an invitation to visit from the Duke of Argyll with whom Livingstone spent three days at Inverary Castle. Livingstone enjoyed the visit greatly and on leaving Inverary immediately went on a steamer to visit Iona, Staffa and Mull. Then a Captain Greenhill took him on his yacht to the Livingstones' ancestral home on Ulva. On the island he found only the ruins of his grandfather's croft in a green, fertile but uninhabited spot. In contrast with his ambiguous, to say the least, reception in London, Livingstone was delighted by the reception given to him by the people of Argyll, who welcomed him everywhere with great enthusiasm as a one of their own.

Livingstone also visited an eminent Edinburgh surgeon, James Syme, about the excruciating suffering he had had to endure during the previous three years from bleeding piles. On one occasion in July 1861 at Mbame's in the Shire highlands Livingstone was in such severe pain caused by a haemorrhoid having prolapsed that something had to be done immediately. Kirk was not available and poor Horace Waller was handed the lancet by Livingstone and instructed how to carry out the necessary incisions. When this condition existed along with dysentery, as it did with Livingstone again and again in Africa, the patient was in grave trouble. Syme told Livingstone that major surgery was necessary to right the situation. Livingstone refused, partly because he was afraid of the operation becoming a matter for discussion in the press, but also for medical reasons. It was still accepted at that time that 'bleeding' was an effective therapeutic technique in some circumstances and Livingstone believed that the loss of blood from bleeding piles had helped him regain good health and vigour after periods of weakness and exhaustion in the bush. His decision, whatever the reason, was a bad one since late twentieth-century medical opinion has concluded that it was a combination of dysentery and massive loss of blood from continuously bleeding piles that was responsible for Livingstone's death.[8]

On 17 September 1864, Livingstone went off to Bath with Agnes, now his constant companion. He was not looking forward to giving his speech. Despite his apparent success in moving audiences, he never felt comfortable giving a formal address to a large audience. Given the bad publicity that had surrounded him for two years, the pressure was greater than usual. He was, however, looking forward to hearing the debate about which everyone was talking. The British Association had scheduled a debate between Richard Burton and John H. Speke about the true source of the Nile. Burton insisted that it flowed from Lake Tanganyika, which he and Speke had visited in 1858. Speke, who on that same trek had gone north without Burton and became the first European to see the vast Lake Victoria, as he named it, insisted that the Nile flowed from it. In 1862 Speke returned to Lake Victoria and found what be believed to be Nile flowing from its northern shore, though he was not able to prove that this river flowed into a known stretch of the Nile.

Burton was looking forward to the debate; he was man who loved conflict while Speke was someone for whom this debate, set up as a gladiatorial contest, was distasteful. Livingstone was interested in the problem of the source of the Nile, in part at least because of his belief, to which he made a series of references in his study of Tswana and other Bantu languages, that the Ancient Egyptians were Africans and that their language was related, if distantly, to the Bantu family of languages. He was also interested because he detested Burton as someone who consistently described Africans as animal-like savages and who scorned the Christian faith. The debate, however, did not take place. Speke was killed in an accident while out shooting on an estate near Bath. Livingstone attended the funeral and later, in the preface to his *Narrative*, declared that Speke had found the source of the Nile.

Livingstone delivered his lecture, which was well received by an audience of something over two thousand people. Lord John Russell was angry when he heard of its content which focused on the nature of Portuguese rule in east Africa, and on the Portuguese involvement with the rapidly increasing trade in slaves that was undermining traditional African societies economically and socially. Livingstone also made some remarks about the Civil War which implied that it could be seen as a punishment on the people of the United States for having condoned slavery for so long. Some commentators have said that these opinions, which he did not keep secret, offended 'the Americans'. Certainly the adjutant of Robert's regiment, through whom Livingstone was hoping get Robert included in an exchange of prisoners, was upset by this opinion.[9] Yet members of President Lincoln's administration could hardly have been offended by the attitude of Livingstone to the Civil War. It was a thoroughly American attitude, movingly articulated by President Lincoln himself in his Second Inaugural Address.

> Fondly do we hope – fervently do we pray – that this mighty scourge of war may speedily pass away. Yet, if God wills that it continue, until all the wealth piled by the bondsman's two hundred and fifty years of unrequited toil shall be sunk, and until every drop of blood drawn with the lash shall be paid by another drawn with the sword, as was said three thousand years ago, so it still must be said 'the judgements of the Lord, are true and righteous altogether'.

Before Livingstone left Hamilton for Bath, he had been invited to stay with William Webb and his family in their house, Newstead Abbey, near Nottingham. Livingstone had rescued Webb when he was seriously ill on the fringes of the Kalahari, and then, with Mary's help, nursed him back to health at Kolobeng. Webb, along with Oswell, Steele and Vardon, the other upper-class hunters from Livingstone's South African years, remained Livingstone's friends and supporters to the end. At first Livingstone had refused the kind offer because he and Agnes did not want to be separated. Mrs Webb, whose eldest daughter, Alice, was the same age as Agnes, insisted that Agnes was also invited and arranged that a governess, able to teach piano, was available to teach the girls, something that Agnes particularly wanted.

Although, after handing in the manuscript of his *Travels* to Murray, Livingstone had vowed never to return to such an onerous task, he had decided before the Bath meeting of the British Association to write a 'blast against the Portuguese'. He knew he could not do that in the crowded house in Hamilton so the invitation from the Webbs came at an opportune time.

Newstead Abbey was a vast house which enabled Livingstone and Agnes to have their own quarters in what was called the Sussex Tower, where Oswell and Tom joined them in the school holidays. Livingstone relaxed in this welcoming atmosphere and romped with Agnes and the children of the house in a way that completely won their hearts.[10] During his time at Newstead, Livingstone met an extraordinary variety of people who also shared the warm hospitality of the Webbs, who loved to hold open house. Sir Henry Rawlinson, later President of the RGS, Edward Denison, the Speaker of the House of Commons, and Thomas Hughes, the author of *Tom Brown's Schooldays*, who was to be one of Livingstone's many biographers, were among a cross-section of British upper-class society who visited the abbey. Many of Livingstone's own friends also came to Newstead and stayed as house guests of the ever hospitable Webbs. Kirk came and stayed for a month, as did Charles Livingstone and his wife Harriet. William Oswell was never able to visit because of his wife's ill health. He and Livingstone, however, wrote to each other at least weekly during the seven months Livingstone spent at Newstead.

One particular visitor has to be mentioned because of what Livingstone's reactions to the visit tell us about Livingstone. This visitor was a lawyer, Abraham Hayward, who was a close friend of Mrs Webb's, but more importantly was one of Lord Palmerston's 'fixers', men who were the Prime Minister's personal agents. Hayward brought a message to Livingstone that a true place seeker would have been overjoyed to hear. 'Could the Prime Minister do anything for Dr Livingstone?' The reply expected by Hayward would usually have been a request for an honour or a pension. What Livingstone asked for was that the Prime Minister should seek Portuguese agreement to the free navigation of the Zambesi and Shire river system. This is the same Livingstone of whom Kirk, so often quoted by twentieth-century writers as someone whose views on Livingstone should be trusted, had written to James Stewart in February that year saying, 'He would give all for a CB or better still a KCB'.[11]

It is difficult now to be sure how Charles Livingstone originally became involved with the production of the new book. The agreement that emerged from some lengthy discussions was that Livingstone was to write the book, making use of Charles's diaries, which Charles had kept assiduously throughout his time on the Zambesi, as well as from Livingstone's own journals and notes. Charles was to be listed as joint author and receive the royalties of the United States edition. Many others, however, also played a part in the production of this book. For example, Livingstone regularly consulted James Stewart. Livingstone's calling on him, on his way back from Argyll to Hamilton, had startled Stewart and provoked a sense of guilt in him. Livingstone called on him as if on an old friend and afterwards Stewart eagerly helped whenever Livingstone asked for his assistance. Rae, Waller and Kirk were also roped in to help. They ran errands for Livingstone as well as helping with details of dates, places and names that Livingstone wished confirmed. Livingstone's daughter Agnes and Mrs Webb both helped write out fair copies of Livingstone's manuscript for the printers. It was, however, Oswell who played the most important role in the production of the book other than Livingstone's own. Oswell proof read and edited the text as Livingstone produced it; as a result in January and February of 1865, he and Livingstone were in touch by letter three or four times a week. Sir Michael Owen also read over the galley proofs of the book. At the end, because of all these consultations, Livingstone was rushing the work and cutting down sharply on the amount he wrote. As a result, his extraordinary feat of sailing the *Lady Nyassa* to Bombay occupies a mere two pages of text.

The *Narrative of an Expedition to the Zambesi* did not appear until after Livingstone had left Britain on his way back to Africa. It had nothing like the success of his *Missionary Travels*. This probably reflects the severe dent Livingstone's image had received with the British public. It may also have resulted from the book having little of the vivid immediacy of Livingstone's first book, except in his description of the trek to Linyanti and of the last march after the expedition had been stood down, when Livingstone went with African companions up the lake shore to Nkhotakhota and across to the Luangwa. It can be argued that only in those episodes had Livingstone been free to be the Livingstone of his march with the Kololo across Africa. The real reason for the book's flatness may also be that so many were involved in the production of the main text. The introduction to the *Narrative* is lively and very direct; it was Livingstone's own and had not been pored over by anyone else.

The book was remarkable for its omissions. Not only did Livingstone omit his utter frustration over the barrier that was the Cabora Basa but also he omitted any significant reference to the many personal conflicts. For example, the names of Bedingfeld and Baines simply do not appear in the text. Perhaps the most extraordinary omission is signalled by the appearance as joint author of his brother Charles, who troubled Livingstone as much as, if not more than any one else. Kirk and the many others all consulted by Livingstone throughout the writing of the book have to be seen as consenting to the form the book took. There is no record in the voluminous correspondence still available of any of them objecting. Of course Livingstone, and this applied to Kirk and Rae also, wanted to reject the attacks made on the expedition, but Livingstone's main aim was to produce concern in Britain about the slave trade in East Africa and also produce a 'blast against the Portuguese'.

Although Livingstone had not asked anything for himself from Palmerston, he did use whatever influence he still had with government to help both his brother Charles and Kirk. Livingstone pursued getting a government post for Kirk consistently throughout the time he was in Britain, even when under strong pressure to get the book finished. It was, however, only when he was in India, in Bombay preparing to re-enter the Rovuma valley, that Livingstone's close friendship with Sir Bartle Frere got Kirk an appointment that the latter was happy to accept. Frere, on Livingstone's recommendation, appointed Kirk as agency surgeon to the British consulate in Zanzibar, where he later became political agent and then consul general.

Livingstone's efforts on behalf of his brother, Charles, bore fruit much sooner. Apparently Charles and his American wife did not want to return to the United States and Charles no longer felt able to continue as a minister. Livingstone suggested to him a government post in Africa and Charles agreed to this. Livingstone's efforts led to Charles being offered the consulship at Fernando Po (now Boiko). This post had become vacant, strangely enough, because of the transfer to Brazil of Richard Burton, whom Livingstone so thoroughly detested. Burton and he had come into direct and bitter conflict in May 1865 as each gave evidence before the House of Commons Committee reviewing British policy in West Africa. Burton gave evidence that missionary activity led to Africans becoming worse than they were before. In doing so he made clear his view that they were lesser beings, congenitally incapable of understanding higher things. Livingstone, at another session of the committee, presented the case for the worth of missionary work and the worth of Africans.[12]

While he was trying to do something for Charles and Kirk, what was Livingstone intending to do himself? Soon after arriving back in Britain Livingstone had noted in his journal that he appeared to be on the shelf, and if so he might as well be 'on the shelf in Africa'. This remark was similar to his insistence in his journal in 1857, soon after arriving in Britain, that if nothing else turned up he would simply go back to Africa and rely on the friendship and hospitality of the Kololo. Neither remark can be taken as any sort of firmly worked out intention. The words were, however, indicative of his unshakeable belief that God had spared him to do something for Africa. What could be more convincing evidence of the guiding hand of Providence than the successful completion of his extraordinary voyage to Bombay? It was while he was still at Newstead that Livingstone began planning his next African journey. In a letter to John Murray he said that, though he had every comfort there at Newstead, 'I often take a sore longing to be in Africa. My family is my only chain'.[13]

It was on the visit to the Abbey by Sir Roderick Murchison that Livingstone and he began serious discussion of Livingstone's return to Africa. Murchison offered to back Livingstone leading an expedition that had a purely geographic nature. Livingstone insisted that he could never do that as there must be always a missionary dimension to what he did. Several twentieth-century writers have declared this hypocritical since they could see little, if anything, that was missionary about his last seven years of wandering in east central Africa. Their remarks represent an attitude close to that of the pious mid-Victorian critics of Livingstone's *Missionary Travels*, who declared them not missionary enough. It is a view which sees missionary work in very conventional terms. Throughout his life Livingstone never ceased to bear verbal witness to his belief that Jesus was his Saviour and to his belief in God's love for all humanity. He was not paid by a missionary society, he did not build new Christian congregations, but he believed that he was opening up the way and sowing the seed. A picture of Livingstone as missionary on these last wandering years is represented, though I am sure not with that intention, by Oliver Ransford, who wrote of Livingstone:

> During this time many Africans became familiar with the haggard, bearded, benign aging man, who was often hungry and sick, yet for some incomprehensible reason wandered from one village to another, halting only to rest and ask innumerable questions or speak of a mysterious redeemer who was his master.[14]

Murchison was still a Livingstone supporter and pressed the RGS to support Livingstone on another expedition. The response of the RGS reflected the new status of Livingstone in Britain; it provided a mere £500. With the grant there also came instructions that Livingstone should map his route carefully and let the secretary of the society see his notes before any publication. This was a dreadful insult to someone who was an outstandingly accurate mapmaker. Livingstone was in no position to do other than to control his temper, where his dignity was concerned, and swallow the insult. Worse was to follow. Lord John Russell, under pressure, reluctantly agreed to allow Livingstone a 'one off' grant of £500 and the unpaid title of consul 'to the tribes between Mozambique and Abyssinia'. The Foreign Office official, Murray, who wrote the letter of appointment, added the sharp instruction that Livingstone was to be sure not to embarrass Her Majesty's Government on this trip.[15] Again, although he was furious and though these insults wounded him deeply, Livingstone could do nothing. His old friend, 'Paraffin' Young, came to his aid, however, with the gift of £1000. Livingstone hoped that he would also be able to raise some money in Bombay when he got there. The two thousand pounds he felt was just enough to let him set out, so he began preparations to depart. Before he could leave, however, he had to make arrangements for his children.

It was to his old friend Young that he turned. Young was given access to all money due to Livingstone from his publisher and with this Young assumed responsibility for Tom and Oswell, who were to continue at Gilbertfield School, and Anna Mary, who was to attend the Quaker school at Kendal under the eye of the Braithwaites. Livingstone had much more difficulty in knowing what to do about Agnes, who had been his close companion all these months. This experience had introduced her to a world very different from that she had known before. Living with her father at Newstead, taking classes with Alice the eldest daughter of the house, dining with the many notable guests whom the Webbs entertained regularly, all meant that, when she and her father left Newstead, Agnes was a very different young woman from the girl who had first arrived there. It was Livingstone's continuing connection to the French Protestant missionaries among the Sotho that provided the solution to his problem. Livingstone had not lost touch with Prosper Lemue, who had performed his and Mary's wedding service in 1845 at Kuruman. Lemue had a niece, a lively bright young woman, Madame Hocédé, who ran a school for British Protestant girls in Paris.[16] It was arranged that, when her father left for Africa, Agnes should go there. Livingstone also made an additional arrangement for Agnes's welfare. With her agreement Livingstone gave Agnes into the care of his old friend Oswell, who became a second father to her. Indeed Oswell always referred to her as his 'adopted daughter' and once wrote to her: 'If you are within a hundred miles of me let me know, and I will come and shake you by the hand. I will always come even to the end of the earth, if I can be of any use to you, or you want me.'[17]

In May Livingstone was in Scotland seeing Tom and Oswell settled at their school and also awaiting his mother's death. She had been failing for some time and often did not know him, asking him what he had done with his brother Robert: 'Where is that puir laddie?' When she appeared to revive somewhat he dashed down to Oxford to deliver a lecture. While there he received a telegram telling him of her death. He was, however, able to get back to Hamilton for the funeral on 23 June 1865. He spent seven weeks in all in Scotland at that time, some of it he spent with James Young, his oldest and perhaps his most devoted friend.

He and Agnes then went to London where they stayed with a fellow Scot, the Reverend Dr James Hamilton, a Presbyterian minister in London. Livingstone was by then eager to get away. He paid a number of farewell visits with Agnes, who also asserted her great influence with her father by dragging him on a round of sightseeing in the capital about which he complained to Oswell. When he went to bid farewell to Miss Burdett-Coutts, he met the Christian Queen of Hawaii, whom he deemed 'a nice sensible person'. He also spent some time with the Webbs and with the Oswells. The Webbs saw Livingstone and Agnes off at Charing Cross station where Kirk and Waller joined them and accompanied them to Folkestone. Here Livingstone and Agnes boarded the ferry to France. Livingstone stayed a few days in Paris to see Agnes settled, then took the train to Marseille, where he boarded the *Massilia* bound for Alexandria. Here he and the other passengers disembarked and went overland to Suez and then took ship to Bombay. Livingstone travelled free of charge as the P & O Company had presented him with a ticket. He arrived in Bombay on 11 September 1865.

13

Bombay to Bangweulu

Livingstone arrived for a second time at Bombay on 11 September 1865. This time, however, he arrived as an honoured visitor whose arrival had been awaited with interest. For the first few days in Bombay Livingstone stayed with William Stearns, a young American merchant he had met on the ship. He then went up to Pune (the British called it Poona), the garrison town in the hills where the Governor, Sir Bartle Frere, and many of his staff were spending part of the hot season. Dr Wilson of the Free Kirk College in Bombay, an active supporter of Livingstone's, introduced him to the European business community in Bombay. Livingstone addressed a gathering of these businessmen at the end of which Wilson called for donations in support of Livingstone's expedition. A thousand pounds was pledged there and then, although in the end only something over six hundred pounds was delivered.

While in Bombay Livingstone wanted first to sell the *Lady Nyassa*, secondly to confirm the Bombay government's interest in helping to end the east African slave trade, and finally to recruit reliable staff for the expedition.[1] He was able to sell the *Lady Nyassa* but not for the £6000 it had cost him to build her; he received a mere £2300. Livingstone invested this in the Bank of Agra, which the very next year collapsed so that Livingstone lost even this sum. As for his second concern, he was assured that as long as Frere was Governor the Bombay government would do all that it could to inhibit if not end the East African slave trade. The third problem was difficult. He had discussed with Oswell the possibility of recruiting some Baluchis to act as porters. These were mercenary soldiers serving the Sultan of Zanzibar, as Livingstone wanted to avoid hiring slave porters. When he mentioned his problem to Frere, the Governor immediately offered him twelve sepoys of the Bombay Infantry, Marine Battalion, under a havildar.[2] These men were sent off as if on Bombay government business; they were not volunteers but a small group of soldiers arbitrarily detached from their regiment with its carefully structured discipline to be under a civilian whose aims appeared pointless to them. Why Livingstone accepted the offer is puzzling. Livingstone also recruited eight young Africans from the Church Missionary Society School for freed slaves at Nassik. One of them, Gardner, became a

personal follower of Livingstone's, one of those Livingstone called his 'faithfuls'. He also sought out four young men who had been with him on the
epic voyage from Zanzibar to Bombay and who were to provide the core
of his 'faithfuls'. Two were Chuma and Wakatini, teenage Yao freed slaves
whom he had left at the Free Kirk College; the other two were Susi and
Amoda, Shupanga men for whom, in 1864, he had found jobs in the Bombay
docks.

The transport of goods in Africa north of the Limpopo in the nineteenth
and early twentieth century was always bedevilled by the impact of the tsetse,
or rather the deadly trypanosomiasis its bite conveyed to draught animals.
As a result, the human being carrying his or her head load was the principal
means of transporting goods.[3] Livingstone decided he should take this
opportunity to try an experiment to discover if this difficulty could be
overcome. As the African buffalo appeared immune to trypanosomiasis,
perhaps its domesticated cousin, the Indian buffalo, might also be immune;
so he purchased some Indian buffaloes to go with the expedition.

The Bombay government was about to gift a steamship, the *Thule*, to the
Sultan of Zanzibar. Livingstone, Frere decided, could travel in it with his
people and act as the Governor's envoy to present the *Thule* formally to the
Sultan. So Livingstone crossed to Zanzibar in the steamer with all his
equipment and recruits, arriving on 28 January 1866. The next day he and
Captain Brebner of the *Thule* went to the palace to pay their respects to the
Sultan and deliver Frere's official letter. In a letter to his daughter Agnes,
written the same day, Livingstone described the event.

> His Highness met us at the bottom of the stair, and as he shook hands a brass
> band ... blared forth 'God save the Queen!' This was excessively ridiculous, but
> I maintained a sufficient official gravity. After coffee and sherbet we came away
> and the wretched band now struck up 'The British Grenadiers' – as if the fact of
> my being only five feet eight, and Brebner about two inches lower, ought not to
> have suggested 'Wee Willie Winkie' as more appropriate.[4]

For his trek Livingstone needed more men and in Zanzibar he met Musa,
a Johanna man who had worked with Lieutenant Young on the *Pioneer* and
gained that officer's bad opinion.[5] Livingstone, however, decided to engage
him and with his help chose nine other Johanna men from among the many
to be found in Zanzibar.[6]

At that time a network of Zanzibari traders was expanding from the coast
over what is now Tanzania, Malawi, Zambia and the eastern Congo. Livingstone used a company at the centre of this business world to send various
supplies to Ujiji to await his arrival there.[7] The company, Jairam Sewrji, was
used extensively by the British Consulate and had done work for Burton

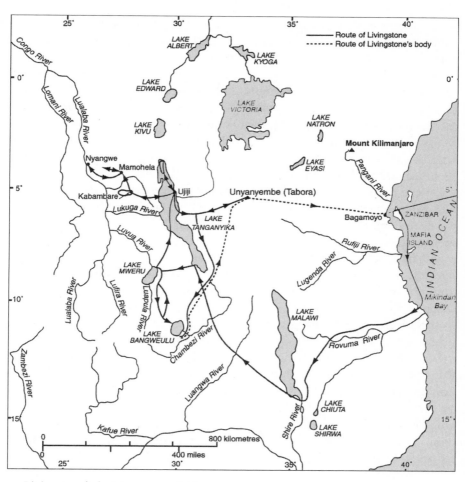

4. Livingstone's last journeys, 1866–73.

and for Speke. It was owned and managed by Indians, who, as British
subjects, were not allowed to own slaves but played an essential financial
role in the Zanzibari slave and ivory trade.

With all this arranged Livingstone then waited for HMS *Penguin*, which
was to carry his expedition to the mouth of the Rovuma. Once he reached
the African mainland, Livingstone had two main aims. The first was to
ascend the Rovuma valley to the highlands on the north-east corner of Lake
Malawi. He hoped that there he could find a suitable place which would
later be his permanent base and a possible site for the kind of 'colony' that
he hoped would begin the transformation of Africa.

Having found such a spot, he intended to travel north to Lake Tanganyika
where he would replenish his supplies at Ujiji. He would then move westwards to complete the task set him by the RGS, to investigate the watershed
west of Lake Tanganyika. Both Murchison and he thought that the Nile
might have its headwaters there rather than further north, as Burton and
Speke had suggested, but they also thought that possibly the sources of the
Zambesi and Congo lay there. With that area thoroughly surveyed and
mapped, Livingstone aimed to return to set up his long-term base as 'Consul
to the tribes beyond the Portuguese dominions' in the area already chosen
near Lake Malawi and the source of the Rovuma.

HMS *Penguin* carried Livingstone and his people from Zanzibar to the
Rovuma, towing behind a dhow with the animals on board – he had added
donkeys and mules to the few remaining buffalo, most of which had died
on Zanzibar. To Livingstone's chagrin the *Penguin* could not land the
animals at the Rovuma, so they sailed north to the good harbour at Mikandani. They landed there on 24 March 1866 and Livingstone was able to
recruit the remaining porters needed for the journey. Two days later he
filled several pages of his journal with his thoughts on setting out again on
an African journey. They have been quoted often and show a man charged
with joy and enthusiasm. On those pages we see him as he was, not as a
tortured lonely man seeking martyrdom as he has been too often portrayed.
The pages echo his enthusiasm for African travel about which he wrote in
his first letters from the Cape in 1841 when he had insisted that he had
found what he felt was his calling.

> Now that I am on the point of starting on another trip into Africa I feel quite
> exhilarated ... Whether exchanging the customary civilities, or arriving at a village,
> accepting a night's lodging, purchasing food for the party, asking for information,
> or answering polite African enquiries as to our objects in travelling, we begin to
> spread a knowledge of that people by whose agency their land will become
> enlightened and freed from the slave trade.
>
> The mere animal pleasure of travelling in a wild unexplored country is very

great. When on lands of a couple of thousand feet elevation, brisk exercise imparts elasticity to the muscles, fresh and healthy blood circulates through the brain, the mind works well, the eye is clear, the step is firm and a day's exertion always makes the evening's repose thoroughly enjoyable ... No doubt much toil is involved ... but the sweat of one's brow is no longer a curse when one works for God: it proves a tonic to the system, and is actually a blessing.[8]

The Rovuma valley was thickly forested and a path had to be cut for the animals at the cost of time and labour. What was worse, Livingstone's complete inability to command paid employees – so apparent on the Zambesi expedition – was soon evident again. He gave up in exasperation trying to organise and supervise his motley crew, which was disastrous since neither Musa nor the havildar were good managers of their men. Livingstone simply pushed ahead with his personal followers, the Nassik men and some of the Mikandani porters, leaving the rest to straggle along behind. As a result, it sometimes took the sepoys, the Johanna men and the porters with them, three weeks to cover the ground that Livingstone and his men had covered in a week. Despite all these difficulties Livingstone still made careful notes on the fauna and flora as well as the geology of the area through which they were travelling.

> Looking at the geology of the district, the plateaux on each side of the Rovuma are masses of grey sandstone, capped with masses of feruginous conglomerate; apparently an aqueous deposit. When we ascend the Rovuma about sixty miles, a great many pieces and blocks of silicified wood appear on the surface of the soil at the bottom of the slope up the plateaux. This in Africa is a sure indication of the presence of coal beneath, but it was not observed cropping out; the plateaux are cut up in various directions by wadys well supplied with grass and trees on deep and somewhat sandy soil: but at the confluence of the Loendi highlands they appear in the far distance. In the sands of the Loendi pieces of coal are quite common.[9]

When they eventually emerged from the wooded valley onto the higher savannah lands, though the terrain was easier their difficulties increased. By this time most of the draught animals were dead through a combination of disease – the Indian buffalo were not immune to tripanosomiasis – together with neglect and ill-treatment. The major difficulty, however, was that food was desperately scarce because the Ngoni had recently raided across these highlands after what had been a poor harvest. The caravan was also crossing the route of Zanzibari slavers going to Kilwa. Along the way they saw the corpses that marked their passing. This all became too much for the Mikandani porters, who refused to go further and were paid off and allowed to go home on 11 June, just two hundred miles from the coast. Soon afterward Livingstone and his advance party arrived at

Mtarika's close to the headwaters of the Rovuma. The news he learned there changes his plans. The Ngoni had stripped clean the countryside between Mtarika's and the north end of Lake Malawi. It would be impossible to get adequate food there and, in addition, most of Livingstone's followers were very apprehensive about meeting an Ngoni raiding party. Mtarika advised Livingstone to go south to Mataka's, where there was plenty of food and whence he could move west to Lake Malawi and sail across the lake to Nkhotakhota.

On 5 July Livingstone led his men towards Mataka's. En route he met a major Zanzibari slave trader, Sef Rupia. The trader gave Livingstone an ox for slaughter and a bag of maize meal and accompanied him to meet Chief Mataka. When he moved on, Rupia took Livingstone's letters and despatches with him and had them delivered to the consulate in Zanzibar. This encounter was the beginning of Livingstone's good relationship at a personal level with some of the Zanzibari slavers, whose trade he was dedicated to stop. Was it that these men, devout Muslims, saw Livingstone as a 'holy man' and treated him as such, just as Malik al Kamil, Sultan of Egypt, is said to have received Francis of Assisi in Damietta with courtesy and hospitality in the midst of the Fifth Crusade in 1219? Many of Livingstone's devout contemporaries in Britain, as we have seen, had begun to doubt his religious commitment but Muslims had a different perception of holiness from that of nineteenth-century mainstream British Protestantism.

At Mataka's Livingstone finally admitted to himself that bringing the unwilling sepoys along had been a bad mistake and that he had to get rid of them. Burton, long before that, would have flogged them into some sort of disciplined behaviour. Livingstone could not. As in the Zambesi expedition, he got on with what he wanted to do with those who would follow him, ignoring routine administrative tasks and the puzzlement and frustration he caused to those not caught up in his vision. He made demands on those around him that comrades might accept but were unacceptable to people who were simply doing a job for pay. The Indian soldiers had not even had the choice of accepting the job or not; they had been sent off on what was to them a wild goose chase with a madman. They wanted to go home. At Mataka's, Livingstone arranged supplies enough for them to get back to the coast in the care of a Zanzibari trader. He then marched off to Lake Malawi.[10]

In the midst of all these troubles Livingstone continued to record careful geographical observations as well as details of African craftsmanship, tribal lore, forms of sexual practice – the refusal of intercourse till after a baby is weaned – and so on. He also made drawings of tribal marks, of the design of African pottery, hairstyles and weapons.

Well supplied by Mataka and freed from the burden of the unwilling sepoys, the column soon reached the shore of Lake Malawi. None of the Zanzibari-owned dhows, however, would take Livingstone and his people across the lake. The *firman* (a sort of passport) granted Livingstone by the Sultan carried no weight at all – an indication that the close relationship some Zanzibari traders struck up with Livingstone had nothing to do with his having this document. Thus balked, Livingstone had no alternative (since the north was still blocked) to marching south and going round the south end of Lake Malawi, which he reached on 13 September. This march along the shores of the lake did not entirely displease him, he wrote:

> It was as if I had come back to an old home I never expected again to see; and pleased to bathe in the delicious waters again, hear the roar of the sea, and dash in the rollers. Temperature 71° at 8 a.m., while the air was 65°. I feel quite exhilarated.[11]

On the march Livingstone encountered many chiefs and headmen whom he knew. They all treated him and his people well. After Livingstone crossed the Shire, Wakatini, whom he had left along with Chuma at the Free Kirk College in Bombay, met members of his family and Livingstone gladly discharged him from any obligation to go on. Livingstone then struck north west towards the mountains he had earlier named the Kirk Range. Before they began their ascent onto the higher ground, he had to deal with another crisis. Musa and his Johanna men refused to go further, as they had been told that the Ngoni were operating ahead. Livingstone was then left with Chuma, Susi, Amoda and eight of the Nassik men.

When Musa and his followers arrived back at Zanzibar they reported that the Ngoni had killed Livingstone and scattered his other followers at the north end of Lake Malawi. Seward, the political agent and Kirk, who had newly arrived in post at Zanzibar, lowered the consular flag to half-mast. In London, however, Waller and Lieutenant Young, who both had known Musa on the Zambesi, refused to believe the story. Lord Clarendon, the Foreign Secretary, financed an expedition to go out to Lake Malawi. Young commanded it and showed that, with vessels properly suited to river travel, one could sail comparatively quickly up the Shire, then portage a light steamer in parts past the cataracts and, having assembled the craft, sail on into Lake Malawi. This was what Livingstone had always claimed could be done, for which claim he was scorned by many contemporaries and, more puzzlingly, by twentieth-century writers. Even if these writers forgot Young, the fact is that the African Lakes Company steamers did that journey on a regular basis in the 1880s and 1890s. Young confirmed from local people that Livingstone had safely passed round the south end of the lake. Even as Young was proving Musa had lied, Livingstone's letters and despatches arrived at Zanzibar, confirming Young's findings.

After Musa's departure, Livingstone was able to recruit enough of Chief Marenga's men as porters to allow him to set off again. He climbed up onto the Dedza plateau, which ascends to the watershed between Lake Malawi and the Luangwa valley. This was a very pleasant time for Livingstone, as the climate of the area is good and the Chewa villagers and their chiefs were exceedingly hospitable and invited him to talk to their people, which opportunity he took to give Christian teaching.[12] He also wrote long notes on Chewa spinning and weaving, on their metalwork techniques and social customs. In discussing Chewa/Mang'anja culture he referred again and again to their relationship to ancient Egypt – all part of his belief, which he had first expressed back in Botswana, that Ancient Egyptian culture was African against the insistence in his day that it had been a Mediterranean culture and emphatically not an African one.

It was at the end of October, with the rains beginning, that Livingstone and his little group of followers began the descent into the Luangwa valley. Normally at that time of the year food was not plentiful, but things had been made much worse by a series of Ngoni raids. The regiments of Mpeseni had emptied the village grain stores and taken away as many good-looking, fit children as they could capture.[13] Livingstone was used to shooting game to feed the men but, as at that time of year most of the game was moving out of the valley onto the high ground, there was almost no game to shoot in the valley. He and his men began to suffer real hunger. Livingstone's personal suffering was made worse by the villagers having only finger millet (*maere*) to offer with which to make *nsima*.[14] For most people *maere* is used only as a last resort and Livingstone's digestive system, which had suffered so much in the past, could not cope. It was all there was, he reported, except for mushrooms.[15] On 3 December, when he was ill and weak through hunger, two young Yao slaves whose master had been killed asked to join his party. Livingstone accepted them and they appeared to work hard and fit in well with his 'faithfuls' Amoda, Chuma, Susi and Gardner, one of the Nassik men. The other Nassik men Livingstone referred to in his journal as the 'lazies'.

On 16 December 1866 they crossed the Luangwa and entered the Bisa country through which Livingstone had to pass to reach the country of the great chief Kazembe. Kazembe was the ruler of the western kingdom of the Luba/Lunda clans who had dominated Katanga and Kasai since the end of the seventeenth century.[16] It was, Livingstone believed, there that the key watershed lay from which rivers flowed north, almost certainly the source of the Congo and, he hoped, also the source of the Nile.

As the climbed out of the Luangwa valley through thick woodland in the heavy rain, lack of food continued to be a problem. As Livingstone reported in his journal on the evening of 30 December:

> In the evening we camped beside a little rill, and made our shelters, but we had so little to eat that I dreamed the night long of dinners I had eaten, and might have been eating.[17]

The next day they were welcomed kindly by an old chief, Chitembo, and stayed a few days at his village since food was available there and they were all very tired. Torrential downpours also made the thought of moving on unattractive. On 6 January they set off through country that in Livingstone's words exhibited 'the extreme of leafiness and the undulations are masses of green leaves; as far as the eye can reach it rests on a mantle of that hue'.[18] January 1867 was to be a dreadful month for Livingstone. On the very first day out of Chitembo's their guides took them down through a deep, soaking wet ravine, full of trees and bamboo. Two porters slipped and fell damaging the chronometers they were carrying, which led to Livingstone getting his reading of longitude wrong for the next few months. This was a serious problem when charting territory through which you might travel again while relying on the accuracy of these charts. On 15 January, Livingstone was saddened by the death of a little dog, Chitane, that had been his companion since Mikandani; it drowned crossing the River Chimbwe. On 20 January he received the most serious blow of all: the two Yao freed slaves deserted with their loads; in the thick forest and heavy rain they could not be tracked and their loads recovered. The desertion of any two carriers with guns and ammunition was a serious loss to the small caravan, but this was a crisis since one of the Yao had been carrying the medical chest with all the quinine. As Livingstone wrote, 'I felt as if I had now received the sentence of death, like poor Bishop Mackenzie'. The little band struggled on nevertheless through appalling difficulties, sometimes wading breast high through bogs, until they crossed the Chambesi near its head. This is in fact one of the two main sources of the Congo, though Livingstone did not know it for certain at that time. Then, two days later, on 31 January 1867, Livingstone became the first European to enter the lands of the Bemba and visit their chief, the Chitimukulu, who at that time was called Chipankwa.

Livingstone and his men were treated very hospitably and filled themselves with good food after their weeks of starvation rations. At the Bemba capital there was a Zanzibari caravan whose leader generously agreed to stay an extra day to allow Livingstone to write letters and despatches, which they then took to Bagamoyo. Livingstone ordered fresh supplies, particularly of quinine, to be sent to Ujiji to await him there with the other stores which should have arrived already. At the Chitimukulu's Livingstone preached publicly on a number of occasions and also had some private words with Chipankwa, showing him 'woodcuts from my Bible which he readily understood'. He and the chief also had some altercations, but the difficulties came from a number of inadequate translations as Livingstone found out in time. The two men parted friends, the Chitimukulu taking a knife in an ivory sheath from his waist and giving them to Livingstone as he was leaving.

As they marched towards Lake Tanganyika, Livingstone was ill and could not be the driving force he had always been on such marches, yet the march went on successfully. This was because of the strong bond between him and his 'faithfuls'; Livingstone's situation was by then like that on the Kololo march across Africa where he had marched with people with whom had a personal bond. When they reached the south end of Lake Tanganyika on 1 April 1867 Livingstone was very ill indeed with malaria, rheumatic fever and loss of blood. It was not until 30 April that he was well enough to start entries in his journal again. Referring to his illness he recorded that: 'The boys had seen the wretched state I was in, and hung blanket at the entrance to the hut, that no stranger might see my helplessness ...' [19] Despite the most debilitating experience of his life, as he got stronger he could write almost poetically about Tanganyika.

> After being a fortnight at this lake it still appears one of surpassing loveliness. Its peacefulness is remarkable, though at times it is said to be lashed by storms. It lies in a deep basin whose sides are nearly perpendicular, but covered well with trees; the rocks which appear are bright red argillaceous schist; the trees at present all green; down some of the rocks come beautiful cascades, and buffaloes, elephants and antelopes wander and graze on the more level spots, while lions roar by night [20]

Once he had recovered somewhat Livingstone started northwards along the lake, hoping to reach Ujiji, but was halted by stories of warfare ahead. He turned aside to get news from a nearby Zanzibari encampment. There he learned that war had broken out between the Tabwa people and the most powerful of all the Zanzibari traders, Tippu Tib. Hamis wa Mtoa, whose camp it was, persuaded Livingstone to stay with him till the fighting was over. Hamis treated Livingstone as an honoured guest during the three months wait. The delay allowed Livingstone to recover his strength and also enabled him to gain some fluency in Swahili. [21]

His health was better but he had only a few resources left. Should he strike north for Ujiji with his handful of men? The alternative was to go west with Tippu Tib and Hamis to explore the area of Lake Mweru of which he had heard and which he thought might be part of the great central African watershed which he hoped to map out for the RGS. Its successful exploration would bring him again, he believed, the prestige that would make the British public listen to his pleas for the transformation of Africa by Christianity and commerce and to free East Africa from the destructive impact of the slave trade and the slave-based ivory trade.[22]

There was a minor earthquake while they were at Hamis's camp which damaged Livingstone's chronometers again, making his reading of longitude even more inaccurate. While waiting for peace to be brought about between the Zanzibaris and the Tabwa of Chief Nsama, Livingstone had the opportunity to observe the Tabwa at various times during the negotiations. He wrote down his reflections in his journal, where he comes back again to his insistence that the Ancient Egyptians were Africans. He wrote:

> Nsama's people are particularly handsome ... all have very fine forms, with small hands and feet ... My observations deepened the impression first obtained from the remarks of Winwood Reade, that the typical Negro is seen in the ancient Egyptian, and not in the ungainly forms which grow up in the unhealthy swamps of the West Coast. Indeed it is probable that this upland forest region is the true home of the Negro. The women ... have fine, well-formed features: their great defect is one of fashion, which does not extend to the next tribe: they file their teeth to points, the hussies, and that makes their smile like that of the crocodile.[23]

The caravans reached the vicinity of Lake Mweru on 6 November, when Livingstone and his men broke away and reached the lake proper on 8 November. To his intense excitement Livingstone learned that a large river flowed northwards from it, the Lualaba.[24] Since he was told that another large river flowed into it from the south, Livingstone put this together in his mind with the Chambesi which flowed into the vast swampy area surrounding Lake Bangweulu. Were they all connected? Were these the headwaters of the Congo or even of the Nile? He decided to go south to Kazembe's and then to Bangweulu or Bemba, as he called it initially, and test his theory.

As he and his comrades marched down the east shore of Mweru he chatted with the fishermen he met on the way and recorded the local names for thirty-nine varieties of fish in the lake. Before reaching the capital of Mwata Kazembe VIII, he passed by, on 18 November, the place where the great Portuguese traveller Jose de Lacerda e Almeida had died in 1797. At his capital Kazembe received him at a formal reception where Livingstone provoked a great deal of giggling and confusion among the retinue of the Mwata's consort. Perhaps the appearance of this skinny, nut-brown stranger with the straggly hair and no front teeth was too much for them.

Livingstone stayed at the capital for nearly four weeks and became friendly
with two Zanzibari traders, Mohammad bin Saleh and Mohammad bin
Gharib.[25] The former had been there for over twenty years, the virtual
prisoner of Kazembe. Livingstone was able to persuade Kazembe to allow
him to leave. Bin Gharib became Livingstone's friend. While in the capital,
Livingstone also spent hours discussing the history of the Luba/Lunda
empire, of which Mwata Kazembe's kingdom was part, with an ancient elder
called Perembe.

In mid December the rains were making the way impossibly difficult as
Livingstone left Kazembe's with bin Saleh and headed back towards Mweru.
The plateau they were crossing had become a large morass, as its African
name Mweru Wantipa, sea of mud, should have warned them. Although
their ultimate destination was Ujiji, where Livingstone could pick up his
stores, Bin Saleh stopped off halfway across the plateau to stay at his son's
encampment. Livingstone pressed on and had two exciting encounters. The
first was to see the Lualaba, as he and local people called this river, pouring
our of the north-west corner of Lake Mweru; the second was to come across
the new home of Said bin Habib, the Zanzibari trader whom he had met
at Linyanti on his return from Loanda.

When bin Saleh returned, Livingstone was frustrated by his insistence that
there was no point in setting off to Ujiji with the heavy rain still falling and
turning all the paths into bogs. So Livingstone decided, if he had to wait to
go to Ujiji, he might as well use the time effectively and go south again and
confirm the Bangweulu/ Chambesi link through the Luapula to Mweru
and the Lualaba. His men, even the 'faithfuls', refused to go back through
the mud and swollen rivers. It took all of his powers of persuasion to
change their minds but, on 20 April, Livingstone was able to set out southwards with Chuma, Susi, Gardner and, out of character, two of the 'lazies',
Abraham and Simon. Amoda stayed behind with the other 'deserters'. In
his journal Livingstone wrote of this incident in tones that were becoming
typical of him and showed a very different attitude to that which he had
shown in the past to those who had failed him. He wrote:

> I did not blame them very severely in my own mind for absconding: they were
> tired of tramping and so verily am I ... consciousness of my own defects makes
> me lenient.[26]

Livingstone and his few companions got to Kazembe's capital in three
weeks, then stayed there a month, Livingstone eating his meals with Mohammad bin Gharib, who was still camped there. They eventually did move
off but completed the journey to Bangweulu very slowly indeed, because of
detours to avoid Ngoni raiding parties and because swamps slowed their

progress dreadfully. Livingstone reached the north-west corner of Lake Bangweulu on 18 July 1868. Tragically, because of the faulty chronometers, he thought himself to be seventy miles further west than he was. This situation was made worse by being unable to get canoes to explore the lake in any detail. Where he reached Bangweulu the shoreline was a sandy beach and he presumed the rest was like that. From questioning informants he accurately gauged the size of Lake Bangweulu together with its swamps, but he understood the whole to be clear water. In fact, of seven thousand square miles, only 20 per cent of the area is clear water while 80 per cent is swamp through which there are a few paths but over almost all of which one can move by canoe.

Despite his emaciated state, Livingstone's spirits were high and he wrote a number of letters and, more importantly, a long despatch to Lord Clarendon.[27] Waller referred to this as a 'scientific treatise': it certainly was an astonishingly detailed study of the climate, geography, fauna and flora of the region. This study of the region and his conclusive explanation of the connected river system have been seen by some as his greatest geographical achievement.[28]

After a fortnight at Lake Bangweulu Livingstone began the march north to rejoin Mohammad bin Saleh. The journey of one hundred and fifty miles took over two months. This time it was not because of difficult terrain, as it was the dry season, but because the territory through which they passed was the scene of violent fighting between Mwata Kazembe, various rebels and Ngoni raiders. When they did link up, Livingstone found bin Saleh waiting to go north to the Manyema country, which pleased Livingstone because by going there he could further explore the Lualaba, which led either to the Congo or the Nile. The Zanzibaris were increasingly alarmed, however, at the anti-Zanzibari violence spreading across the countryside. Along with other Zanzibari traders, bin Saleh decided to retreat out of the area in one large caravan. Their servants and retainers were all Nyamwezi, confident and effective warriors whose prowess saved their Zanzibari paymasters on a number of occasions on their retreat. Livingstone took careful notes of the Nyamwezi techniques for smelting and working copper and other aspects of their culture. When the caravan met up with Mohammad bin Gharib, Livingstone found the rest of his original band waiting for him and seeking to re-enter his service, to which he agreed with the remark in his journal, 'I have faults myself'.

Many Zanzibari traders joined together and formed a militarily formidable caravan. It was also a very rich caravan with, as well as slaves, a large amount of copper from Katanga and much ivory. In his journal Livingstone recorded that, even on this difficult journey, the Zanzibari were the attackers as well as the object of attacks. Of one particular encounter with the Bemba on 20 November, Livingstone wrote praising the bravery of the Bemba in battle, especially the way they sought to carry away their wounded even when under heavy fire: 'Victoria-cross fellows truly many of them were'.[29]

As the long line of Zanzibaris, porters, slaves and Manyema escorts wound their way towards Lake Tanganyika, the rains began. Livingstone, though often ill, was able to march independently of (but in touch with) the caravan. He was able to purchase only the cheapest and coarsest food. He was getting wet through again and again. His clothes had often to be put on damp, which meant that his body became the host to the maggots of the fly, called *putsi* in Chewa, which lays its eggs in wet clothing. The emerging maggots burrow under the skin of the wearer causing severe pain. On 3 January 1869 he wrote:

> I marched one hour, but found I was too weak to go further. Moving always good in fever; now I had a pain in the chest, and rust of iron sputa: my lungs, my strongest part, were thus affected. We crossed a rill and built sheds, but I lost count of the days of the week and month after this. Very ill all over.[30]

The caravan caught up with him on 7 January 1869 and Mohammad bin Gharib's kindness undoubtedly saved Livingstone's life. He fed Livingstone well, gave him medicine and had a litter made on which Livingstone was carried all the way to Tanganyika. Throughout all this Livingstone still contrived to make some entries in his journal on the geography of the area, but there are gaps of several days with no entries. That he made any entries at all is astonishing when we read his description of his condition:

> carriage is painful; head down and feet up alternates with feet down and head up; jolted up and down and sideways – changing shoulders involves a toss from one side to the other of the *kitanda*. The sun is vertical blistering any part of the skin exposed, and I try to shelter my face and head as well as I can with a bunch of leaves, but it is dreadfully fatiguing in my weakness.[31]

Arriving at Lake Tanganyika, Livingstone had to put moral pressure on Said bin Habib to provide canoes for him and his people, chiding him that all the other Zanzibari had aided him except Habib and asking whether he, bin Habib, was going to let him down at the last. The canoes were provided and took them from near the mouth of the Lukuga up the coast and then across to Ujiji. Muhammad bin Gharib found Livingstone a house to stay in but that was the only good thing Livingstone found in Ujiji.

Jairam Sewrji Company had let Livingstone down badly. Most of his goods had not been delivered. Wine, cheese and medicine, including the vital quinine, had been left at Unanyembe (today's Tabora) two hundred miles away, and most of the cloth that had been ordered, vital currency for

Livingstone, had been looted. The buffaloes that he had ordered from Stearns in Bombay had been sent but all had died before reaching Ujiji. Livingstone was still very weak, and the only currency with which to buy necessities was what little poor quality cloth had been left him.

Livingstone remained four months in Ujiji and discovered that most of the Zanzibaris there saw him as a threat, despite his near destitution. He had contacts with the British Government and with the Sultan. The Sultan allowed the buying and selling of slaves but he forbade raiding and killing to capture free men and women to make them slaves. So the Ujijians prevented any letters Livingstone attempted to send – and he wrote many – from reaching the coast (though two letters did get through, we do not know by what means). One was to the Sultan exposing the deeds of the Zanzibari traders, confident of the Sultan's disapproval of their actions. He specifically exonerated bin Saleh and bin Gharib from these complaints.

At that time the Zanzibaris at Ujiji were beginning a new expansion of their activities to the north west, west and south west, where they had discovered there were large quantities of ivory available at what were very cheap prices in the light of the international market price. Things were made worse, for the African peoples of those areas, by a cholera epidemic which killed thousands of slaves in the coastal plantations and those on Zanzibar and Pemba in 1869. Market forces quickly drove the price of slaves sky high, so these new ivory-producing lands also became a massively profitable source of slaves. The economic pressure, which some have likened to that of a 'gold rush', drove many Zanzibaris in 1870 and 1871 to forego any attempt to trade. They simply raided for slaves and ivory in an utterly ruthless fashion. At this time Livingstone was in constant contact with men and women enslaved in this fashion. He recorded one encounter with some slaves which he felt to be revealing of the African understanding of reality:

> Six men slaves were singing as if they did not feel the weight and degradation of the slave-sticks. I asked the cause of their mirth, and was told that they rejoiced at the idea 'of coming back after death and haunting and killing those that had enslaved them'. Some of the words I had to enquire about; for instance, the meaning of the words 'to haunt and kill by spirit power'; then it was, 'Oh, you sent me off to Manga (sea-coast), but the yoke is off when I die, and back I shall come to haunt and kill you'. Then all joined in the chorus, which was the name of each vendor. It told not of fun, but of the bitterness and tears of such as were oppressed, and on the side of the oppressors there was power: there be higher than they! [32]

The near destitute Livingstone, served by Chuma, Susi, Amoda and Gardner (all the other Nassik men had by that time taken service with Zanzibaris), could not get any porters to help him investigate the north end of Lake Tanganyika. That investigation was necessary to clear up the suggestions that had been made that the Nile or some other major river flowed from the north end. Livingstone felt frustrated and, more significantly, he felt let down by the way his requests to the consulate at Zanzibar for support had been dealt with. His mood changed when bin Gharib arrived at Ujiji. Livingstone's old friend was willing to take him into the Lualaba basin so that Livingstone could further investigate that great river which he hoped was the Nile, but he in his heart knew (in his journal he said 'feared') was the Congo. Livingstone hoped the trip would last about six months and that he would find, when he returned to Ujiji, that the porters and supplies for which he had again asked Kirk would have arrived.

On 12 July 1869 Livingstone and his ally started off across the lake, leaving Amoda in charge of Livingstone's house. Livingstone attempted to check the lake's depth. His line broke at 1965 feet and he noted that he believed the lake was even deeper. This was an important indicator of the special nature of the lake for other researchers afterwards. The lake is in fact the second deepest in the world. The land into which they were moving was called Manyema – and still is – and Livingstone referred to its various peoples by that name.[33] On this trek Livingstone reached further west than any European had gone previously in east Africa.

During the march it was clear Livingstone had not recovered from his previous illnesses. He was unwell, which was to be his condition from then until his death. Sometimes he was a little better than at others but he was never really well again. Dysentery and anal bleeding were steadily wearing him down. On 10 August he recorded that 'any ascent, though gentle makes me blow since the attack of pneumonia; if it is inclined to an angle of 45°, a 100 or 150 yds makes me stop to pant in distress'.[34] What was worse was that he no longer had any serviceable shoes or boots. On 21 September they reached Bambarre (now Kabambare), which was one of the new Zanzibari forward bases. It lay in the middle of the Manyema country halfway as the crow flies between Tanganyika and the Lualaba. Bin Gharib then decided to go north for his own commercial reasons, leaving Livingstone and his tiny band of followers at Kabambare. No other Zanzibari, because of their suspicion of Livingstone, would help him get to the Lualaba. While at Kabambare he began to study the Manyema people. Although in one letter he referred to the women as pretty and the men ugly, when he settled down he came to admire both men and women. He describes their land as both beautiful and rich. Indeed he described the Manyema country in terms that were almost idyllic, yet containing accurate observation.

The villages are very pretty, standing on slopes. The main street generally lies east and west, to allow the bright sun to stream his clear hot rays from one end to the other, and lick up quickly the moisture from the frequent showers which is not drained off by the slopes. A little verandah is often made in front of the door, and here at dawn the family gathers round the fire, and, while enjoying the heat needed in the cold that always accompanies the first darting of the light or sun's rays across the atmosphere, inhale the delicious air, and talk over their domestic affairs. The various shaped leaves of the forest all around their village and the near nestlings are bespangled with myriads of dewdrops. The cocks crow vigorously, and strut and ogle; the kids gambol and leap on the backs of their dams quietly chewing the cud; other goats make believe fighting. Thrifty wives often bake their new clay pots in a fire, made by lighting a heap of grass roots: the next morning they extract salt from the ashes, and so two birds are killed with one stone. The beauty of this morning scene of peaceful enjoyment is indescribable. Infancy gilds the fairy picture with its own lines, and it is probably never forgotten, for the young, taken from slavers, and treated with all philanthropic missionary care and kindness, still revert to the period of infancy as the finest and fairest they have known. They would go back to freedom and enjoyment as fast as would our own sons of the soil, and *be heedless to the charms of hard work and no play which we think so much better for them if not for us.*[35]

The Manyema had plenty of ivory but would not sell to the Zanzibaris unless offered the precise goods they desired. If the Zanzibaris offered that for which they felt no need they turned them down and insisted that the ivory could stay and rot rather than accepting such rubbish for it. This infuriated the Zanzibaris and led to the traders taking ivory by force from the weaker and more vulnerable villages.

While waiting at Kabambare, Livingstone wrote a number of long letters which have survived, to his brother John, to his children Agnes and Tom, to W. C. Oswell, and to Maclear and Frere. In these letters he showed a very jealous and critical attitude to the work of Burton, Speke and Grant. He also described for the first time his new obsession which was that somewhere in the watershed he was exploring were the sources of the Nile, Zambesi and Congo. Herodotus had reported the Nile rising from a place where there were three fountains. Livingstone believed that this lay to the west in Katanga.[36] There also, he believed, might be the remains of the city of Meroe which Josephus declared had been founded in Ethiopia by Moses in honour of his foster mother Merr when he went deep into Africa with her.[37]

His letters to Tom and to Agnes are of particular importance because of what they reveal about his attitude to issues as important at the beginning of the twenty-first century as they were in the late nineteenth, race and the role of women. In a long letter to Tom, which covered many issues from possible cannibalism among the Manyema to advice on marriage, Livingstone focused on the righteousness of Lincoln's freeing of the slaves and of the cause of Reconstruction. In direct contrast, he deplored the support of the British establishment for Governor Eyre, perpetrator of the Morant Bay massacre in Jamaica.[38] In this he was communicating to Tom a realistic view of Britain and the British which he does not express in his published writings where he was seeking to build up British interest in and care for Africa and its peoples. His letters to Tom and Agnes reflect his musings recorded in his journal for 19 May 1869:

> The emancipation of our West-Indian slaves was the work of but a small number of the people of England – the philanthropists and all the more advanced thinkers of the age. Numerically they were a very small minority of the population, and powerful only from the superior abilities of the leading men, and from having the right, the true, and the just on their side. Of the rest of the population an immense number were indifferent, who had no sympathies to spare for any beyond their own fireside circle. In the course of time sensation writers came up on the surface of society, and by way of originality they condemned almost every measure and person of the past. 'Emancipation was a mistake'; and these fast writers drew along with them a large body, who would fain be slaveholders themselves. We must never lose sight of the fact that, though the majority perhaps are on the side of freedom, large numbers of Englishmen are not slaveholders only because the law forbids the practice. In this proclivity we see a great part of the reason for the frantic sympathy of thousands with the rebels in the great Black war in America. It is true that we do sympathize with brave men, though we may not approve of the objects for which they fight. We admired Stonewall Jackson as a modern type of Cromwell's Ironsides; and we praised Lee for his generalship, which, after all, was chiefly conspicuous by the absence of commanding abilities in his opponents, but, unquestionably, there existed besides an eager desire that slaveocracy might prosper and the Negro go to the wall. The would-be slaveholders showed their leanings unmistakably in reference to the Jamaica outbreak.[39]

He was still holding to the essential oneness of humanity and was urging it upon his son at the very time when humanity was being divided by the science of the day into mutually exclusive groups placed on an hierarchic scale, with Africans near the very bottom. In the letter to Agnes he describes a small incident to amuse her but which again is typical of his taking as given the full humanity of Africans.[40]

> The door is shut, all save a space to admit light ... eager heads sometimes crowd the open space, and crash goes the thin door, landing a Manyema beauty on the floor. 'It was not I,' she gasps out, 'It was Bessie Bell and Jeannie Gray that shoved me in and -', and as she scrambles out the lion's den, 'see they're laughing'; and fairly out she joins the merry giggles too.

In response to her assertion in a letter that she could travel as well as Mrs

Baker, he not only agreed but went on to praise the role of women who challenged the ideas of men as to what were appropriate activities for women. He praised Miss Tinne, who had explored the Nile without any accompanying European men, and went on to point out that, after all, 'the death knell of American slavery was rung by a woman's hand'. He was undoubtedly an exponent of racial equality. It would be going too far to see him as an exponent of sexual equality but his letter to Agnes certainly challenged conventional Victorian attitudes in that area.

At the beginning of November Livingstone had had enough of waiting and he set off for the Lualaba, escorted by his few 'faithfuls'. He soon found it impossible to go on as he had what he called 'choleric dysentery', accompanied by bad haemorrhoids which resulted in massive anal bleeding. So the bedraggled little party returned to Kabambare on 19 November to find that bin Gharib had returned. Bin Gharib gave Livingstone a substantial quantity of opium to deal with the pain he was suffering as well as food for his party. Later he sent over a goat so that Livingstone and his little band could celebrate Christmas. Tragically for the Manyema, Livingstone reported that a caravan of Zanzibaris able to mount a force of five hundred guns had come to Kabambare to exploit the new source of what they had heard was cheap and abundant ivory.

By this time Livingstone had come to admire the Manyema people for their good looks and for their skills, though he was unhappy with their careless attitude to human life. He despaired that their lack of any sort of political unity meant that they had no chance of uniting to repel the Zanzibari raiders.[41] These remarks about their looks reflected his awareness of the growing influence of 'scientific racism' in Britain and its espousal by the Anthropological Society. At one point, while discussing whether the Manyema were cannibals or not, he went on:

And yet they are a fine-looking race; I would back a company of Manyema men to be far superior in shape of head and generally in physical form too against the whole Anthropological Society.[42]

This was a riposte to the branch of scientific racism, popular at the time, which used craniometry and general physical appearance as signs of the moral and intellectual superiority of one so-called race over another.

On 26 December 1869, with the rainy season well begun, he decided to set off again for the Lualaba and wrote:

I get fever severely, and was down all day, but we march, as I have always found that moving is the best remedy for fever: I have, however, no medicine whatever.[43]

Dysentery soon struck with heavy anal bleeding again, but a new problem also arrived. Because he had no satisfactory shoes he developed tropical ulcers on his feet. These ulcers developed not laterally but by penetrating deeper and deeper through to the bone and were extremely painful. The miserable situation of the little party was made worse by villagers refusing to serve as guides because they feared that the expedition was an advance party for the Zanzibaris. The rain continued to pour down while they slogged on soaking wet through the mud. Eventually Livingstone decided to turn away and seek help and rest at the nearest Zanzibari encampment. The going was still utterly exhausting, often in mud up to mid thigh and in the interminable rain. Despite fear of the Zanzibaris, some villages still received him with traditional African hospitality. Of one of these days he wrote:

> Caught in a drenching rain which me fain to sit, exhausted as I was, under an umbrella for an hour trying to keep the trunk dry. As I sat in the rain a little tree-frog about half an inch long, leaped onto a grassy leaf, and began a tune as loud as that of many birds, and very sweet ... I drank some rain-water as I felt faint – in the paths it is now calf deep. I crossed a hundred yards of slush waist deep in mid channel ... I stripped off my clothes on reaching my hut in the village, and a fire during the night nearly dried them. At the same time I rubbed my legs with palm oil, and in the morning had a delicious breakfast of sour goat's milk and porridge.[44]

In March the Zanzibaris welcomed him at Mamohela and, after gathering strength, he and his few stalwarts struggled back to Kabambare where he remained till the end of the year. During this time he became even more enamoured of the Manyema. He also read his Bible through from beginning to end four times. It must also be said that this was a time when he indulged in what can only be called intellectual rambling, desperately trying to show the Lualaba was the Nile, while all the time knowing deep down that it was the Congo. If he could have escaped from his Nile fixation, his discovering one of the two main sources of the Congo so far from its entry into the Atlantic would have been success enough for anyone.[45] But it was no longer the simple geographic matter of the Nile source, it was Meroe and Herodotus's fountains and the travels of Moses that all had to be authenticated. The description by Zanzibaris of the place from which rivers flowed northwards and southwards confirmed to him he was pursuing reality not a fantasy.

Zanzibari friends gave him powdered malachite, which slowly but surely cleared up his tropical ulcers, while he remained in his house from July until 10 October 1870. This rest helped to build up his strength again to some degree. His spirits were sorely tried, however, by the stories of villages destroyed and Manyema killed by Zanzibaris and their servants. The months of sitting idle finally created in him a terrible sense of frustration which boiled over in bitter condemnatory words about the very Manyema for whom, though most of this period, he had consistently expressed admiration.

The entry for 1 January 1871 reads 'O Father! Help me finish this work to thine honour'. Livingstone was still stuck at Kabambare because he had no resources and only Chuma, Susi and Gardner as followers. Amoda was back at Ujiji. However, on 4 February the men and supplies promised by Kirk arrived, or rather a group of the men arrived with some supplies, the rest having been left with their overseers at Ujiji. Livingstone welcomed the tea, coffee and quinine they brought but the men disappointed him. They were all slaves hired by the Jairam Sewrji Company and they insisted that Kirk had instructed them to bring Livingstone back to Zanzibar. This apparent interference by Kirk in his affairs distressed Livingstone and he began to worry about Kirk's attitude towards him.

After bin Gharib threatened to shoot them if they did not march west with Livingstone, the new men joined Livingstone in yet another attempt to reach the Lualaba, which he eventually did at Nyangwe on 29 March 1871. At Nyangwe he saw that the Lualaba truly was a mighty river flowing north, already three thousand yards broad and so deep that it was never fordable at any time of the year. Despite this confirmation of his hopes, he was depressed, because throughout the journey he had seen how the Manyema country was being devastated by the Zanzibaris. The Manyema were cheated, insulted and many killed or taken into slavery. The Zanzibari traders had become marauders.

Livingstone was determined to report all that was being done to the outside world, hoping to provoke international efforts to stop this destructive process. As he had said to his son Tom in his letter of September 1869, he held to his belief that 'The day for Africa is yet to come', and that he was going to play his part in its coming. His intention was only too clear to the Zanzibaris at Nyangwe, who decided they would do nothing to help him. He wanted to go further west to see if he could find the fountains of Herodotus, which he saw as the western source of the watershed he was investigating, but Zanzibaris denied him the necessary canoes. He was stuck again. He and his men built a house and he settled down to study the society of Nyangwe, which was the site of an important traditional market for the African people on both sides of the Lualaba. He soon began to enjoy his stay in this bustling African market centre, where he spent hours in the market. Of it he wrote in his journal 10 April:

I counted upwards of 700 passing my door. With market women it seems to be a pleasure of life to haggle and joke, and laugh and cheat: many come eagerly, and retire with careworn faces; many are beautiful and many old; all carry very heavy loads of dried cassava and earthen pots, which they dispose of very cheaply for palm-oil, fish, salt, pepper and relishes for their food. The men appear in gaudy lambas, and carry little save their iron wares, fowls, grass cloth and pigs.[46]

He reset his chronometers and began studying the fish in the river, drawing them and comparing them with those of Lake Malawi and what he knew of Nile fish. He still would not admit to himself that this was the Congo.

Livingstone also began to cultivate Dugumbe bin Habib, the most important Zanzibari, and in the end unashamedly begged him for help to go on over the river. While awaiting Dugumbe's answer there occurred an event that was definitive for the next stage of Livingstone's life and in the long run definitive for future of the East African slave trade.

On 15 July 1871 there was an appalling massacre of the people, mainly women and children, gathered at the market at Nyangwe. The morning began with Livingstone noting that three servants of the Zanzibaris had gone into the market carrying their weapons, which was contrary to market rules. Livingstone thought of checking them when suddenly one of them shot and killed a stallholder with whom he was quarrelling. This appeared to have been a signal, for almost immediately, from around the perimeter of the market, armed Zanzibaris and their men fired into the crowded market. Within minutes their fellows began firing into the canoes packed with people fleeing the carnage, while across the river other Zanzibari groups began to burn houses and shoot their inhabitants. Livingstone, who was watching with Dugumbe, went to shoot the nearest riflemen with his pistol. Dugumbe persuaded him of the pointlessness of this. Livingstone was horror-struck as never before in his life. As the firing began to die down in the market proper and on the canoe beach, he and his 'faithfuls' went into the shambles holding the consular Union Jack above them, the only time he appears ever to have used the flag. The desultory firing that had been continuing now stopped and he and his men rescued thirty women still cowering among the market stalls. Across the river the killing and burning went on until the next day. Livingstone appealed to Dugumbe to punish those who had initiated this terrible event, which saw at least 400 dead for certain with an unknown number drowned trying to get away. Dugumbe insisted he was powerless to do anything.

Livingstone's graphic report of this massacre when it reached Britain had a widespread impact. It was used again and again in Britain and elsewhere and did more than any other single thing to awaken a British concern about the east African slave trade. A delegation of village headmen from the other side of the river, to whom he restored the thirty women saved, came to meet him the next day. They invited him across the river to stay with them. His presence they thought would prevent further attacks. They also wanted his help to reorganise their villages in the face of the Zanzibari threat. What they meant exactly Livingstone does not make clear in his journal but, as an outsider to their feuds, he might have been able to help them to unite and better defend themselves against the Zanzibaris.

This was the opportunity he had been waiting for but Livingstone said he was so ashamed he could not look any Manyema in the face. Despite their pleas for him to come over, he insisted that he was leaving. He did, however, arrange for the chiefs to meet with Dugumbe, at which meeting he helped them come to a treaty arrangement with Dugumbe which he hoped would afford the Manyema some protection.

The slave porters sent by Kirk, Livingstone recorded in his journal, would have liked to join with the Zanzibaris. He felt he had no alternative but to return to Ujiji and send these unsatisfactory fellows back to Zanzibar then await more supplies and better porters so as to go back and finish exploring the watershed beyond the Lualaba. The problem was the emotional impact upon him of the slaughter was such that he was unable to travel immediately. On 18 July the Manyema headmen were still visiting him and entreating him to stay with them. He wrote:

> The terrible scenes of man's inhumanity to man brought on severe headache, which might have been serious had it not been relieved by a copious discharge of blood; I was laid up all yesterday afternoon with the depression the bloodshed made, it filled me with unspeakable horror.[47]

When he felt a little stronger, Livingstone started off for Ujiji on 21 July 1871. Dugumbe gave Livingstone and his men a generous gift of supplies. When they arrived back at Ujiji on 23 October, after a very difficult and dangerous journey, Livingstone was warmly welcomed by a number of the Zanzibari leaders. After the initial euphoria of the welcome came the devastating news that the £600 worth of supplies sent up by Kirk were all gone. The head of the caravan, Sherif, had been assured by divination that Livingstone was dead so had used the supplies to obtain ivory and slaves for himself. The Zanzibari authorities in Ujiji said there was no way that they could obtain compensation for Livingstone. He was left destitute in the same town where Sherif, the agent of Jairam Sewrji and indirectly of Kirk, was enjoying the profits of having cheated him. All that he and his loyal followers, Chuma, Susi, Gardner and Amoda, had to live on was the small stock of cloth and beads Livingstone had left with bin Saleh for safekeeping. These supplies would not last long. Their only other possible source of support was an offer of Said bin Majid, who privately assured Livingstone he would sell some ivory and give him the proceeds. Livingstone replied 'not yet', hoping against hope that he would not be reduced completely to what he called 'beggary'. This was probably the low point of all Livingstone's years in Africa, other than the day Mary died. After his insistence that he could no longer be associated with the Zanzibaris, he was on the verge of complete dependence upon them with little hope of help, since he had had no word from Britain for over a year and his link to Britain, Kirk at Zanzibar, appeared unable to render him any effective assistance.

14

Last Journeys

When Livingstone and his little band arrived back at Ujiji, on 23 October 1871 by his calculations, the future appeared impenetrably dark. Had he exchanged the bloody 'hell' of Nyangwe for the humiliation of beggary at Ujiji? At this darkest hour, help came. Livingstone wrote:

> But when my spirits were at their lowest ebb, the good Samaritan was close at hand, for one morning Susi came running at the top of his speed and gasped out, 'An Englishman! I see him!' and off he darted to meet him. The American flag at the head of a caravan told of the nationality of the stranger. Bales of goods, baths of tin, huge kettles, cooking pots, tents &c., made me think 'This must be a luxurious traveller and not one at his wits end like me'. It was Henry Morton Stanley, the travelling correspondent of the *New York Herald*, sent by James Gordon Bennett, junior, at an expense of more than £4000, to obtain accurate about Dr Livingstone if living, and if dead to bring home my bones.[1]

Henry Morton Stanley, his solar topee freshly chalked and his riding boots brightly polished, entered Ujiji in a state of highest excitement with his men flying the Sultan's as well as the American flag. He described the meeting as follows:

> I pushed back the crowds, and, passing from the rear, walked down a living avenue of people, until I came in front of the semicircle of Arabs, in front of which stood the white man with the grey beard. As I advanced slowly towards him I noticed he was pale, looked wearied, and had a grey beard, wore a bluish cap with a faded gold band round it, had on a red-sleeved waistcoat, and a pair of grey tweed trousers. I would have run to him, only I was a coward in the presence of such a mob – would have embraced him, only, he being an Englishman, I did not know how he would receive me; so I did what cowardice and false pride suggested was the best thing – walked deliberately to him, took off my hat, and said:
> 'Dr Livingstone, I presume?'
> 'Yes,' said he with a kind smile, lifting his cap slightly.
> I replace my hat on my head, and he puts on his cap, and we both grasp hands, and then I say aloud:
> 'I thank God, Doctor, I have been permitted to see you.'
> He answered, 'I feel thankful that I am here to welcome you'.[2]

This most theatrical event has been drawn by artists and reproduced in books and magazines for over a hundred years. It has, however, a symbolism that was not seen by contemporary commentators nor by most writers on Livingstone since. Although to Livingstone the meeting was a reassurance that Providence still guided his affairs, it was a symbol of the coming of the new approach to Africa which would postpone Livingstone's dream of 'a good day coming yet for Africa'. Although Stanley had more respect for individual Africans than most of the Europeans who were about to open up Africa in the next twenty-five years, he, not Livingstone, represented the immediate future for Africa. Stanley was the vanguard of those who, in the Scramble for Africa, would parcel Africa up into European colonies and bring its peoples into the modern world by means of the whip and the machine gun.[3] Stanley who, in his *How I Found Livingstone*, promoted the image of the old Protestant saint who treated Africans as fellow human beings, was also a key figure in the creation of the most brutal and repressive colonial regime in Africa, that of King Leopold's Congo Free State. This is not to pillory Stanley as a unique monster as has been done in the past; Stanley was not untypical of many European actors on the African stage between 1870 and 1914. What brought him disrepute in the eyes of the British establishment, then and since, was his honesty.[4] As General Gordon wrote in a letter to Sir Richard Burton: 'He is to blame for *writing* what he did (as Baker was). These things may be done but not advertised.'[5]

H. M. Stanley was a leading reporter for the *New York Herald*.[6] An illegitimate child, born John Rowlands, who had spent his childhood in a workhouse in north Wales, he went to the United States before the Civil War. There he adopted the name by which we now know him. He enlisted in the Confederate army, was captured at Shiloh, and volunteered from prison camp to serve in the Union army, from which he was discharged as medically unfit. After a brief return to Wales, he joined the US Navy, from which he deserted, and then became a journalist. He first came to prominence in 1868 by getting his reports back to New York and London before any one else while reporting on the British invasion of Ethiopia. This gained him a long-term contract with the *New York Herald* of James Gordon Bennett, one of the first of the new breed of newspaper owners always seeking a 'scoop'. In 1868 Bennett sent Stanley to Aden to begin enquiries about Livingstone, who had disappeared from outside view. With no news of Livingstone there, Stanley was then sent to cover the civil war in Spain. In October 1869, however, Bennett decided that it would make a great story if his star reporter went into Africa and 'found' Livingstone. Strangely, although Bennett authorised Stanley to draw as much money as he needed for the expedition and treated this task with the utmost seriousness, he first sent Stanley off on a long journey beginning with the opening of the Suez Canal and ending up at Bombay via the Black Sea and the Caucasus. As a result it was not until 7 January 1871 that Stanley arrived at Zanzibar. No one has yet satisfactorily explained why Bennett deliberately manufactured this delay.

The editorial in the *Herald* of 23 December 1871, however, made clear what Bennett was aiming for in initiating the expedition. In the editorial Bennett insisted that the he sought to give modern journalism a new role. It was to be a 'bold new venture in the cause of humanity, civilisation and science'. Late twentieth-century complaints about the media making the news, instead of simply reporting it, were perhaps a hundred years too late. This prickly Scots-American also made it clear that he wanted to show up the British authorities for their neglect of Livingstone.[7]

When Stanley arrived at Zanzibar, he consulted the United States consul; more oddly, however, he deliberately withheld the purpose of his expedition from Kirk. The two men met on a number of occasions and disliked each other instantly. This has usually been explained by reference to Stanley's dislike of British officials, who, in the past, had treated him with cold and arrogant indifference. That Stanley was looking for trouble and had a chip on his shoulder is undoubtedly true, but most biographers of Livingstone have ignored Bishop Tozer's comment on Kirk: 'He is a great hand at contradicting you flat, and aims at being the authority on all points under debate.'[8] Stanley insisted that, when he asked Kirk how Livingstone might react if he 'ran across him' on his trip, Kirk had replied that:

> He was eccentric ... nay, almost a misanthrope, who hated the sight of Europeans; who, if Burton, Speke, Grant or anybody of that kind were coming to see him, would haste to put as many miles as possible between himself and such a person. He was a man also whom no one could get along with – it was almost impossible to please him ...[9]

Some time later, when Stanley went across to Bagamoyo to begin the final stages of organising his caravan, he found Kirk there. Kirk had to delay a hunting trip because he was having to hurry on Livingstone's supply caravan that was, to his surprise, still there three weeks after it was supposed to have left. That extraordinary situation was, for Stanley, final confirmation that Kirk was indifferent to Livingstone's fate. When Stanley arrived at Ujiji and found Livingstone upset by the failure of Kirk to get supplies and reliable men through to him, Stanley made things much worse by implying to Livingstone that Kirk was perhaps hostile to him.[10]

Kirk, however, was not at all the principal thing that Stanley and Livingstone talked about. This pair of outsiders soon developed a remarkable rapport; Stanley described that first afternoon together:

> The hours of that afternoon passed most pleasantly – few afternoons of my life

more so. It seemed to me as if I had met an old friend. There was a friendly or good-natured abandon about Livingstone which was not lost on me. As host, welcoming one who spoke his language, he did his duties with a spirit and style I have never seen elsewhere. He had not much to offer, to be sure, but what he had was mine and his. The wan features which I had thought shocked me at first meeting, the heavy step which told of age and hard travel, the grey beard and stooping shoulders belied the man. Underneath that aged and well spent exterior lay an endless fund of high spirits, which now and then broke out in peals of hearty laughter – the rugged frame enclosed a very young and exuberant soul. The meal – I am not sure but what we ate three meals that afternoon – was seasoned with jokes and pleasant anecdotes, interesting hunting stories, of which his friends Webb, Oswell, Vardon and Cumming were always the chief actors.[11]

The eating went on apace, which provoked Halima, Amoda's wife who cooked for them, to come out onto the veranda and watch in amazement. Before Stanley's arrival, she had been trying hard but failing to get Livingstone to eat. From then on Stanley arranged for Livingstone to eat four meals a day.

In the days that followed they engaged continually in long conversations. Occasionally, however, Livingstone would sit quietly gazing into space, Stanley usually left him alone when in that mood but once he asked 'A penny for your thoughts doctor?' Livingstone's sharp reply was 'They are not worth it, my young friend, and let me suggest that, if I had any, possibly I should wish to keep them.'

The two men became close and, while there may be something in the suggestion that Livingstone had found a son he needed and Stanley the father he never had, there were reasons for this closeness other than those drawn from a presumption of psychological need. Livingstone was very open to the visitor because, understanding himself to be forgotten by the outside world, he felt himself vindicated by the fact that an American newspaper thought enough of him and his cause to mount an expensive expedition to find him. Also this young man, who was so eager to help him and listen to his ideas, was an extraordinarily effective means of publicising his findings and exposing to the world the devastation that the east coast slave trade was causing Africa and her peoples. At many levels, Stanley was a gift from God.

Stanley was clearly personally attracted to the older man. Even had this personal link not developed, Livingstone and his story was the basis of the 'scoop' of the century and everything he could learn from Livingstone was material for his despatches. His reports to the *Herald* would be repeated in other papers round the world – this was a journalistic triumph. All of that was in addition to kudos to be gained by the achievement of his effectively executed African trek to find Livingstone. He had done what the Royal Geographical Society and the British Government had failed to do, indeed what they apparently had not been particularly interested in doing.[12]

After a fortnight on these new generous rations Livingstone felt so well, the anal bleeding having stopped, that he wanted to be on the move again. He enquired if Stanley was willing to come with him across Lake Tanganyika and beyond the Lualaba to investigate the western watershed of the Congo – Livingstone still insisted on calling it the Nile – and chart the area where four rivers rose. Stanley insisted that there was no way his men would go across to the other side of the lake. He did suggest, however, that they might explore the north end of the lake and find out whether the Rusise flowed out of or into Lake Tanganyika. Burton had at one time suggested it as the headwater of the Nile in opposition to Speke's suggestion of Lake Victoria. The Zanzibaris in Ujiji had never explored the north of the lake. Livingstone agreed and they set off with some of their followers including Halima, Livingstone's cook, in a sixteen-paddle canoe hired from Said bin Majid. Twice on the trip Stanley had to be nursed through a bout of malaria; more ominously, Livingstone had a severe attack of dysentery which he dismissed in one sentence in his journal.

When they returned to Ujiji, Livingstone decided to go back to Tabora with Stanley and wait there in Stanley's comfortable house for the new porters whom Stanley would send up from Zanzibar. Stanley tried very hard to persuade Livingstone to return to Britain to recoup his health and only then return to finish the task of investigating the western watershed. Livingstone insisted, however, that returning to Britain was inappropriate since with new supplies and the reliable freemen porters promised by Stanley, not the useless slaves of Jairam Sewrji that Kirk had been sending, he could accomplish the task in a very few months. While in Ujiji Livingstone wrote up his journal, as was his wont, from the material in his smaller notebooks and also wrote one of the two long letters that were published in the *Herald*.

Stanley accepted Livingstone's plan and, on 27 December 1871, Stanley and his men, along with Livingstone and his faithfuls, began their trek to Tabora. They divided their people into a smaller party going south on the lake in canoes while the larger party marched on the shore. The intention was that when they had reached a sufficient distance south they could then strike across country on a diagonal route to Tabora, avoiding the continuing Mirambo war. Once the whole party had left the lake on 5 January 1872, they had a hard 250-mile march to Tabora. Although Stanley had provided a donkey for him, Livingston marched all the way. Whether this was because of a recurrence of anal bleeding or his characteristic pugnacious insistence on his fitness, or a combination of both, is not clear. Stanley wrote at the end of the journey: 'The expedition suffered considerably from famine, and your correspondent from fever, but these are incidentals to the march in this country. The Doctor tramped it on foot like a man of iron.'[13]

Livingstone and his followers then settled down in Stanley's large Arab style house where Livingstone and Stanley spent a month together and where their relationship grew even closer. When Stanley left for the coast on 14 March, his parting with Livingstone was very emotional and both men were close to tears. Stanley had, the night before, wept at the thought of parting. Of that night he wrote in his diary:

> The last day of my stay with Livingstone has come and gone, and the last night we shall be together is present and I cannot evade tomorrow! I feel as though I would rebel against the fate which drives me away from him ... we are both busy with our own thoughts. What his thoughts are I know not. Mine are sad ... I regret to surrender the pleasure I have felt in this man's society, though so dearly purchased. And I cannot resist the sure advance of time, which flies this night as if it mocked me, and gloated on the misery it created.[14]

Once on the road Stanley wrote a letter to Livingstone which was another extraordinary expression of deep affection. In all his published writing Stanley praised Livingstone for many qualities, particularly his ability to relate to Africans, which time and time again had diffused potentially dangerous situations with chiefs they encountered. This skill of Livingstone's extended also to relations within the camp where, for example, Livingstone once stopped Stanley beating his cook and had them shaking hands and apologising to each other. In private correspondence Stanley added one caveat: when he asked too many questions about the past, Livingstone would sometimes indulge in bitter recriminations about Bedingfeld and Baines.

Stanley took back with him to Zanzibar Livingstone's letter to be published in the *Herald*; also Livingstone's journal, which was sealed and was to be handed to the publisher Murray. In fact Stanley gave it to Agnes, Livingstone's daughter, with a large number of other letters. Perhaps most important of all, he took with him Livingstone's despatch to the Foreign Office, describing the Nyangwe massacre.

Because of the failure of the three efforts to send him men and supplies from the consulate in Zanzibar, Livingstone asked Stanley to recruit the porters to be sent to him at Tabora. In this connection Livingstone also sent three letters to Kirk, two complaining of Kirk's failures to help him and another instructing him to give the £500 pounds he held on Livingstone's behalf to Stanley to cover the cost of Stanley's efforts. Livingstone had been upset before Stanley arrived and with reason: none of the Zanzibar consulate's efforts to help him had worked and Sherif's selling of all Livingstone's goods at Ujiji while Livingstone languished at Nyangwe had been intolerable. There is no doubt that Stanley made the situation worse by implying that these failures were directly due to Kirk's lack of concern for (or perhaps even antagonism towards) Livingstone. Kirk was not only hurt by Livingstone's letters but also furiously angry. He denounced Livingstone to the Foreign Office in very strong language. His argument was that he had done his best. He had used Jairam Sewrji, as the consulate and other Britons had always done. In any case he had so many other duties and, in addition, slave porters were the only porters available. Modern writers since have come to his defence, accepting what he said and adding that without a European to supervise it no caravan could get goods into the interior without pilfering or worse.[15]

Stanley, when back in Britain, began a series of attacks on Kirk for having deliberately let Livingstone down. Apart from its effect on the reputations of Kirk and Stanley, the ensuing public controversy kept Livingstone very much in the public eye. Stanley undoubtedly attributed to Kirk motives and attitudes that were unfounded. In Britain, however, many leapt to Kirk's defence so enthusiastically as to exonerate him of any fault whatsoever, as have a majority of Livingstone biographers since. That is going too far. Stanley was able to raise a party of *free* porters (making Kirk's insistence that slave porters were the only ones to be had puzzling) under disciplined African leadership that successfully made their way to Livingstone at Tabora with all their goods intact. Why had Kirk not able to do that? Perhaps Agnes Livingstone summed up the sorry affair best when she said of Kirk, 'I do not think he wilfully neglected Papa, but I do not think he exerted himself as he should have done'.[16] When Kirk's conduct in this matter was formally investigated, he was completely exonerated of all fault and went on to have a distinguished official career. While Kirk was not guilty of the extreme charges made by Stanley, Agnes's judgement is perhaps overgenerous.

Back at Tabora, Livingstone was living well on the supplies left by Stanley and under the care of Halima, who was now joined in the small elite of Livingstone's personal following by another woman. Ntaoeka had been associated with someone in Stanley's staff but stayed behind and was welcomed into the Livingstone household, shortly after which Livingstone married her to Chuma. He wrote in his journal 'I did not like a fine looking woman among us unattached'.[17] While he waited at Tabora, Livingstone wove a new sounding line to replace the one he had lost in the lake. He bought some cattle and had the household make cheeses from their milk for the coming journey, and he read the books and newspapers that Stanley had left with him and prepared himself for the last great effort to 'finish his work'. Livingstone had chosen to ignore that, as soon as they had hit hard times on the journey from Ujiji to Tabora, he had had a number of bad bouts of anal bleeding. He should have taken this as a warning that Stanley had been correct to insist that he should have gone to Britain to recoup his health.

During his four months waiting at Tabora, Livingstone had frequent meetings with a number of Ganda traders and learned of their well-organised kingdom on the western shores of Lake Victoria. In his journal in July and August 1872 he discussed the potential of the Ganda kingdom as a site for a new mission. It was to the Ganda kingdom that the Church Missionary Society went only four years after his death, inspired by an appeal from Stanley. After a visit to the Ganda capital in 1876 Stanley wrote to British newspapers calling on the missionary community to take advantage of the opportunity offered by this sophisticated society open to new ideas. It is also to be noted that the success the CMS and Catholic missions achieved among the Ganda was based on what Livingstone had always insisted was the key to the growth of Christianity Africa, reliance on 'native agency'.[18]

Livingstone wrote a second letter published in the *New York Herald*; this was the letter where he made the famous appeal:

> All I can say in my loneliness is may heaven's rich blessing come down on every one – American, English, Turk – who may help to heal this open sore of the world.[19]

After the Nyangwe massacre his overriding concern had become the ending the east African slave trade but that did not remove his concern for Christian mission. Indeed in his journal, which he hoped would be published, he made a direct appeal for missionaries to come to the inland tribes. He made the appeal in a long passage where he refuted in detail Speke's assertion that African mothers had no maternal feelings. His words were heard but his profound belief in human equality which they displayed was not understood in an English-speaking world which was becoming, on both sides of the Atlantic, increasingly convinced that science had proved the immutable biological inferiority of African people. Livingstone wrote:

> I would say to missionaries, Come on, brethren, to the real heathen. You have no idea how brave you are till you try. Leaving the coast tribes, and devoting yourself heartily to the savages, as they are called, you will find, with some drawbacks and wickedness, a very great deal to *admire and love*.[20]

Speke, Burton and Stanley all hated Tabora but Livingstone liked it. Amid all the preparations for the next trek, he studied the geology of the area as well as the fauna and flora, and started to learn yet another African language, Nyamwezi. It was then that he looked at the tradition that said the Nile originated in the Mountains of the Moon. Nyamwezi means the place of the moon and the territory stretched across to the mountains in the west where the Kagera river rises and flows northwards into Lake Victoria and is therefore the ultimate source of the Nile. He did not know of the Kagera but he wrote in his notebook that the source of the Nile probably did lie there. He still insisted for public consumption that his Lualaba and its western twin watershed were the sources of the Nile. In his heart he knew they were the sources of the Congo.

When the band of free porters marched into Tabora on 15 August 1872, they included six Nassik men, two of whom were the brothers Jacob and John Wainwright. Fifty-six men had set out and fifty-six men arrived with their loads intact under the leadership of an African, Manwa Sera. Livingstone bestowed on them his ultimate praise: they had done as well as if they were Kololo. This success was a stark contrast to the three efforts with slave porters mounted by the British consulate in Zanzibar. The men brought mail and more news of the search and relief expedition mounted by the RGS, of which he had already heard. It was led by three Europeans, two naval officers, Lieutenants L. S. Dawson and W. Henn, and Livingstone's youngest son, Oswell.

Stanley's arrival at Bagamoyo had persuaded the two naval officers that there was no more point in mounting an expedition and they had abandoned it. It had then been suggested that Oswell might go up to Tabora with Stanley's new recruits, but he declined, apparently on Kirk's advice and on the grounds of weak health. The letter he had written to his father on first arriving on the coast casts a different light on his refusal.

When Livingstone had received his son's letter he had been deeply upset. In his journal on 27 June 1872, however, all he wrote was 'Received a letter from Oswell yesterday, dated Bagamoyo 14 May, which awakened thankfulness, anxiety and deep sorrow'. Its contents and the profound anger they aroused were revealed later in two letters, one to his brother John and the other to his sister Janet.[21] From them we learn that Oswell had told his father that he had come out to bring him back to Britain, to obtain money to complete his medical education, and force his father to face up to his family responsibilities. Since now he, Oswell, had heard that his father was to receive money from the government and from public subscriptions, he was returning to Britain in order to try to obtain some of it for his education. What a contrast with the letter Livingstone had received from his daughter Agnes somewhat earlier when he was arguing with Stanley about returning to Britain. In his journal for 18 February 1872 Livingstone had written:

My daughter Agnes says, 'Much as I wish you to come home, I would rather that you finished your work to your own satisfaction than return merely to gratify me.' Rightly and nobly said my darling Nannie.

Giving the men who had arrived from Bagamoyo some days rest, Livingstone got on with the preparations for this last trek which would 'finish his work'. His aim was to go south along the coast of Lake Tanganyika then south west towards Bangweulu, passing down its east side before turning west to Katanga and the place where the four rivers rose. In doing this he was fulfilling his original agreement with Sir Roderick Murchison. He was also seeking fame, but fame as a means to an end – a platform from which to make his words heard about the horrors of the slave trade and Africa's future. He made this point in a series of letters he wrote at the time. How he expressed the idea in a letter to his daughter Agnes is revealing of his own self-understanding:

> No one can estimate the amount of God-pleasing good that will be done, if, by Divine favour, this awful slave-trade, into the midst of which I have come, be abolished. This will be something to have lived for, and the conviction has grown in my mind that it was *for this end* I have been detained so long.[22]

On 25 August 1872 Livingstone led his assembled men and women out of Tabora and marched towards Lake Tanganyika. They had with them ten cattle, some goats and two donkeys. On the second day they lost the best milker among the cattle. When a week or so later they discovered they had left the dried milk behind, Livingstone realised that a potentially serious situation was developing as, when he was weak from dysentery, milk was one of the few things he could digest. Nothing daunted, however, he marched on despite dysenteric attacks that often left him unable to eat solid food for days on end. They reached sight of Lake Tanganyika on 8 October. Unfortunately for Livingstone, slavers had devastated the whole area and most people had withdrawn from the lake into stockaded villages in the mountains. As Livingstone and his people made their way down the coast, there were very few people around and little food. It was also the hottest part of the year, just before the rains broke. As a result his people, as good as the Kololo though they were, had to be given extra rest periods. Livingstone, as ever, kept a careful record of the journey. His records allow the researcher to identify each camping site, village, hill, stream and island that they passed.[23] This was done while he was ill and the marching conditions terrible. He wrote of this situation in his journal and the entry is archetypical Livingstone.

> I sent some to find a path out from the Lake mountains for they will kill us all; others were despatched to buy food, but the Lake folks are poor except in fish.

Swifts in flocks are found on the Lake when we came to it, and there are small migrations of swallows ever since. Though this is the hottest time of the year, and all the plants are burnt off or quite dried, the flowers persist in bursting out of the hot dry surface, generally without leaves. A purple ginger, with two yellow patches inside, is very lovely to behold, and it is alternated with one of a bright canary yellow; many trees too put on their blossoms. The sun makes the soil so hot that the radiation is as if it came from a furnace. It burns the feet of the people and knocks them up ... I too was ill, and became better only by marching on foot.[24]

What few people they met were still unfriendly because of the ravages made by Livingstone's old acquaintance, Tippu Tib. Then on 11 November they reached village of Kampamba at the foot of the lake and at last received a warm and hospitable welcome from the chief, who remembered Livingstone from his visit in 1868. As they marched on southwards towards Bangweulu, the villagers were friendly and hospitable, so progress was good, but then the rains began. On 28 November he wrote how they came to the River Lofu which was very deep and sixty feet across. They made a bridge across the river. Two days later they constructed another bridge across another stream swift flowing and deep because of the rains. He followed his old route of 1868 in reverse till he reached the village of chief Chibwe. There he made an important decision. He could continue on the old route down to the headquarters of the Bemba and then go due west round the south of Lake Bengweulu towards Katanga and the place where the four rivers rose, or he could go through territory he had not previously crossed directly to where he believed the Chambesi entered Lake Bangweulu. The tremendous sense of urgency that possessed Livingstone at this time and the real speed with which the journey had gone so far, despite it having been hard going, all contributed to his deciding not to follow the longer Bemba route.

He embarked on a march directly towards Bangweulu in persistent rain. It was a march upon which, for the first time in all his African travels, he became frequently lost. Because of the overcast weather he could only take readings occasionally. As a result, when these did not square with the readings he had taken in 1868, he trusted the 1868 readings. Those readings, however, had been taken with faulty chronometers so that Livingstone, by trusting them, was always sixty to seventy miles further east than he thought he was. When guides took him in a westerly direction he thought they were trying to trick him. What was worse he was operating with the mistaken understanding of Lake Bangweulu gained in 1868 – he thought of it as a large lake with some swampy verges instead of an enormous swamp with a small lake which was and is little more than appendage to the swamp. From

January until near the end of March 1873 Livingstone and his people
wandered about lost in the midst of vast swamplands frequently under cold,
driving rain. An entry for a typical day was that of 13 February:

> In four hours we came in sight of the Luena and Lake, and saw plenty of elephant
> and other game, but very shy. The forest trees are larger. The guides are more at
> a loss than we are, as they always go in canoes in the flat rivers and rivulets. Went
> E., then S.E. round to S.[25]

It was on 18 March that they finally reached the banks of the Chambesi,
which they crossed, and made camp 'on the left side'. However it took two
more weeks for the party to assemble together again since progress had
become one of relays of people moving forward in the few canoes they could
rent. As they moved on it was still water, water everywhere, as he noted in
his journal for 6 April. By this time Livingstone was becoming weaker and
weaker as a result of heavy anal bleeding. He who had marched 'like a man
of iron', as Stanley had put it, had to be carried on a *machila*.[26] When crossing
deep rivers he was carried on the shoulders of relays of his men.[27] He was
in fact bleeding to death but he continued to make entries in his journals,
as on 20 April, a Sunday:

> Service. Cross over the sponge, Moenda, for food and to be near the headman of
> these parts, Moanzambamba. I am excessively weak. Village on Moenda sponge,
> 7 a.m. Cross Lokulu in canoe. The river is about thirty yards broad, very deep,
> and flowing in marshes two knots from south south east to north north west into
> Lake.

Intense pain in the lumbar region now added to his suffering. After
reaching firm if not dry land they began to make better progress but he was
weak and in intense pain when, on 29 April 1873, he was carried into the
village of Chief Chitambo of the Lala people. The chief welcomed them and
granted Susi permission to build a small house for Livingstone and shelters
for his people. Chitambo came to pay a formal visit early on the 30 April
and was shown into the house where Livingstone lay. Livingstone begged
Chitambo's pardon saying he was so unwell that they could not talk together,
but he asked the chief to return the next day when he hoped to be much
better. His followers already knew very well that he was not going to get
better. They kept careful watch over him through the night during which
Livingstone, on several occasions, sent his personal attendant, a youngster
called Majwara, to get Susi. On one of these occasions Livingstone asked
Susi in Swahili, 'how many days to the Luapula?' When Susi answered that
he thought it might be three days, he sighed deeply and muttered 'O dear,
dear'. Majwara then dozed off for a time. Awakening around four in the

morning, he ran to tell Susi he was not sure if Livingstone was alive or dead. Susi called Chuma and three others and they all entered the house. They found Livingstone kneeling beside the bed with his head in his hands on the pillow. They touched his cold cheek and knew that he was dead.

It was then that the preparations began for Livingstone's last and most unusual African journey. The immediate problem that faced Chuma and Susi, whom the rest saw as their leaders, was that created by the widespread taboos and fears of ritual and spiritual contamination associated with dead bodies in the culture of all central and southern African peoples. Initially Chuma and Susi followed ritual practice by taking Livingstone's body through a gap broken through the back wall of the house, not the door. They then took his body across the river away from the village and quickly built a reed enclosure to house the corpse, saying Livingstone had been taken there to help him recover. Chitambo, however, realised what had happened and came to pay his respects to the dead. The chief's attitude freed Livingstone's people to break into the wild weeping, shouting and volleys of gunfire that were the due of a great man.

It is clear that Susi and Chuma had no hesitation about what was to be done next, Livingstone's papers and instruments in their special tin trunks must be got back to the coast and so must his body. Jacob Wainwright, who was the most competent in writing English, was deputed to make a complete inventory of Livingstone's belongings. Two others, who had served a doctor in Zanzibar, removed the heart and entrails from Livingstone's body. Wainwright recorded their findings; the most significant of which was a massive blood clot the size of a fist found in the lower bowel.[28] Livingstone's heart and viscera were placed in an iron box and ceremonially buried, Wainwright reading the funeral service from the Book of Common Prayer.

Then they had to decide how to get the body to Zanzibar, through the hundreds of villages that lay on the route. They decided to mummify the body then bend the legs up onto the chest so that body could be encased in a tube made of bark covered in tarred sailcloth and so resembling a trade load. Within the reed enclosure Livingstone's body was slowly mummified by exposure to the sun. When preparations were complete, the body was made up into a two-man load ready for the march. They set off on their fifteen hundred mile journey, flying the Union Jack and the banner of the Sultan at the front and with Majwara beating a drum. They would try to use this impressive front on approaching major villages to give the impression they were an important commercial caravan. Despite a month's delay near the Luapula, due to many of the company falling ill, they marched steadily on. Close to the south end of Lake Tanganyika they had to open fire on the people of one petty chief in order to get through but usually their progress was straightforward. A strange event happened, however, near Chief Nsama's which puzzled the caravan leaders. When passing a large Zanzibari caravan encamped near the chief's village, the Zanzibaris turned out and fired a number of volleys in salute. There seemed no other explanation than that they had guessed that this was Livingstone's body on its way home.

The first target of the caravan was Tabora, where they intended to pick up the stores and other belongings of Livingstone that had been left there. As they approached Tabora in early October they heard that a new Livingstone search expedition was there. They thought that one of Livingstone's sons was with the expedition, which was in fact headed by Lieutenant V. L. Cameron of the Royal Navy, so Chuma went ahead to meet the Europeans with a letter written by Wainwright.[29] The encounter there was a disconcerting and unpleasant one for Chuma and Susi. Cameron tried to take charge and insisted that Livingstone be buried forthwith. Chuma and Susi and the others refused but were not able to stop Cameron, who shouted down their opposition, from opening Livingstone's boxes and taking all his instruments.[30] Cameron wrote two reports on this meeting and sent them on with Chuma.

After a rest and collecting Livingstone's belongings, the column marched on. They took under their wing two Europeans from Cameron's staff, who had had enough, one of whom, a Dr Dillon, shot himself on the way to Bagamoyo. Despite enormous difficulties, the column reached Bagamoyo in the first week of February 1874. Ten men and women had died on the way but seventy-nine completed this extraordinary march where their leaders had displayed intelligence and diplomacy, and during which they all had displayed great courage and extraordinary loyalty. The first Europeans they encountered on reaching the coast were some French priests who put Livingstone's mummified body into a zinc container inside a wood coffin, which the Fathers then painted black. The acting British consul, Lieutenant Prideaux, Kirk having gone on leave, came across to Bagamoyo to take charge. He paid the men the precise wages due to them and summarily dismissed them. The women received nothing, presumably Prideaux viewing them as mere camp followers. Thus Ntaoeka, Livingstone's 'fine looking woman', went away with nothing, as did Livingstone's 'dear Halima', to whom he had promised a house and a garden in Zanzibar.

Completely misunderstanding the situation, Prideaux took Jacob Wainwright to be the leader of the trek and arranged for him to accompany Livingstone's body to London. It was a year later that the situation was corrected in part. Waller arranged that Chuma and Susi should come to Britain, their tickets and kit paid for by 'Paraffin' Young. They helped Waller greatly in producing the two-volume edition of Livingstone's journal; the second half of the second volume is based primarily on their oral testimonies. Some time later special medals were struck and sent out to Africa but by then most of the men could not be found and there were no medals for the women.

Prideaux had the coffin put aboard the first available mail ship. Wainwright guarded the coffin and was aided in his care from Alexandria onwards by Thomas Livingstone, the great man's son who boarded the ship there. At Southampton the coffin was received in great state. It was carried in procession through packed streets to the sound of minute guns and muffled church bells. A special train conveyed the coffin to London where it was opened at the headquarters of the Royal Geographical Society. Sir William Fergusson led a team of doctors who performed there the task of formal identification. Robert Moffat, W. C. Oswell, William Webb and a few other old friends were also there. Although the doctors formally recorded the false joint in the left humerus, of which they made a cast, as the proof that the mummy was that of David Livingstone, both Webb and Oswell insisted that, despite the long hair and beard, they recognised the face to be Livingstone's.

After lying in state in the rooms of the RGS, the funeral, paid for by the government, took place on 18 April 1874. The streets between the society's rooms and Westminster Abbey were thronged with a massive crowd and the coffin and the carriages of the principal mourners were followed by a long queue of carriages led by the empty carriages of the Queen and the Prince of Wales.[31]

The Abbey was packed and eight pallbearers, Stanley and Wainwright, Waller and James Young, Kirk and Webb and lastly General Steele and W. C. Oswell, carried the coffin down the aisle. Behind the coffin walked the seventy-nine-year-old Robert Moffat, and Livingstone's two sons, Tom and Oswell. Livingstone's two sisters were seated with his daughter, Agnes, near the burial spot. Agnes's two aunts were outside Scotland for the first time in their lives and their broad Scots accents were the subject of a great deal of comment. Of course Chuma and Susi should have been there, as should Halima and Ntaoeka, but they had been at the real funeral along with Majwara, Gardner and Amoda and the others who had served Livingstone so well. There is reason to suppose Livingstone would have seen it that way in keeping with what wrote in his journal on 25 June 1868:

> We came to a grave in the forest; it was a little rounded mound as if the occupant sat in it in the usual native way: it was strewn over with flour, and a number of the large blue beads put on it: a little path showed that it had visitors. This is the sort of grave I should prefer: to lie in the still, still forest, and no hand ever disturb my bones. The graves at home always seemed to me to be miserable, especially

those in the cold damp clay, and without elbow room; but I have nothing to do but wait till He who is over all decided where I have to lay me down and die.[32]

15

Livingstone and Imperialism

Mythic status has been thrust upon Livingstone: as a saintly hero of Protestantism, as an icon of imperialism, as a leading embodiment of resurgent Scottish self-consciousness, and lastly, in the 1960s, as the patron saint of African nationalism.[1] At the dedication of the new monument to Livingstone at Chitambo's, President Kaunda of Zambia led the singing and dancing and referred to Livingstone as 'the first freedom fighter'. This image has lasted into the twenty-first century and is marked by the towns of Livingstone in Zambia and Blantyre in Malawi continuing to bear these names, in stark contrast with the hundreds of African towns and cities whose European names were changed, in the middle third of the twentieth century, to the old African name for the locality.

David Livingstone was a more complex person than can be captured by any of these myths, but Livingstone as patron saint of African nationalism is closer to who he was than the others. For ordinary mortals to be made into heroic figures by others there must at least be something in the potential hero to build on. Secondly, there must be an audience wanting to hear the hero's story. There were obvious signs of such readiness within British society, even before Livingstone died. Stanley, whose *How I Found Livingstone* went through three editions in its first year of publication, 1872, went on a very popular speaking tour of Britain and was met generally with a widespread hunger for stories of Livingstone. In Scotland the public response was particularly impressive. It was small donations by ordinary Scots that financed the creation of the Livingstone Memorial Centre in Blantyre, Lanarkshire.

By the time news reached London of the efforts to return Livingstone's body to Britain, popular biographies of Livingstone had already begun to appear. Ranged from folio-sized volumes with a profusion of illustrative line drawings to cheaply produced publications that were little more than tracts, they sold well. The mounting of eight different expeditions to find Livingstone in the previous four years had led various publishers to realise that material about him was likely to attract sales.

This widespread interest in Livingstone, however, appears to have take Disraeli's newly formed Tory administration completely by surprise.[2] The government view was that they were responsible for getting the body of this eccentric British consul to Southampton. Thereafter what was done with it was the responsibility of the Livingstone family and their friends. Unknown to the government, A. P. Stanley, the Dean of Westminster Abbey, had already written to the Royal Geographical Society informing them that he had arranged a burial place in the abbey for Livingstone, should the family and the RGS wish him to be buried there. With this encouragement the President of the RGS, Sir Bartle Frere, asked the government for a grant to pay for a suitable funeral for Livingstone in the abbey.

The government was at first inclined to refuse this. Some of its members still believed that the story of the body brought to the coast by an African-led expedition was probably a hoax, perpetrated, the Chancellor of the Exchequer suggested, by Bennett and Stanley. Pressure on the government, however, increased as their own backbenchers entered the fray, led by Russell Gurney, MP for Southampton, who, in the House of Commons, called on the government to provide a public funeral for Livingstone. Finally the government agreed reluctantly to a grant of £250 to the RGS towards Livingstone's funeral, which the society arranged with the eager cooperation of Dean Stanley.[3] At Southampton, the corporation, the local Volunteer Regiment and the general public gave Livingstone's body a hero's welcome entirely on their own initiative.[4] In London there followed a lying-in-state at the headquarters of the RGS, with flowers from Queen Victoria herself on the coffin. Then came the virtual 'state' funeral, again with a personal wreath from the Queen on the casket, as it was borne to the abbey through massive crowds who had gathered along the route, followed by the royal carriage as mark of her grief and concern.

A flood of publications then appeared, many of them of a more substantial nature than the first efforts of 1873–74. Horace Waller's two-volume edition of Livingstone's *Last Journals* and W. G. Blaikie's *The Personal Life of David Livingstone* are the fundamental texts upon which the subsequent popular works have been based. These works, complemented by countless sermons, lectures, magazine and newspaper articles, created the iconic Livingstone, patron saint of imperialism and the ideal Protestant missionary. H. M. Stanley's lectures and publications had been a powerful element in the creation of the image of the Protestant saint, but the foremost and most effective propagator of this image was Waller. In addition to editing and publishing *The Last Journals*, Waller also maintained a regular and purposeful correspondence in the *Times* and other publications to keep the dead hero in the public eye.

There was no one key figure in the creation of Livingstone as patron saint of imperialism. In some ways it was the leading imperialist politicians of

Europe who seized on his popularity and used it. In the decade of the Scramble for Africa, 1885 to 1895, when Africa was parcelled up by the powers of Europe, leading imperialist statesmen and political commentators were agreed in describing the movement as Europe's response to Livingstone's famous appeal to the outside world to intervene to end the east African slave trade. The whole effort was one intended to fulfil Livingstone's dream of a peaceful and prosperous development of Africa. Even King Leopold of the Belgians made this claim as he carved out his massive private fiefdom, the Congo Free State, with appalling abuse and cruelty.

This was an era of sordid exploitation but also of genuine paternalism epitomised by Kipling's 'Take up the whiteman's burden'. Both Leopold's ruthlessness and the paternalism of the liberal imperialists, with their ideal of 'trusteeism', were shaped by the intellectual dominance in European and American thought of an amalgam of ideas developed from Social Darwinism, Scientific Racism and Anglo-Saxonism. The overwhelming authority of these ideas penetrated into mainstream Christian and missionary thinking.[5] Their impact was such that Livingstone as the patron saint of liberal imperialism and Livingstone the patron saint of Protestantism became almost one. Thus a writer for a prominent non-political Protestant organisation, the Sunday School Union, could, in 1910, publish a life of Livingstone which presented Livingstone as the ideal missionary and patron saint of liberal imperialism. The author, Edward Hume, ended the preface to his biography thus:

> It is not too much to say that the work of exploration and development carried on by his successors has been made easier by the perfect frankness with which he dealt with the coloured races of Africa.
>
> In such a sense, therefore, Livingstone still lives. And as confidence in the honesty of purpose of the governing race will need to be the foundation of British rule in South and Central Africa, as it has been in India, so the man whose labours resulted in strengthening this reputation for fairness has a claim on Anglo-Saxon gratitude which each year should see deepened and extended.[6]

For a hundred years the literature relating to Livingstone has been either of the iconic kind or, when aiming to be critical, of a style which still focused on the icon. Too often what has been written about Livingstone has dominated the discussion of Livingstone, not what he wrote himself. In the intellectual quest of the early twentieth century for the 'Historical Jesus' the problem was that all scholars had to study were sources that were written by others about Jesus, so they agonised over whether it was possible to encounter the 'historical Jesus'. In the case of Livingstone there is a mass of material written by him to work from, but so much has the iconic literature shaped the agenda that much of what he wrote has been ignored

or overlooked. Much of what he wrote did not fit into the picture writers
wanted to paint, even writers close to him like Waller. Waller, for example,
edited out Livingstone's sympathetic references to the work of the Jesuits.
Waller was not alone. Most writers working with Livingstone's letters and
journals have relegated to the periphery his admiration for the Jesuits,
expressed on many occasions from the time of his visit to Loanda onwards.
Livingstone's explicit adoption of Boniface's ninth-century missionary approach to Germany as the model for the Christian mission to central Africa
has never been discussed at all. Livingstone was fitted into a conventional
Protestant image to which he did not conform. Astonishingly, in the late
twentieth century distinguished scholars were still referring to his Scottish
Calvinism, when, in fact, he grew up in an evangelical atmosphere where
some of the key tenets of Scottish Calvinism had been specifically rejected.
Livingstone was Scottish but never a Calvinist.

In the matter of imperialism, the widespread understanding of Livingstone
that could produce Hume's biography is all the more puzzling because it
contradicts what Livingstone stood for throughout his life. Hume wrote at
the beginning of the twentieth century, but as late as the hundredth anniver-
sary of his death Livingstone could still be described as a liberal paternalist
and colonialist.[7] This was said of a man who left southern Africa to get away
from the impact on Africans of white settlers, who sided with the Xhosa in
the War of Mlanjeni, a man who acted as an *nduna* of the Kololo *morafe*,
and who wept over the deaths of 'some fine young men whom I knew and
loved' after the Transvaalers attack on Sechele and the Kwena.[8]

The misunderstanding of what Livingstone wrote and said was also created
in part by the difference between the unconscious presuppositions in the
minds of those who read his words in the four decades after 1880 and the
presuppositions which shaped his thinking. Livingstone took as given the
equality of all humankind and their shared basic human rights. After 1880
people came to take immutable divisions between different kinds of humans
as proven. This also affected the language with which Africans were described. To Livingstone 'savage' was a cultural condition that could apply
to whites as well as Africans. By the 1880s, 'savage' or 'native' had become
code words for the darker-skinned peoples of the earth. These different
presuppositions and changes in understanding can excuse some confusion
about what Livingstone meant, yet much that he wrote was utterly unambiguous. No later colonialist would have written as Livingstone wrote of the
Xhosa attempt to defend their autonomy, at a time when an official British
document referred to them as 'irreclaimable savages':

But while England had been sympathising with the struggles for freedom which she herself knows so well how to enjoy, she has been struggling to crush a nation fighting as bravely for nationality as ever Magyar did ... We are no advocates for war but we would prefer perpetual war to perpetual slavery. No nation ever secured its freedom without fighting for it. And ever nation on earth worthy of freedom is ready to shed blood in its defence. In sympathising with the Caffres we side with the weak against the strong.[9]

Nevertheless the Livingstone of Hume's book and of many others about him did appear as a paternalist and a colonialist. These writers portrayed a patron saint who was needed not only morally to justify but also morally to glorify the British Empire. This attitude of mind helped create an ideal that made the British colonial administration, at its best, a not unworthy institution. This was attested to by the conflicts between colonial administrators and white settlers. It was also endorsed by the crowds of Africans who, in the early 1900s, left good agricultural land in Mozambique on the Ntcheu border of Mozambique and Malawi to crowd onto the agriculturally less attractive hillsides on the British side of the border. When the only choice available was between the British and the Portuguese colonial administrations, the people showed their preference by voting with their feet.

Except for a few months in 1857 when he appeared to have toyed with the idea in discussions with the Duke of Argyll and some Cambridge dons, Livingstone was a consistent opponent of white rule in Africa and of large-scale white settlement. The Cambridge episode was an aberration and the idea of 'colony' he used from 1860 until his death was best exemplified by the Blantyre Mission in southern Malawi in the 1880s and 1890s. It operated as one community among neighbouring African communities; David Scott led it as its chief, recognised as such by the neighbouring chiefs.[10] Scott's Blantyre Mission was Livingstone's idea of a 'colony', a small Christian missionary community intended to act, with the cooperation of the African Lakes Company, as a cultural and economic as well as religious catalyst within African society.

Livingstone's dream of Christianity and commerce, combining to produce what W. W. Rostow has called 'take-off' in terms of Africa's development, we now agree was not capable of being fulfilled. The demand of the industrialised countries for ivory, combined with the East African slave trade, was barrier enough to the achievement of that hope being realised, even before the powerful worldwide imperialist expansion of the industrialised countries in the last decades of the nineteenth century finally killed it. That Livingstone's dream was an impossible one does not alter the fact that spontaneous 'take-off' was his dream for Africa, with no place or need for 'Rhodesian' European settlement or for European rule. The truth underlying what he said of himself in South Africa in 1852 was still true at his death:

> There is not a native in the country but knows now for certain whose side I am on.[11]

Notes

Notes to Introduction

1. In effect, within a few decades of the crushing of the rebellion which ended the old way of life for all Highlanders, rebel or not, clan chiefs were transformed into landowners who sought profits from the land not warriors.

Notes to Chapter 1: The Displaced Gael

1. The family name was spelt with and without a final e at different times in David's lifetime but, except in direct quotations, it will be spelt with a final e throughout this text. A 'single-end' was a one room flat with bed recesses in a tenement building and could still be found in Glasgow and other Scottish cities in the 1940s.
2. R. J. Campbell, *Livingstone* (London, 1929), p. 35, where he quotes a letter from Chamberlin asserting that the tradition was still strong in Appin.
3. Archibald McArthur was a leading Gaelic scholar and one of the translators of the Bible in 'modern' Scots Gaelic that was published in 1801.
4. Reproduced in Campbell, *Livingstone*, p. 31. The original is in the hands of the Livingstone family.
5. David Livingstone, *Missionary Travels and Researches in South Africa* (London, 1857), pp. 1–2.
6. NLS, MS 10767, Janet Livingstone's notes for Dr Blaikie.
7. Classical or Literary Gaelic was the written form of the language used by the literate elite in both Scotland and Ireland into the eighteenth century, though the spoken forms of the language in the two areas had begun to deviate one from the other in the late middle ages.
8. Livingstone, *Missionary Travels*, p. 11.
9. NLS, MS 10767, Janet Livingstone's notes for Dr Blaikie
10. The Hunters were Seceders and Agnes, David's mother, had been put off religious controversy forever because of their constant quarrelling about the Covenants, so central to Scottish political as well as religious history.
11. NLS, MS 10767.
12. NLS, MS 10767. The Relief Church was part of an earlier Calvinist secession from the Established Church.
13. Livingstone, *Missionary Travels*, p. 3.
14. David Livingstone to J. S. and Emily Moffat, 20 October 1858, recorded in J. P. R. Wallis (ed.), *The Matabele Mission* (London, 1945).

15. Livingstone, *Missionary Travels*, p. 15.
16. NLS, MS 10767.
17. The 'sister' organisation of the London Missionary Society. For the beginning of medical missions, see Andrew C. Ross, 'The Scottish Missionary Doctor', in D. A. Dow (ed.), *The Influence of Scottish Medicine* (Park Ridge, New Jersey, 1988).
18. SOAS, CWM Archives, Africa Odds, box 3, Neil Livingstone to Tidman, 26 April 1838.
19. Now Strathclyde University, which deliberately named the building in which it housed its Centre for Development Studies, Livingstone House.
20. James Graham, James Young of Paraffin Oil fame, Lyon Playfair, James Thompson and William Thompson were all there at that time.

Notes to Chapter 2: A Student in Glasgow and London

1. In the western Highlands and Islands the sheer size of the parishes meant that a school in every parish was gravely inadequate to the needs of the population.
2. T. C. Smout, *A History of the Scottish People, 1560–1830* (London, 1990), pp. 424–32.
3. David Livingstone, *Missionary Travels and Researches in South Africa* (London, 1857), pp. 3, 4, 6, 7.
4. R. D. Anderson, *Education and Opportunity in Victorian Scotland* (Edinburgh, 1989), p. 4.
5. NLS, MS 10767, Janet Livingstone's notes for Dr Blaikie.
6. SOAS, CWM Archives, Africa Odds, box 3, Neil Livingstone to LMS, 26 April 1838.
7. NLS, MS 10767, Janet Livingstone's notes.
8. 'So-called' because it dealt with areas of study which would now be in a Physics or Electrical Engineering department. James and William Thomson, two of Britain's leading physicists of the second half of the century, had their interest in science aroused there.
9. Playfair was later Professor of Chemistry, University of Edinburgh, 1858–69, then a Liberal MP and member of Gladstone's third administration. He became Deputy Speaker of the House of Commons in 1880 and was elevated to the House of Lords in 1890.
10. Livingstone, *Travels*, p. 455; M. Gelfand, *Livingstone the Doctor: His Life and Travels* (Oxford, 1957), p. 96.
11. Timothy Holmes (ed.), *David Livingstone, Letters and Documents: The Zambian Collection* (London, 1990), p. 40.
12. Richard Lovett, *The History of the London Missionary Society* (London, 1899), i, p. 50.
13. 'Essay on Holy Spirit', submitted to the directors of the LMS. Included in the Rev. John Moir's letter to the LMS, 10 September 1837. SOAS, CWM Archives, Africa Odds, box 3.

14. He explains the meaning of this phrase very clearly in the preface to his book, *Researches in South Africa* (London, 1828).

15. Livingstone passionately defended Finney against his close friend D. G. Watt's conservative condemnation, in Livingstone to Watt, 27 September 1843, CWM Archives, Livingstone Papers, box 11.

16. See George Shepperson, 'The Free Church and American Slavery', *Scottish Historical Review*, 30 (1951), pp. 126–43. Shepperson describes the controversy about money raised in America to support the Free Church, some of it raised from slaveholders. The appeal to 'send the money back' from a Finneyite minority of evangelicals was rejected by the majority.

17. W. G. Blaikie, *The Personal Life of David Livingstone* (London, 1880), pp. 26–27.

18. NLS, MS 1707, Moore's notes for Blaikie.

19. SOAS, CWM Archives, Africa Odds, box 3, Richard Cecil to directors of LMS, 26 January 1839.

20. SOAS, CWM Archives, Africa Odds, box 3, David Livingstone to John Arundel, 2 July 1839.

21. Livingstone wrote to her regularly for the next twelve years.

22. Blaikie, *Personal Life*, pp. 34–35.

23. Ibid., pp. 31–32.

24. NLS, MS 10707, David Livingstone to Arthur Tidman, April 1840.

25. NLS, MS 10707, David Livingstone to Henry Dickson, 8 May 1840.

26. Livingstone, *Travels*, p. 16.

27. NLS, MS 10767, Janet Livingstone's notes.

28. This is most fully developed in T. Holmes, *Journey to Livingstone* (Edinburgh, 1993).

29. The correspondence can be found in NLS, MS 10779.

30. All of these letters can also be found in T. Holmes (ed.), *David Livingstone: Letters and Documents* (London, 1990), pp. 6–24.

31. Exeter Hall was a large hall in the Strand where the Antislavery Society, the LMS and other philanthropic and evangelical groups held their annual general meetings. This name became a shorthand among white settlers in South Africa, Australia and New Zealand and their supporters for what they saw as meddlesome liberal interference in their dealings with indigenous peoples.

Notes to Chapter 3: The LMS and Southern Africa

1. See John de Gruchy (ed.), *The London Missionary Society in Southern Africa, 1799–1999* (Cape Town, 2000).

2. Known in older literature as Hottentots, an unacceptable term in the eyes of people of Khoi ancestry.

3. Andrew C. Ross, *John Philip: Missions, Race and Politics in South Africa, 1775–1851* (Aberdeen, 1986); W. M. Macmillan, *Bantu, Boer and Briton* (Oxford, 1963).

4. See Ross, *John Philip*, pp. 102–11.

5. Some groups waited till the end of the Xhosa war, but the planning of this emigration had started in 1830.

6. This whole episode is known in South African historiography by its Xhosa name *difaqane* or the Tswana equivalent *mfecane*.

7. The *Grahamstown Journal* was the newspaper of the British settler community in the eastern part of the colony and its editor was one of the leaders of that community.

8. The Griquas of Philippolis and Griquatown were organised as two independent mini-states led by Christian mixed race families but attracted runaway slaves and marginalised Tswana groups to join them, creating a new nation.

9. Rheinische Missiongesellschaft, a missionary society supported by the Protestant churches of the Rhineland.

Notes to Chapter 4: Kuruman and Mabotsa

1. NLS, MS 10779 (20), Livingstone to Prentice, 27 January 1841.

2. Ibid.

3. NLS, MS 10779 (20) Livingstone to Prentice, 17 March 1841.

4. Tim Jeal, *Livingstone* (London, 1973), p. 25.

5. Livingstone to D. G. Watt, 7 July 1841, NLS, MS 10778.

6. Livingstone, *Missionary Travels*, pp. 12, 16.

7. Blaikie, *Personal Life*, p. 38.

8. NLS, MS 10779 (20), Livingstone to Prentice, 3 August 1841.

9. SOAS, CWM Archives, Africa Odds, box 3, Livingstone to D. G. Watt, 7 July 1841.

10. See Ross, *John Philip*, pp. 133–34.

11. SOAS, CWM Archives, Africa, wooden box of Livingstone letters, Livingstone to D. G. Watt, 7 July 1841.

12. Ibid.

13. SOAS, CWM Archives, Africa, wooden box of Livingstone letters, Livingstone to D. G. Watt, 17 January 1847.

14. NLS, MS 10778, letters to J. J. Freeman and John Arundel of the LMS and to Dr J. Risdon Bennett and Benjamin Pyne, all dated 22 December 1841.

15. NLS, MS 10778, Livingstone to Arthur Tidman, 30 October 1843.

16. NLS, MS 10777 (19), Livingstone to H. M. Dyke, 24 February 1843.

17. Livingstone, *Missionary Travels*, pp. 21–22.

18. NLS, MS 10778, Livingstone to Watt, 27 September 1843.

19. NLS, MS 10701, fos 14–15, Livingstone to Janet and Agnes Livingstone, 8 December 1841.

20. NLS, MS 10779 (8), Livingstone to Richard Cecil, 13 May 1841.

21. NLS, MS 10780 (3), Livingstone to Mary Moffat, 1 August 1844.

22. NLS, MS 10780 (3), Livingstone to Mary Moffat, 12 September 1844.

23. NLS, MS 3650, fos 151–52, Livingstone to Pyne, 28 January 1845.

24. SOAS, CWM Archives, Africa, wooden box of Livingstone letters, Livingstone to Tidman, 30 December 1847.

25. Bertram Wyatt-Brown, *Southern Honor* (New York, 1982), is a study of this phenomenon among the whites of the Southern States and its impact on the history of the South.
26. This phenomenon is well illustrated William McIlvaney's novel *Docherty*, and in plays based on working-class culture in the west of Scotland such as *Just Another Saturday*, *The Slab Boys* or Peter Mullan's award-winning 1997 film *Orphans*.
27. Oliver Ransford, *David Livingstone: The Dark Interior* (London, 1978), pp. 1–5.

Notes to Chapter 5: Kolobeng and the North

1. See P. Sanders, *Moshoeshoe, Chief of the Sotho* (London, 1975).
2. NLS, MS 10701, fos 42–43, Livingstone to Mrs N. Livingstone, 4 May 1847.
3. SOAS, CWM Archives, Africa Odds, box 3, Livingstone to Arthur Tidman, 17 March 1847.
4. NLS, MS 10779 (20), Livingstone to D. G. Watt, 13 February 1848.
5. Steele ended his career as General Sir Thomas Steele. He was a pallbearer at Livingstone's funeral. Pringle died young.
6. Copies of these letters, which are held in private hands, are now available in NLS, MS 10777 (10aa). They were not available to early biographers of Livingstone.
7. Livingstone to Oswell, 22 March 1847, reproduced in Timothy Holmes (ed.), *David Livingstone Letters and Documents: The Zambian Collection* (London, 1990), pp. 24–25.
8. The Portuguese knew this already but their reports were not widely available.
9. NLS, MS 10780 (6), Livingstone to Moffat, 18 September 1850.
10. The full text of the letter can be found in I. Schapera (ed.), *Livingstone's Private Journals, 1851–1853* (London, 1960), pp. 70–71.
11. See Schapera, *Private Journals*, entry for 6 August 1851, p. 46.
12. Schapera, *Private Journals*, pp. 16–22, 56–60.
13. The Botletle was also known to some as the Zouga and this was name by which the child was known to the rest of the family.
14. Later some Protestant churches recognised an existing polygamous relationship, baptising all its members and accepting them at communion though none so baptised could hold office in the church. At the same time they insisted that an already baptised Christian could not legitimately enter a polygamous marriage.
15. NLS, MS 10780 (6), Livingstone to Moffat, 29 November 1851.
16. The original of this is lost. Blaikie preserved some of it in his *The Personal Life of David Livingstone* (London, 1880), p. 131, but he cut out what followed the extract above until the formal and pious end paragraph of the letter, which was dated 5 May 1852 at Cape Town.

Notes to Chapter 6: South African Politics

1. Andrew C. Ross, *John Philip: Missions, Race and Politics in South Africa, 1775–1851* (Aberdeen, 1986), pp. 199–209.
2. The principal chief among the Xhosa was, as with the majority of the peoples southern and eastern Africa, the ultimate judge in all disputes among the lesser chiefs and headmen. He did not have the kind of authority that made the Zulu 'king' an exception among the peoples of southern Africa.
3. NLS, MS 10778, Livingstone to Thompson, 6 September 1852.
4. Ibid.
5. I. Schapera (ed.), *David Livingstone's Private Journals, 1851–53* (London, 1960), p. 82.
6. National Archives of Zimbabwe, MS L 1/1/1.
7. Many of Livingstone's biographers have not noted its existence, let alone dealt with the ideas it contains. Some have suggested it was not sent, but it was. See NLS, MS 10778, Livingstone to Thompson, 24 November 1842, where Livingstone explicitly stated that he had posted the article to the *British Quarterly*.
8. In the Zimbabwe National Archives at Harare, several sheets of alternative drafts of different parts of the article have survived, as well as the final text, further indicating that its writing had been a long process.
9. Hogge to Grey, 19 December 1851, quoted in J. S. Galbraith, *Reluctant Empire: British Policy on the South African Frontier* (Los Angeles, 1963), p. 287.
10. *Speeches, Letters and Selections from Important Papers of the Late John Mitford Bowker*, facsimile reprint (Cape Town, 1962), pp. 116–25.
11. Quoted in J. J. Freeman, *A Tour of South Africa*, (London, 1851), pp. 212–13.
12. See T. F. Gossett, *Race: The History of an Idea in America* (New York, 1996); and K. Malik, *The Meaning of Race* (London, 1996).
13. Schapera, *Private Journals*, pp. 187–88.
14. See Christine Bolt, *Victorian Attitudes to Race* (London, 1971); Gossett, *Race*; and K. Malik, *The Meaning of Race*.
15. John Wesley, *Thoughts on Slavery* (London, 1792), p. 4.
16. In 1833 the constitution of the American Anti-Slavery Society called for immediate abolition and the immediate granting of civil rights to the freed slaves while by 1890 it would be difficult to find a white proponent of equal civil rights for African-Americans.
17. NLS, MS 10778, Livingstone to William Thompson, July 1852. This remark is not without its implications as to why Mary and the children went to Scotland in 1851 and not to Kuruman.
18. This is a reference to Dr Robertson, one of the many Scots ministers then serving the Dutch Reformed Church of South Africa, the state-supported church of the colony, who had several times visited the Transvaalers, baptising children and serving communion. Livingstone had met him and been deeply upset by Robertson's complete support of the Transvaalers.

19. NLS, MS 10778, Livingstone to William Thompson, 30 September 1852.
20. National Archives of Zimbabwe, L 1/1/1.
21. NLS, MS 10701, Livingstone to parents and sisters, 28 July 1850.
22. NLS, MS 10778, Livingstone to Arthur Tidman, 2 November 1852.
23. The eighteenth-century exploration by Portuguese travellers of parts of the area to which he was going was virtually unknown outside Portugal. The arrival of the Portuguese speaking slave traders at Sebitwane's at the time of Livingstone and Oswell's visit to Sebitwane's made Livingstone feel that it was all the more urgent that he open up the area to Christianity and civilisation.

Notes to Chapter 7: Coast to Coast

1. These extracts are to be found in William Monk, *Dr Livingstone's Cambridge Lectures* (London, 1860), pp. 251–53.
2. I have found no record of whether it was ever sent to either of these publications.
3. In his *Missionary Travels and Researches in South Africa* (London, 1857), Livingstone wrote that the Portuguese traders who had penetrated the area had been of mixed race and not true Portuguese, so he was the first European to enter the region and to cross Africa. This strange assertion does not appear in his journals. It was a transparent piece of nonsense but his mid-Victorian readers appear not to have cared; at least no one objected.
4. John Leyden, *Historical Account of Discoveries and Travels in Africa* (Edinburgh, 1817); Hugh Murray, *Narrative of Discovery and Adventure in Africa* (Edinburgh, 1832); and Mrs Holland, *Africa Described in its Ancient and Present State* (London, 1834). I owe this information to my colleague Dr Jack Thompson.
5. NLS, MS 10780 (6), Livingstone to Mary Moffat, 26 September 1855.
6. There is no original copy of this letter available. It can be found in W. G. Blaikie, *The Personal Life of David Livingstone* (London, 1880) pp. 180–81.
7. NLS, MS 10707, Livingstone to Charles Livingstone, 6 February 1853.
8. I. Schapera (ed.), *Livingstone's Private Journals* (London, 1960), pp. 97–98.
9. Ibid., p. 261.
10. Ibid., p. 105.
11. Webb, whom Livingstone had nursed back to health after Webb had come near to death in the Kalahari, was the owner of Newstead Abbey where in 1864–65 Livingstone spent several happy months with his daughter Agnes.
12. D. Livingstone, *Missionary Travels and Researches in South Africa* (London, 1857), p. 175.
13. Schapera, *Private Journals*, p. 128. Here Schapera notes that 'the words are pure Tswana'.
14. Livingstone, *Travels and Researches*, pp. 195–96.
15. The Mambari were the agents of the Angolan slave trade.
16. *Morafe* is the Sotho/Tswana word for a major autonomous political unit. It is more appropriate to use it in conjunction with the Kololo than nation or

state. These English words carry connotations not present in *morafe*, which represents a much less structured and more loosely defined entity.

17. Schapera, *Livingstone's Private Journals*, p. 212.

18. *Nduna* is an officer of a principal chief whose authority is given by the chief and not one he has in his own right.

19. The slaves had been shipped from Benguela to Brazil until 1850, when British cruisers had cut off this trade. Slaves brought from the interior were after that used to develop plantation agriculture in Angola itself.

20. NLS, MS 10780 (6), Livingstone to Moffat, 16 September 1853. The incident is also described in Schapera, *Private Journals*, pp. 181–84.

21. Livingstone, *Missionary Travels*, p. 516.

22. NLS, MS 10777 (10aa), Livingstone to Steele, 23 September 1853.

23. Livingstone, *Missionary Travels*, p. 272.

24. Ibid., pp. 252–53.

25. Ibid., p. 289.

26. I. Schapera (ed.), *Livingstone's African Journal, 1853–1856*, 2 vols (London, 1963), i, p. 57.

27. The *Forerunner* sank on the trip to Britain and Bedingfeld was one of the very few who survived. All Livingstone's notes were lost but he recreated them from memory while staying with Colonel Pires in December 1854.

28. Livingstone, *Missionary Travels*, p. 408.

29. NLS, MS 10775 (1), 23 July 1855, reproduced in Schapera (ed.), *Livingstone's African Journal*, ii, p. 278.

30. Livingstone referred to Habib as Rya Side.

31. NLS, MS 10775 (1) 2 September 1855, reproduced in Schapera (ed.), *Livingstone's African Journal*, ii, pp. 196–96.

32. NLS, MS 10778, Livingstone to Arthur Tidman, 12 October 1855.

33. Ibid.

34. Andrew C. Ross, *A Vision Betrayed: The Jesuits in Japan and China, 1542–1742* (New York, 1994), pp. 143–45.

35. Schapera has pointed out in a footnote in his *Livingstone's African Journal*, ii, p. 326, that the first hint of using this name appeared in a letter to Lord Clarendon, sent from Tete on 19 March 1856 at a later stage of this journey.

36. Livingstone, *Travels and Researches*, pp. 520–21.

37. Schapera, *African Journal*, ii, pp. 346–47.

38. Schapera, *African Journal*, ii, p. 373.

39. Livingstone, *Missionary Travels*, p. 590.

40. Temperatures of over 100 degrees are common in the Zambesi valley in the hot season, the season in which Livingstone was travelling.

41. Livingstone, *Missionary Travels*, p. 504.

42. These peoples were matrilocal in that the husband went to stay at his wife's village and matrilineal in that titles and other important matters of ancestry were cheifly always traced through the mother's family.

43. 'A hundred thousand welcomes', with which every verse of the poem opens, is a translation of the traditional Gaelic welcome, *cued mile failte.*

Notes to Chapter 8: Years of Triumph

1. It was this kind of endorsement that led to Livingstone's being made a Fellow of the Royal Society in 1858, the scientific community's highest accolade.
2. Report in the *Times* of 16 December 1856, my italics.
3. W. Monk (ed.), *Dr Livingstone's Cambridge Lectures* (Cambridge, 1858), p. vii. Monk had to insist at this point in his preface that human equality was basic to everything Livingstone said and did. Monk was clearly aware that people were not hearing though they had ears to hear.
4. It seems that he went without Mary on this visit.
5. Neil Livingstone to Arthur Tidman, 24 June 1853, CWM Archives.
6. Richard Owen, *The Life of Sir Richard Owen* (London, 1894), ii, pp. 25–26.
7. Governor Eyre suppressed a rebellion in Jamaica with great ferocity. The missionary and humanitarian lobby sought to have him tried for murder. Dickens was one of a powerful lobby led by the Anthropological Society which supported Eyre, who was tried but acquitted.
8. This tradition was carried into the 1960s in Eric Stokes and Richard Brown (eds), *The Zambesian Past* (Manchester, 1966).
9. NLS, MS 10709, David Livingstone to Lord Clarendon, 19 March 1857.
10. David Livingstone, *Missionary Travels and Researches in South Africa* (London, 1857), p. 677, my italics.
11. *Dr Livingstone's Cambridge Lectures*, p. 168.
12. The UMCA joined with the Society for the Propagation of the Gospel in 1970 to form the United Society for the Propagation of the Gospel (USPG).
13. Quoted in Blaikie, *Personal Life*, p. 216.
14. SOAS, CWM Archives, Africa, wooden box of Livingstone letters, Livingstone to D. G. Watt, 17 January 1847.

Notes to Chapter 9: The Zambesi Expedition

1. *Hansard*, third series, vol. cxlviii (1857/58), p. 558.
2. David Livingstone, *Missionary Travels and Researches in South Africa* (London, 1857), p. 677.
3. NLS, MS 10709 (43), Livingstone to Lord Clarendon, 19 March 1857.
4. NLS, MS 10779 (20), Livingstone to H. E. Stephens, 11 December 1857.
5. Livingstone and Washington became friends, despite Livingstone's rejection of the latter's plan.
6. NLS, MS 10780 (6), Livingstone to Clarendon, 7 January 1858.
7. The letter is reproduced in W. G. Blaikie, *The Personal Life of David Livingstone* (London, 1880), pp. 487–89.
8. The status of the Zambesi as an international waterway remained an area of

controversy between Portugal and Britain until 1889. See A. C. Ross, *Blantyre Mission and the Making of Modern Malawi* (Blantyre, Malawi, 1996), pp. 107–8.

9. NLS, MS 10777 (19), Livingstone to Hudson Gurney, 6 December 1857.

10. Sir Joseph Hooker was Director of Kew Gardens; his son, Dr J. D. Hooker, was his assistant and successor.

11. NLS, MS 10780 (6), Livingstone to Lord Clarendon, 7 January 1858.

12. Zimbabwe National Archives, L1 1/1/1, Livingstone to Thomas Maclear, 10 September 1858.

13. NLS, MS 10780 (6), Livingstone to Lord Clarendon, 7 January 1858.

14. The sole exception is Timothy Holmes, who in his *Journey to Livingstone* (Edinburgh, 1993), p. 151, commented on 'Baines's pride in having been a good Kaffer-shooter' without any reference for his authority for the statement.

15. J. P. R. Wallis, *Thomas Baines of King's Lynn* (London, 1941), pp. 64 and 70.

16. Ibid., p. 83.

17. The other children were under the care of trustees, with a trust fund of over £5000 pounds at their disposal for the care of the children. Agnes was left in the care of Grandmother Livingstone and the two aunts in Hamilton, while Robert and Thomas were left in boarding school.

18. Reginald Foskett (ed.), *The Zambesi Journal and Letters of Dr John Kirk* (Edinburgh, 1965), i, p. 4.

19. Foskett, *Zambesi Journal*, ii, p. 602.

20. Mary's brother, in his biography of their parents, reported that Mary was too seasick to go on and it was decided she should join Livingstone later on the Zambesi by an overland route. J. S. Moffat, *The Lives of Mary and Robert Moffat* (London, 1886), p. 313.

21. Livingstone and Kirk consistently refer to this building as the 'iron house', even though only the roof was made of corrugated iron.

22. Ship's carpenter Robert Fayers and Mrs Livingstone.

23. The Portuguese landed goods at Quilemane and sent them up the Kwakwe river to a point where it was very close to the Zambesi proper. Then the goods were transferred across a narrow neck of land to canoes on the main river.

24. Foskett, *Zambesi Journal*, i, p. 31, entry for 26 May 1858.

25. Ibid., i, p. 47, entry for 27 June 1858, my italics.

26. Bedingfeld, back in Britain, demanded an enquiry into his 'dismissal'. One was granted but found in Livingstone's favour.

27. Whatever the authorities in Lisbon thought, on the Zambesi, at this time, Livingstone was aided consistently by the local Portuguese authorities.

28. Livingstone to Sir Morton Peto, 17 September 1858, reproduced in Timothy Holmes (ed.), *David Livingstone: Letters and Documents, 1841–1872* (London, 1990), pp. 55–56.

29. J. P. R. Wallis (ed.), *The Zambesi Expedition of David Livingstone* (London, 1956), i, p. 42, entry for 8 September, 1858.

30. Foskett (ed.), *Zambesi Journal*, i, p. 115, entry for 3 November 1858.

31. Foskett, *Zambesi Journal* i, p. 134, entry for 1 December, 1858. Kirk mentions a Kruman but Livingstone recorded that all Africans on that trip were Kololo.

32. J. P. R. Wallis (ed.), *The Zambesi Expedition of David Livingstone* (London, 1965), i, p. 69, entry for 3 December 1858.

33. Wallis, *Zambesi Expedition*, i, p. 86. Entry for 20 February 1859. My italics.

34. The district is known as Chikwawa today.

35. Foskett, *Zambesi Journals*, i, pp. 213–14, entry for 23 June 1859.

36. Ibid., i, p. 156, entry for 17 March 1859.

37. Thornton later rejoined the expedition in 1861.

38. The classic example is Wallis, *Thomas Baines*, p. 180, but it is also found in Jeal, *Livingstone*, pp. 225–29, and Holmes, *Journey to Livingstone*, pp. 179–80. The most thorough treatment of the dismissal of Baines is to be found in G. W. Clendennen (ed.), *David Livingstone's Shire Journal* (Cardiff, 1992), appendix 4.

39. Wallis, *Zambesi Expedition*, i, p. 125, entry for 15 August 1859.

40. Wallis, *Zambesi Expedition*, ii, p. 332, despatch to Lord Malmesbury, 15 October 1859.

41. Foskett, *Zambesi Journal*, i, pp. 263–66, entries for 25 October to 1 November 1859.

Notes to Chapter 10: Linyanti

1. Later the Universities Mission to Central Africa (UMCA) amalgamated in the 1970s with the Society for the Propagation of the Gospel (SPG) to become the USPG.

2. Wallis, *The Zambesi Expedition*, i, p. 156, entry for 6 April 1860.

3. Charles Livingstone is listed as joint author of the *Narrative*, but most authorities agree that his contribution was no more than allowing David to use his diaries and journals.

4. Of the Kololo who had survived, only sixty decided they wished to go back. They set off with Livingstone, but very quickly more than twenty slipped back to Tete.

5. David and Charles Livingstone, *Narrative of an Expedition to the Zambesi and its Tributaries* (London, 1865), p. 210.

6. The witch-finder, *mbisalila* in Nyanja, was a functionary consistently confused with the *ngaka* or *nganga* by European commentators throughout the nineteenth and twentieth centuries. The *ngaka* or *nganga* was and is a healer, whom Livingstone always treated as a medical colleague. The witch-finder is simply he or she who smells out the sorcerers who are deemed to have caused otherwise inexplicable evil events.

7. Foskett, *Zambesi Journal*, ii, appendix 1.

8. Max Gluckman, the *doyen* of anthropologists of the Zambesi region, in a radio broadcast in 1955, suggested that Livingstone probably was not to blame for the mission disaster. What was incontrovertible, Gluckman went on, was rather

that he let down the Kololo *morafe*. This broadcast was printed in the *Listener* of 22 September 1955.

9. SOAS, CWM archives, South Africa, box 31, Robert Moffat to Arthur Tidman, 20 August 1858.
10. NLS, MS 10778, Livingstone to Arthur Tidman, 6 March 1858.
11. See John Mackenzie, *Ten Years North of the Orange River* (Edinburgh, 1871), p. 39.
12. Gelfand, *Livingstone the Doctor*, pp. 159–61, and Ransford, *David Livingstone*, pp. 171–72.
13. See Jeal, *Livingstone*, pp. 176–78, and George Seaver, *David Livingstone: His Life and Letters* (London, 1957), pp. 374–75.
14. One of these, Ramakukane, later became an important chief in the Shire valley and cooperated with the first Scottish missionaries in Malawi. See Ross, *Blantyre Mission*, chapter 3.
15. This has been strongly contested, however, by Gary Clendennen in his persuasively argued doctoral thesis, submitted to Edinburgh University in 1978, 'Charles Livingstone: A Biographical Study'.
16. NLS, MS 10775 (7).
17. Zimbabwe National Archives, ST1/2.

Notes to Chapter 11: Failure and Defeat

1. The Gazankulu Nguni were, like the Ndebele, a people who had broken with Chaka's kingdom and marched north, dominating much of what is now Mozambique south of the Zambesi. They are sometimes referred to as Shangaan or Landeen.
2. The most famous was the article by Bandiera published in Lisbon in January 1861, a translation of part of which can be found in Holmes, *Journey*, pp. 187–89.
3. It was their reports that were the basis of the maps referred to in Chapter 7.
4. He had often tried to get his parents to emigrate to Canada or the USA because of his pessimism about the prospects for working-class people in Britain.
5. Quoted in Seaver, *David Livingstone*, pp. 341–42, from a letter in the Zimbabwe National Archives to be found in L1 1/1/1. Seaver wrongly dates the letter to 5 February; it was 15 February 1859.
6. Livingstone to Miss Burdett-Coutts, Tete, 5 July 1859, reproduced in Monk, ed., *Cambridge Lectures*, pp. 368–70.
7. NLS, MS 10768, Livingstone to Palmerston, 15 January 1861. The Oxford and Cambridge Mission had included in the definition of its objectives 'to encourage the advancement of science and the useful arts'.
8. Kazembe was a powerful chief whose people straddled what is now the border between Zambia and the Congo province of Katanga, south of Lake Mweru.
9. NLS, MS 10768, Livingstone to Palmerston, 20 October 1859.

10. See Ross, *Blantyre Mission*; also J. McCracken, *Politics and Christianity in Malawi* (Cambridge, 1977), which concentrates on Livingstonia Mission.
11. Foskett, *Zambesi Journal*, i, pp. 314–15.
12. Despite his condemnation of the Portuguese in general and their increasing antagonism to him, Livingstone and a number of Portuguese, including Ferrao, Sicard and Nunes, remained good friends to the end.
13. Owen Chadwick, *Mackenzie's Grave* (London, 1959), p. 30.
14. At that time the island was referred to as Johanna by the British.
15. D. and C. Livingstone, *Narrative of an Expedition to the Zambesi and its Tributaries* (London, 1865), p. 352.
16. His writings when he returned to Britain had a devastating effect on Livingstone's reputation.
17. Their route via Mbame's did not vary much from the line of the modern road from Chikwawa on the Shire up to Blantyre in the Shire highlands.
18. H. Goodwin, *Memoir of Bishop Mackenzie* (London, 1865), p. 275.
19. Foskett, *Zambesi Journal*, ii, p. 351, entry for 16 July 1861.
20. It has been asserted that this resulted in the Yao in Malawi becoming Muslim not Christian. This is hardly the case: though many Yao are Muslim, there are also many Yao Christians in Malawi and some of the leaders of the Blantyre Synod of the Church of Central Africa Presbyterian come from Yao families associated with the church since the 1880s.
21. At a spot near Nkhotakhota they burned nearly a thousand slave sticks stockpiled there for further use.
22. They were an Nguni group related to the Ndebele who had broken with Chaka and moved north like the Ndebele and the Gazankulu Nguni.
23. Livingstone, *Narrative*, p. 284.
24. Foskett, *Zambesi Journal*, ii, facing p. 564.
25. J. M. Schoffeleers, 'Livingstone and the Mang'anja Chiefs', in B. Patel, *Livingstone: Man of Africa* (London, 1973).
26. After her return from the Zambesi, Miss Lennox became one of the pioneers of modern nursing and a friend of Florence Nightingale's.
27. The expedition's health record was still extraordinary. From the forty-two Europeans who served with the expedition at one time or another between 1858 and 1863, two only died from malaria. This is to be compared with many other European expeditions which had death rates approaching 90 per cent. The UMCA at Magomero had a 50 per cent death rate.
28. The island no longer exists because of changes in direction taken by the Shire.
29. Charles Livingstone, the newly arrived James Stewart and various naval officers are quoted by most modern biographers of Livingstone, deploring the confusion and his 'woeful want of arrangements'.
30. One of the best treatments of relationship of Mary and Stewart is Sheila Brock, 'James Stewart and David Livingstone', in Patel, *Livingstone*, pp. 86–110.
31. Foskett, *Zambesi Journal*, ii, p. 423, entry for 5 March 1852.
32. Clendennen, *Livingstone's Shire Journal*, entry for 27 April 1862.

33. Ibid., entry for 31 May 1862.
34. Magomero, though surrounded by hills, is three thousand feet above sea level. It became an unhealthy site because a large population lived within a limited area in a siege-like atmosphere without adequate hygienic arrangements so that it was intestinal infections that rendered it unhealthy not malaria. See Kirk's judgement in Foskett, *Zambesi Journal*, ii, p. 423, entry for 4 March 1862.
35. George Shepperson, (ed.) *David Livingstone and the Rovuma* (Edinburgh, 1965). On pp. 28–29, Shepperson shows that Livingstone had decided on the Rovuma trip in July before leaving the Zambesi.
36. Rae, to Livingstone's disgust, insisted after two days that he was too ill to go on and was taken back in a boat to the *Pioneer*.
37. Foskett, *Zambesi Journal*, ii, p. 475, entry for 18 September 1862.
38. As late as the 1950s I knew of African schoolteachers from the Shire highlands who resigned the service rather than accept posting to that district and take their families there.
39. J. P. R. Wallis (ed.), *The Zambesi Journal of James Stewart, 1862–63* (London, 1952), p. 189, entry for 1 February 1863.
40. Ransford, *David Livingstone*, p. 220, 'Livingstone was once again the man of 1854'.
41. Jumbe is the hereditary title of the ruler of Nkhotakhota.
42. At this time Livingstone referred to the African sailors as 'Shupanga men' or 'Zambesians' but they appear to have been seven from the larger group on the Shire whom he had called earlier 'my Mazaro men'.
43. Donald Simpson, *Dark Companions: The African Contribution to the European Exploration of East Africa* (London, 1975), p. 52. Susi, Chuma and Amoda were with Livingstone when he died.
44. *London Missionary Society Chronicle*, December 1912 issue.
45. See plate 7.
46. Seaver, *David Livingstone*, p. 449. Seaver reproduces long extracts from Livingstone's log for the voyage, pp. 440–49.

Notes to Chapter 12: Home and Family

1. Printed in R. Foskett (ed.), *The Zambesi Doctors: David Livingstone's Letters to John Kirk* (Edinburgh, 1964), pp. 63–64.
2. Quoted in W. G. Blaikie, *The Personal Life of David Livingstone* (London, 1880), p. 341.
3. Zimbabwe National Archives, L1 1/1/1.
4. Schapera, *Family Letters*, Livingstone to Charles Livingstone 8 November 1854.
5. The original is in the Zimbabwe National Archives and is reprinted in Seaver, *David Livingstone*, p. 454 (slightly modified), and in Holmes, *Journey*, pp. 209–10. Holmes argues persuasively that, since for a British citizen to join either of the American armies was a criminal offence, Robert was attempting to

cover his criminal act by a claim of having been kidnapped. After all Robert said that he wanted to bring no more shame on the Livingstone name.

6. Seaver, *David Livingstone*, pp. 453–55.

7. Blaikie, *Personal Life*, p. 289.

8. Ransford, *Livingstone*, p. 227.

9. NLS, MS 10779, Livingstone to Oswell, 23 March 1865.

10. See A. K. Fraser, *Livingstone and Newstead* (London, 1913). A. K. Fraser was Alice Webb.

11. James Kirk to James Stewart, 11 February 1864, quoted in Seaver, *Livingstone*, p. 461.

12. Burton had been, in 1863, one of the founding members of the Anthropological Society, which was dedicated to propagating and developing the ideas now referred to as scientific racism.

13. Livingstone to Murray, 30 January 1865. This letter is quoted in Ransford, *Livingstone*, p. 230, and is cited as being in 'the archives of John Murray, publisher'; the letter, however, is not listed in Clendennen and Cunningham's *Catalogue* or in Cunningham's *Supplement*.

14. Ransford, *Livingstone*, p. 238.

15. Some late twentieth-century biographers have misunderstood the mid Victorian use of the word 'clerk' of someone like Murray. He was not a junior but a senior civil servant.

16. Mme Hocédé had been a governess in Queen Victoria's household but had been dismissed when letters from her to her relations in France about Prince Albert's illness were leaked to the press.

17. Fraser, *Livingstone and Newstead*, p. 165.

Notes to Chapter 13: Bombay to Bangweulu

1. Because so many Gujerati businessmen operated out of Zanzibar, the Governor of Bombay exercised some responsibility there through the British consul, who acted as the political agent of the Bombay government.

2. Strangely, however they might differ on other matters, all of Livingstone's biographers agree to translate havildar as corporal, but a havildar in the Indian infantry was the equivalent of sergeant, naik was the equivalent of corporal. This small detachment also included a naik.

3. This was still the case in the First World War where thousands of *tenga-tenga* from Malawi and *kariokor* from Kenya died serving the British forces in German East Africa

4. NLS, MS 10704, Livingstone to Agnes Livingstone. This letter is sometimes dated as 22 January 1865, so how could it tell of events on 29 January? The anomaly is created by Livingstone's habit of starting a letter on one day, then adding another page or so a couple of days later, and even a third section appropriately dated, before the whole was sent off. This letter has three sections dated 22 January, 29 January and 6 February 1866.

5. 'Johanna men' was how the British referred to the porters recruited on Anjoan to work in east Africa.

6. Much earlier Livingstone had written to his old acquaintance Sunley, the British consul on Anjoan, asking him to recruit men for him, but he had received no reply to his letters.

7. These traders in slaves and ivory Livingstone refers to as Arabs but almost all were Muslims from the coast, mostly of mixed Arab-African ancestry, whose native language, Swahili, rapidly became a *lingua franca* in Tanzania, southern Kenya, Uganda and eastern Congo. Swahili is a Bantu language with a large Arabic addition to its vocabulary. I will refer to them as Zanzibari throughout since they were all subjects of the Sultan of Zanzibar.

8. H. Waller (ed.), *Livingstone's Last Journals*, 2 vols (London, 1874), i, pp. 13–14.

9. Ibid., i, p. 84.

10. The havildar begged to be allowed to stay with Livingstone, to which Livingstone agreed. He stayed on until 22 September 1866.

11. Waller, *Last Journals*, i, pp. 90–91.

12. One young boy, who met Livingstone then and never forgot him, became a Christian in the 1880s. Before his baptism he had already composed what has become one of the most popular hymns in Malawi called 'Chibanzi' after the village of which he was chief, no. 21 in the 1954 edition of *Nyimbo Za Mulungu*, the principal Protestant hymnbook in Malawi.

13. The Ngoni did not deal in slaves but captured such children to be adopted into their own families.

14. *Nsima* is thick porridge made usually with maize or millet; it has the consistency of a kind of sticky mashed potato and is the staple food in most of Mozambique, Malawi, Zambia and Zimbabwe.

15. Normal *nsima* made with maize or millet flour and eaten with meat or vegetables is pleasantly filling, but I can testify that eating *nsima* made from *maere*, finger millet, is like eating wet sand.

16. Kazembe's country was that to which the great Portuguese traveller Lacerda had gone in the 1790s. His diary of the trip was translated and annotated by Richard Burton and included in his The *Lands of Cazembe* (London, 1873).

17. Waller, *Last Journals*, i, p. 167.

18. Ibid., i, p. 171.

19. Waller, *Last Journals*, i, p. 205.

20. Waller, *Last Journals*, i, p. 204.

21. He was a fluent speaker of Tswana and he clearly gained reasonable fluency in Nyanja/Chewa – in his notebooks he produced a reasonably good translation of Jesus meeting the Samaritan woman at the well. He was soon to become fluent in Swahili and later competent in Manyema.

22. It has been suggested that the new middle-class prosperity in Britain, with its vastly increasing demand for pianos and billiard tables, greatly contributed to the profitability of this ivory market and so to the east African slave trade.

23. Waller, *Last Journals*, i, p. 259. Modern scholars use the word negro only of west African peoples.
24. It is now referred to on maps by an alternative old local name, the Lovua, since in the mid twentieth century geographers decided that the primary source of the Lualaba or Congo is Livingstone's 'western source' see map on page 201, As late as 1955 Professor Debenham, Professor of Geography at Cambridge, still referred to the Lovua as the Lualaba in his *The Way to Ilala*.
25. Livingstone always referred to him as Bogharib.
26. Waller, *Last Journals*, i, p. 287.
27. *Proceedings of the Royal Geographical Society*, 14 (1869–70), pp. 8–12.
28. F. Debenham, *The Way to Ilala: David Livingstone's Pilgrimage* (London, 1955), p. 234.
29. Waller, *Last Journals*, i, pp. 349–50.
30. Waller, *Last Journals*, ii, p. 2.
31. Ibid. ii, p. 3.
32. Waller, *Last Journals*, i, pp. 306–7.
33. In reality a number of different peoples live in the area, but Livingstone spent most of his time among people of the principal group, the Lega or Rega.
34. Waller, *Last Journals*, ii, p. 21.
35. Ibid., ii, pp. 104–5. The italics are mine.
36. To the west a number of large rivers do rise in close proximity, the Lualaba, Lufira , Zambesi and Kafue. He was told of this place by a number of Zanzibaris, a place of hills from whence rivers flowed to the north and to the south.
37. NLS, MS 10779, Livingstone to W. C. Oswell, October 1869.
38. Eyre had put down a freedman rebellion with unparalleled ferocity. Although criticised by some in Britain, where he was tried and acquitted of wrongdoing, he was supported by such luminaries as the Anthropological Society, Matthew Arnold, Carlyle, Dickens, Tennyson and Ruskin. Eyre retired on a state pension.
39. Waller, *Last Journals*, ii, pp. 9–10.
40. NLS, MS 10780, Livingstone to Agnes Livingstone, September 1869.
41. Waller, *Last Journals*, ii, pp. 32–34.
42. Ibid., ii, p. 118
43. Ibid., ii, p. 37.
44. Waller, *Last Journals*, ii, p. 42, entry for 3 February 1871.
45. The Chambesi, Luapula, Luvua complex of river and lake is one source of the Congo. The other is one that Livingstone posited but did not get to see, which is two small rivers, the Lualaba and Lufira, entering Lake Upemba and emerging as a major river also called Lualaba which the Luvua joined. See map on p. 201.
46. Waller, *Last Journals*, ii, p. 115. Years later European visitors to Nyangwe found he was still remembered as the old man Daoud.
47. Waller, *Last Journals*, ii, p. 139.

Notes to Chapter 14: Last Journeys

1. Waller, *Last Journals*, ii, p. 156.
2. H. M. Stanley, *How I Found Livingstone* (London, 1872), pp. 410–11. Both men realised that they had lost track of the days and, after consulting the Zanzibaris, decided the date was 10 November. Recently Mr I. C. Cunningham of the National Library of Scotland has shown that it was 27 October that Stanley arrived, almost the date 28 October recorded in Livingstone's journal, Livingstone had lost track earlier but had somehow got nearly on track again. I. C. Cunningham, *David Livingstone: A Catalogue of Documents. A Supplement.* (Edinburgh, 1985), pp. 37–41.
3. Rhodes's troops as they attacked Lobengula's Ndebele kingdom in 1893 had the British army's latest machine guns, which the British had not yet used in anger.
4. As late as 1945 Reginald Coupland wrote his *Livingstone's Last Journey* as much to vindicate Kirk and denigrate Stanley as to further understanding of Livingstone.
5. Quoted in N. R. Bennett, *Stanley's Despatches to the New York Herald* (Boston, 1970), p. xxxvi.
6. He later completed a brilliantly and ruthlessly executed crossing of Africa from east to west reported in his *Through the Dark Continent*, 2 vols (London, 1878). He was a pioneer administrator in the Congo Free State. He then returned to Britain, became an MP and was later made a Knight Grand Cross of the Order of the Bath.
7. J. Gordon Bennett bore exactly the same name as his father, a Scots immigrant to the USA, who had founded the *Herald*.
8. Tozer to Steere, 30 September 1869, in USPG Archives, quoted in Bennett, *Stanley's Despatches*, p. 29.
9. Stanley's despatch of 26 December 1871, in Bennett, *Stanley's Despatches*, p. 93.
10. Stanley started off from Bagamoyo with six tons of equipment and 192 men, including two British assistants who both died on the way. He was held up at Tabora by involving himself in the Zanzibari war with Mirambo, which cost him the loss of men as well as time. He reached Ujiji with only fifty-two men.
11. Stanley's despatch of 26 December 1871, reproduced in Bennett, *Stanley's Despatches*, p. 96.
12. Sir Henry Lawrenson, who succeeded Murchison as President of the RGS, on four public occasions after rumours arrived in London that Stanley had 'found' Livingstone, insisted that the 'well supplied' Livingstone had almost certainly 'found' the young American who had lost most of his men in the Arab/Mirambo war. His attitude is a sign that there was a certain complacency that everything needed by Livingstone had been done and that Stanley's criticism of British concern about Livingstone was simply a product of the chip on his shoulder. It was after news of the *Herald*'s initiative that the RGS sponsored a British expedition to find Livingstone.

13. Stanley's despatch of 21 February 1872, reproduced in full in Bennett, *Stanley's Despatches*, p. 120.
14. H. M. Stanley, *How I Found Livingstone* (London, 1872), pp. 622–23.
15. See R. Coupland, *Livingstone's Last Journey* (London, 1945).
16. Agnes to John Murray, 4 January 1873, in the Murray Archives, quoted in Ransford, *David Livingstone*, p. 286.
17. Waller, *Last Journals*, ii, p. 203.
18. See J. V. Taylor, *The Growth of the Church in Buganda* (London, 1958).
19. For some reason the word 'solitude' was inserted instead of 'loneliness' on the inscription on Livingstone's tomb in Westminster Abbey.
20. Waller, *Last Journals*, ii, p. 190. The italics are mine.
21. These letters are listed in Clendennen and Cunningham, *David Livingstone: A Catalogue of Documents* (Edinburgh, 1979), who do not indicate where they may now be found. The contents of the letter to Janet are discussed by George Seaver, who apparently had access to it in the 1950s when preparing his *David Livingstone*. The contents of the letter to John are discussed in Ransford, *David Livingstone* without indicating where he saw the letter.
22. Livingstone to Agnes, 15 August 1872, Clendennen and Cunningham, *A Catalogue*, do not record any location for this letter so all we have available now are the quotations from it in Blaikie, *Personal Life*, p. 444. The italics are mine.
23. Ransford, *David Livingstone*, p. 298.
24. Wallis, *Last Journals*, ii, p. 246 entry for 8 November 1872.
25. Waller, *Last Journals*, ii, p. 275.
26. A hammock slung on a long pole.
27. Livingstone's devoted friend, Waller, did him a disservice when, on the cover of both volumes of his *Livingstone's Last Journals*, he portrayed Livingstone being carried on Chuma's shoulders. This perpetuated an image of the arrogant European and the African as a beast of burden utterly untypical of Livingstone and how he travelled normally.
28. A medical colleague has suggested that this may have been a cancerous tumour. This would have produced arterial blood and in turn fits in with an entry late in his journal where Livingstone says that he found he had passed arterial blood. Haemorrhoids produce venous blood.
29. The text of the letter is reproduced in Campbell, *Livingstone*, p. 332.
30. Cameron then marched on across Africa to Angola and later published *Across Africa* (London, 1877), an account of his adventures.
31. I have to thank my friend from student days in Edinburgh, Sir Kenneth Scott, for the information that the Royal Archives contain the formal note instructing the Royal Mews to provide the two-horse carriage with coachmen in 'full epaulettes' for Dr Livingstone's funeral.
32. Waller, *Last Journals*, i, p. 308. Livingstone added 'Poor Mary lies on Shupanga brae, "and beeks fornent the sun [and basks in the sun]".' I have translated the Scots words which Waller was not able to do. 'Beeks fornent the sun' is very old Scots but the use of the verb 'beek' with regard to the sun can be

found in Gavin Douglas's translation of the *Aeneid* where it is used of 'warriors basking in the sun'. Waller and other writers since have seen this passage as lamenting Mary's place of burial and a sign of deep depression on Livingstone's part. When the old Scots words are understood then his meaning is clear: an assertion of his preference to be buried in Africa rather than Britain and his envy of Mary and her resting place. The adjective 'poor' attached to Mary refers to his recognition of what a hard life she had led and does not refer to her resting place, where she 'basks' in the African sun.

Notes to Chapter 15: Livingstone and Imperialism

1. John M. Mackenzie, 'David Livingstone: The Construction of the Myth', in G. Walker and T. Gallagher, *Sermons and Battle Hymns* (Edinburgh, 1990), pp. 24–42.
2. Disraeli came into office in February 1874.
3. The elaborate arrangements associated with the funeral cost much more than this grant. The vast turnout and massive popular interest in Livingstone forced the government reluctantly to cover the shortfall subsequently.
4. The unwillingness of Disraeli's government to provide a hero's funeral and the massive popular support for the idea are described in John Wolffe, *Great Deaths: Grieving, Religion and Nationhood in Victorian and Edwardian Britain* (London, 2000), pp. 138–45.
5. See P. Curtin, *Images of Africa* (Madison, Wisconsin, 1964); and A. C. Ross, 'The Impact of Scientific Racism on Missionary Policy in Africa', in Andrew Porter, *The Imperial Horizons of British Protestant Missions, 1880–1914* (London, 2002).
6. Edward Hume, *David Livingstone* (London, 1910), p. viii.
7. C. Northcott, *David Livingstone* (London, 1973), pp. 74–78, 121–22.
8. I. Schapera (ed.), *Livingstone's Missionary Correspondence* (London, 1961), letter 43, Livingstone to Thompson, 30 September 1852.
9. National Archives of Zimbabwe, MS L 1/1/1. See above Chapter 6 passim.
10. See Ross, *Blantyre Mission*, Chapter 3.
11. NLS, MS 10778, Livingstone to Thompson, 30 September 1852.

Bibliography

More than two thousand letters of David Livingstone can be found in the National Library of Scotland's collection in photocopy or original form, along with a large number of his notebooks and journals. Similarly in the Library of the School of Oriental and African Studies in London almost all of his letters can be found in original or photocopy form. The standard guides to Livingstone's letters are Clendennen, G. W. and Cunningham, I. C., *David Livingstone: A Catalogue of Documents* (Edinburgh, 1979) and Cunningham, I. C., *David Livingstone: A Catalogue of Documents: A Supplement* (Edinburgh, 1985).

Adams, H. G., *David Livingstone: His Life and Adventures in the Interior of Africa* (London, 1857).

Agar-Hamilton, J. A. I., *The Road to the North* (London, 1937).

Anderson-Morshead, A. E. M., *The History of the UMCA* (London, 1909).

Anstruther, I., *I Presume: Stanley's Triumph and Disaster* (London, 1956).

Bennett, N. (ed.), *Stanley's Despatches for the New York Herald* (Boston, 1970).

Blaikie, W. G., *The Personal Life of David Livingstone* (London, 1880).

Boucher, M. (ed.), *Livingstone Letters* (Johannesburg, 1985).

Cairns, H. A. C., *Prelude to Imperialism* (London, 1965).

Campbell, R. J., *Livingstone* (London, 1929).

Chadwick, O., *Mackenzie's Grave* (London, 1959).

Chamberlin, D. (ed.), *Some Letters from Livingstone* (London, 1940).

Clendennen, G. W., 'Charles Livingstone: A Biographical Study' (unpublished Edinburgh Ph.D dissertation, 1978).

Clendennen, G. W. (ed.), *David Livingstone's Shire Journal* (Aberystwyth, 1990).

Coupland, R., *Kirk on the Zambesi* (Oxford, 1928).

Coupland, R., *Livingstone's Last Journey* (London, 1945).

Debenham, F., *The Way to Ilala* (London, 1955).

De Gruchy, J. (ed.), *The London Missionary Society in South Africa, 1799–1999* (Cape Town, 1999).

Du Plessis, J., *A History of Christian Missions in South Africa* (London, 1911).

Duffy, J., *Portuguese Africa* (Boston, 1961).

Foskett, R. (ed.), *The Zambesi Doctors: David Livingstone's Letters to John Kirk* (Edinburgh, 1965).

Foskett, R. (ed.), *The Zambesi Journal and Letters of Dr John Kirk* (Edinburgh, 1965).

Frazer, A. Z., *Livingstone and Newstead* (London, 1913).

Galbraith, J. S., *Reluctant Empire: British Policy on the South African Frontier* (Berkeley, 1963).

Gelfand, M., *Livingstone the Doctor* (Oxford, 1957).

Gosset, T. F., *Race: The History of an Idea in America* (New York, 1965).

Hall, R., *Stanley: An Adventurer Explored* (London, 1974).

Hall, R., *Zambia* (London, 1965).

Healey, E., *Lady Unknown: The Life of Angela Burdett-Coutts* (London, 1978).

Holmes, T. (ed.), *David Livingstone Letters and Documents: The Zambian Collection* (London, 1990).

Holmes, T., *Journey to Livingstone* (Edinburgh, 1993).

Hughes, T., *Life of David Livingstone* (London, 1902).

Jeal, T., *Livingstone* (London, 1973).

Johnston, H. H., *Livingstone and the Exploration of Central Africa* (London, 1912).

Livingstone, D., *Analysis of the Language of the Bechuanas* (London, 1858).

Livingstone, D., *Missionary Travels in South Africa* (London, 1857).

Livingstone, D. and C., *Narrative of an Expedition to the Zambesi and its Tributaries* (London, 1865).

Macnair, J. I., *Livingstone the Liberator* (London, 1940).

MacPherson, F., *The British Conquest of Northern Rhodesia* (London, 1976).

Martelli, G., *Livingstone's River: A History of the Zambesi Expedition* (London, 1970).

Moffat, J. S., *The Lives of Robert and Mary Moffat* (London, 1886).

Monk, W., *Dr Livingstone's Cambridge Lectures* (Cambridge, 1860).

National Portrait Gallery, *Livingstone and the Victorian Encounter with Africa* (London, 1996).

Oswell, W. E., *William Cotton Oswell: Hunter and Explorer* (London, 1900).

Pachai, B. (ed.), *Livingstone: Man of Africa* (London, 1973).

Parsons, J. W., *The Livingstones at Kolobeng* (Gaberone, Botswana, 1997).

Ransford, O., *David Livingstone: The Dark Interior* (London, 1978).

Roberts, J. S., *The Life and Explorations of David Livingstone LL.D.* (Glasgow, 1875).

Ross, A. C., *A Vision Betrayed: The Jesuits in Japan and China, 1542–1742* (Edinburgh and New York, 1994).

Ross, A. C., *Blantyre Mission and the Making of Modern Malawi* (Blantyre, Malawi, 1996).

Ross, A. C., *John Philip, 1775–1851: Christianity, Race and Politics in South Africa* (Aberdeen, 1986).

Ross, A. C., *Livingstone: The Scot and the Doctor* (Glasgow, 1990).

Schapera, I. (ed.), *David Livingstone: Family Letters, 1842–1856*, 2 vols (London, 1959).

Schapera, I. (ed.), *Livingstone's African Journal 1853–1856*, 2 vols (London, 1963).

Schapera, I. (ed.), *Livingstone's Missionary Correspondence, 1841–1856* (London, 1961).

Schapera, I. (ed.), *Livingstone's Private Journals, 1851–1853* (London, 1960).

Seaver, G., *David Livingstone: His Life and Letters* (London, 1957).

Shepperson, G., *David Livingstone and the Rovuma* (Edinburgh, 1965).

Simmons, J., *Livingstone and Africa* (London, 1955).

Stanley, H. M., *How I Found Livingstone* (London, 1872).

Waller, H. (ed.), *The Last Journals of David Livingstone*, 2 vols (London, 1874).

Wallis, J. P. R. (ed.), *The Zambesi Journal of James Stewart* (London, 1953).

Wallis, J. P. R. (ed.), *The Zambesi Expedition of David Livingstone*, 2 vols (London, 1956).

Wallis, J. P. R., *Thomas Baines of King's Lynn* (London, 1941).

Index

OCT 1 3 2005